Rêverie

THE ART OF **SIBYLLINE MEYNET**

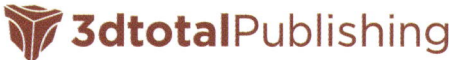

3dtotal Publishing

Website: www.3dtotal.com
Correspondence: publishing@3dtotal.com

Rêverie: The Art of Sibylline Meynet
© 2021 3dtotal Publishing.

First published in the United Kingdom, 2021, by 3dtotal Publishing.

Address: 3dtotal.com Ltd, 29 Foregate Street, Worcester, WR1 1DS, United Kingdom.

Hard cover ISBN: 978-1-912843-38-1
Printing and binding: Leo Paper Products Ltd.
www.leo.com.hk

Visit www.3dtotalpublishing.com for a complete list of available book titles.

Managing Director: Tom Greenway
Studio Manager: Simon Morse
Lead Editor: Samantha Rigby
Lead Designer: Fiona Tarbet
Editorial Project Manager: Sophie Symes

MIX
Paper from responsible sources
FSC® C020056

ONE TREE PLANTED FOR EVERY BOOK SOLD

OUR PLEDGE

From 2020, 3dtotal Publishing has pledged to plant one tree for every book sold by partnering with and donating the appropriate amounts to reforesting charities. This is one of the first steps in our ambition to become a carbon-neutral company with carbon-neutral publications, giving our customers the knowledge that by buying from 3dtotal Publishing, they are working with us to balance the environmental damage caused by the publishing, shipping, and retail industries.

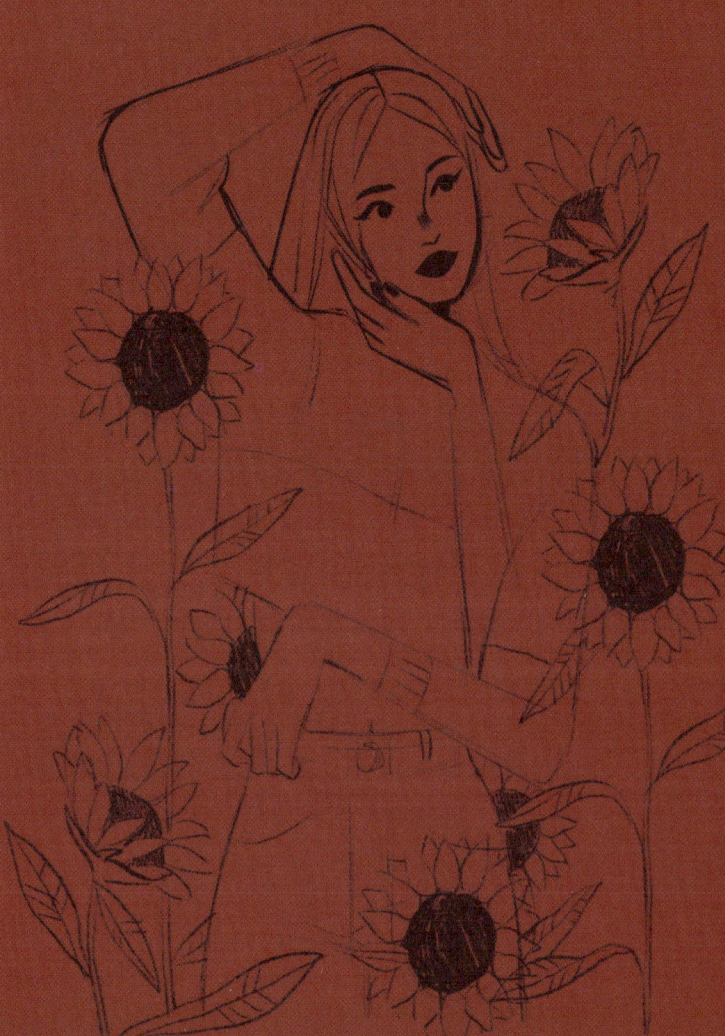

CONTENTS

FOREWORD

Sibylline and I met a few years ago, just before the opening of our joint gallery show. I remember being nervous and overwhelmed, but for the brief moment that we met and talked, I was happy to connect with a person with such warmth, calmness, and genuineness. I believe this impression of Sibylline is also felt by those admiring her gorgeous art.

I have been creating paintings with colored inks and watercolors for many years, and while I have learned to understand the restrictions of traditional mediums and the amount of patience that is needed to work with paints on paper, I have always felt that those quirks are what makes me love working with them. I can sense from Sibylline's works that there must have been a great deal of trial and error while she discovered the quirks of her medium. Having undertaken just a handful of experiments with opaque paint mediums, I can hardly fathom the amount of practice it must have taken to master gouache the way she has.

I am always amazed and inspired by Sibylline's ability to create clean and simple-looking art that appears effortless, as if everything has fallen harmoniously into its correct place. This displays how well she understands the importance of composition and can utilize that knowledge to create interesting rhythm in her works. The way she stylizes different objects, whether it be plants, animals, or everyday items, makes them look like they belong in a "Sibylline" painting. And when it comes to the use of color, her paintings demonstrate that palettes are always thoroughly considered, and her combinations always look playful and true to her style.

In her latest works, Sibylline experiments with creating beautiful settings and environments for her characters that are full of life. It is a joy to witness how Sibylline has her sights set on personal improvement in her craft — something that I strive for in my own work. Seeing how much Sibylline's artistic voice has developed and grown over the years she has been sharing her art, I can only imagine what heights she will reach in the future.

Since you are holding this book, you probably already know what unique and inviting works of art lie within. I warmly invite you to travel into the mind of Sibylline and see for yourself how much thought goes into creating each of her artworks. I truly believe her art and words will inspire!

HEIKALA

Cloak Maker, 2020, Heikala

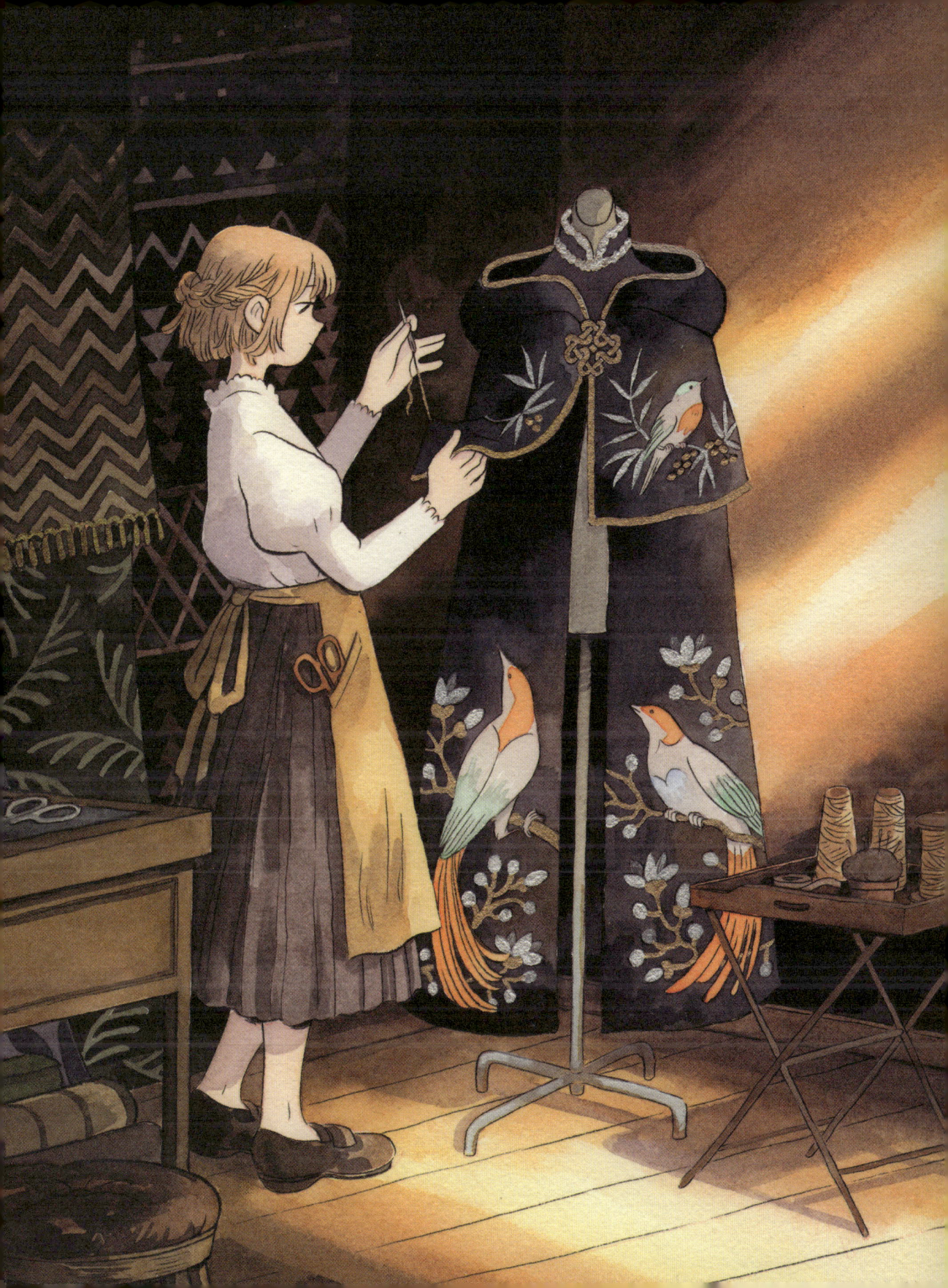

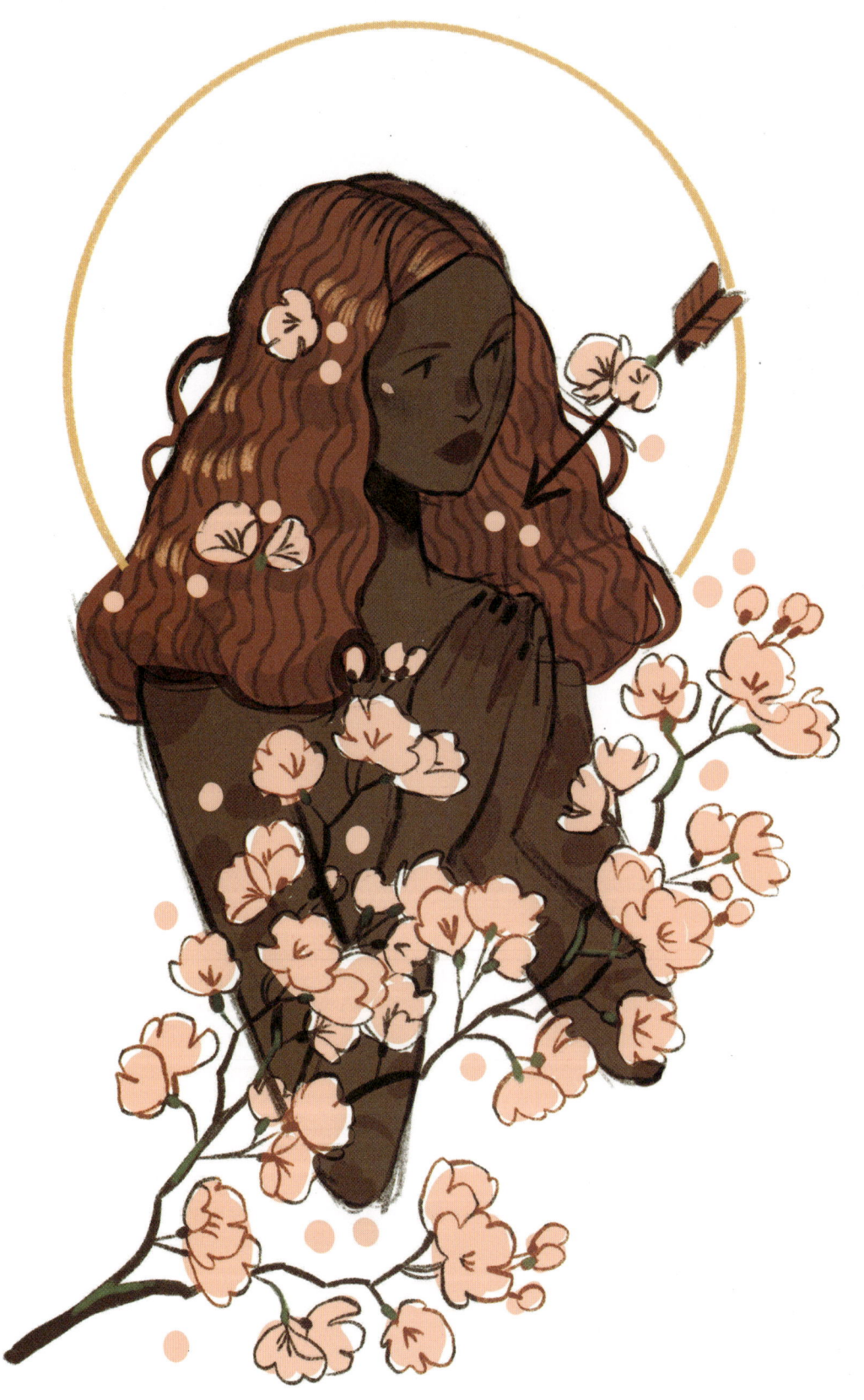

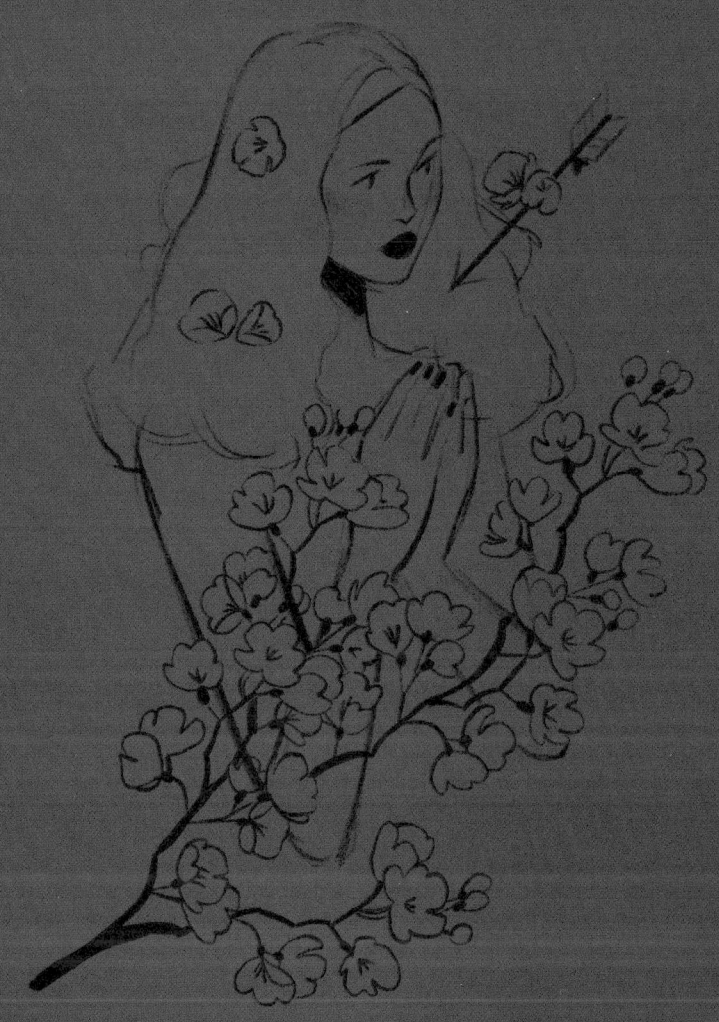

INTRODUCTION

I was born in the French Alps, France. Books, films, drawing, and music have always had an important place in my household. I grew up in the mountains surrounded by animals, trees, and all different types of flowers. At the time there wasn't much to do except run around in the fields and draw, so I spent my days drawing with my sisters and my best friend. They were good times!

I have always been shy and reserved, which is probably why I have never stopped drawing. Painting and telling stories allows me to express myself. I want to create beautiful things, but I also want the viewer to interpret my adventures in their own way, in their own vision, so my stories can become theirs. Art is personal. It's an intimate journey, but it's something that needs to be shared.

I mostly draw women, because I have always looked up to them while growing up. They inspire me to be the best version of myself. I feel that drawing women is my way of paying homage to them, my heroes. And at the same time, these women are all a part of me.

I also always find simple moments interesting to analyze, interpret, and draw. I love depicting aspects of life and combining them with classic fairy tales, to add a dash of magic. Everyone should be able to take a walk in the woods with their familiar, don't you think?

Making a book is a very important step for me because it is my child-self's dream come true! I have always cherished the artbooks of my favorite artists, and buying artbooks for myself is my favorite treat! Holding a book in my hands and reading its contents again and again is a magical and inspirational experience.

The times in which we live are wonderful, but also strange. At a time when social networks move and change quickly, and artists are anxious to constantly create so as not to be forgotten, I think it is good to stop and contemplate what we have succeeded to build. To take a deep breath. Having spent years drawing and posting my work online, realizing my drawings could interest people, and building an engaged community around my drawings, I really liked the idea of creating a book to document the entire experience. What I love most about an artbook is discovering more about the artist behind the works we see on social media. Because sometimes we forget that the art does not just happen by magic! We forget that an actual person is on the other side of the screen, and spends days drawing, working, creating new things to give to the world. Making a book is a great way to humanize the artist.

It's also a way for me to say thank you. *Rêverie* has given me the perfect opportunity to share even more about my art and creative story with the people who have followed and supported me for years. I want to use this book to offer more personal, in-depth information about myself and my art than I share on social media. I receive questions daily about how I create, organize myself, and make everything work, so I will also answer those questions.

I hope *Rêverie* can provide a source of motivation for those who would like to make a living from their passion. And I would like aspiring artists to understand that the road is long, sometimes painful, but anything is possible. Finding your style, identity, and flair, takes time and it's a journey that you do on your own. It's a wonderful trip!

I hope you will enjoy looking at my illustrations as much as I enjoyed creating them.

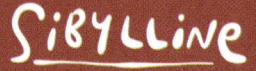

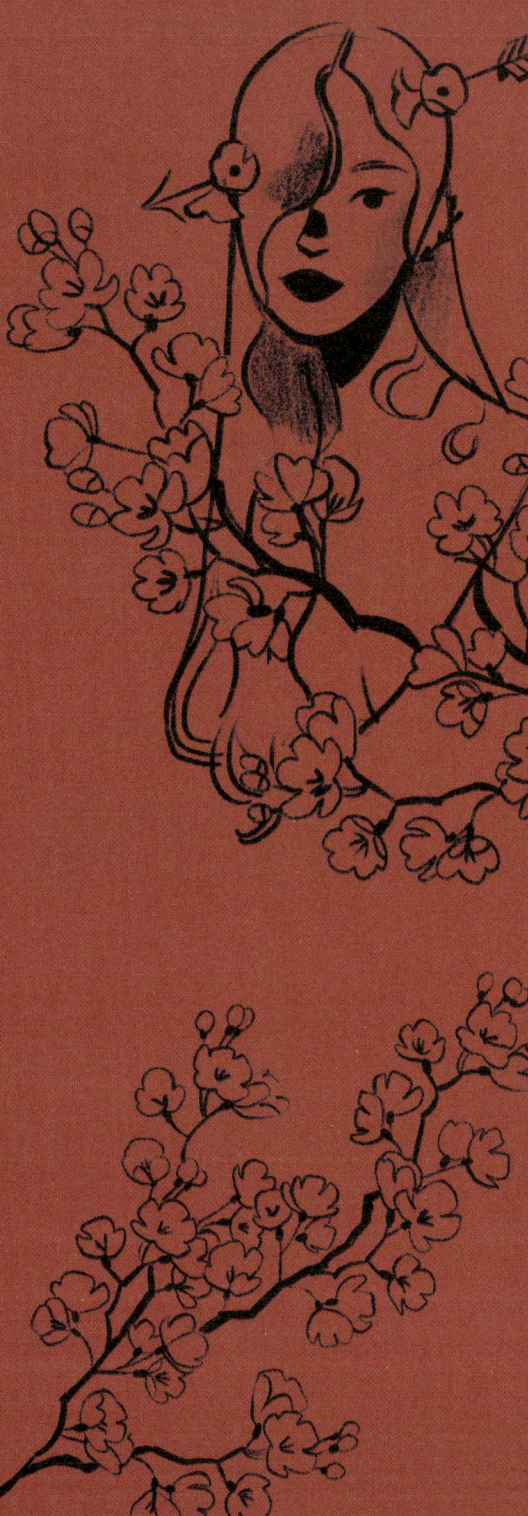

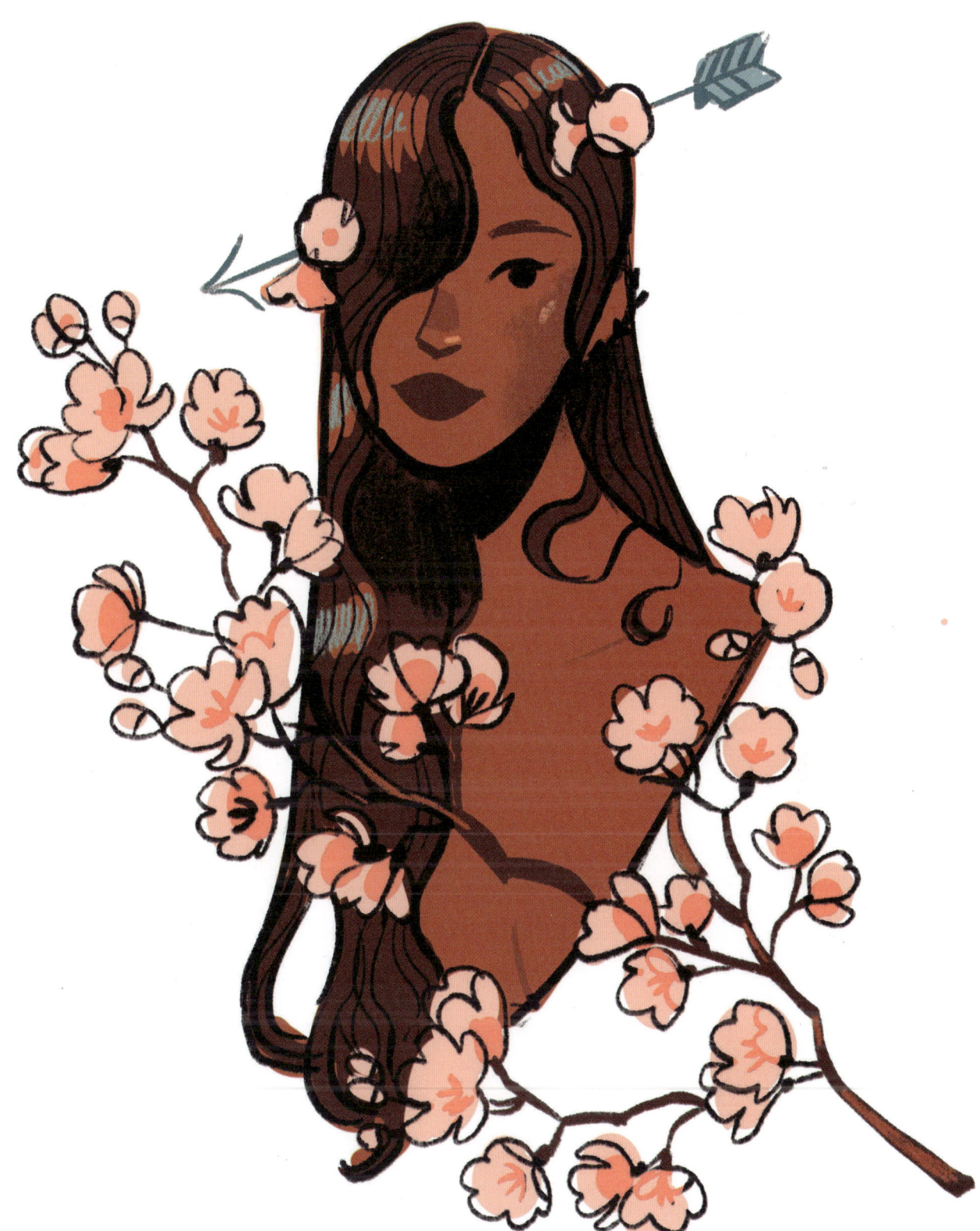

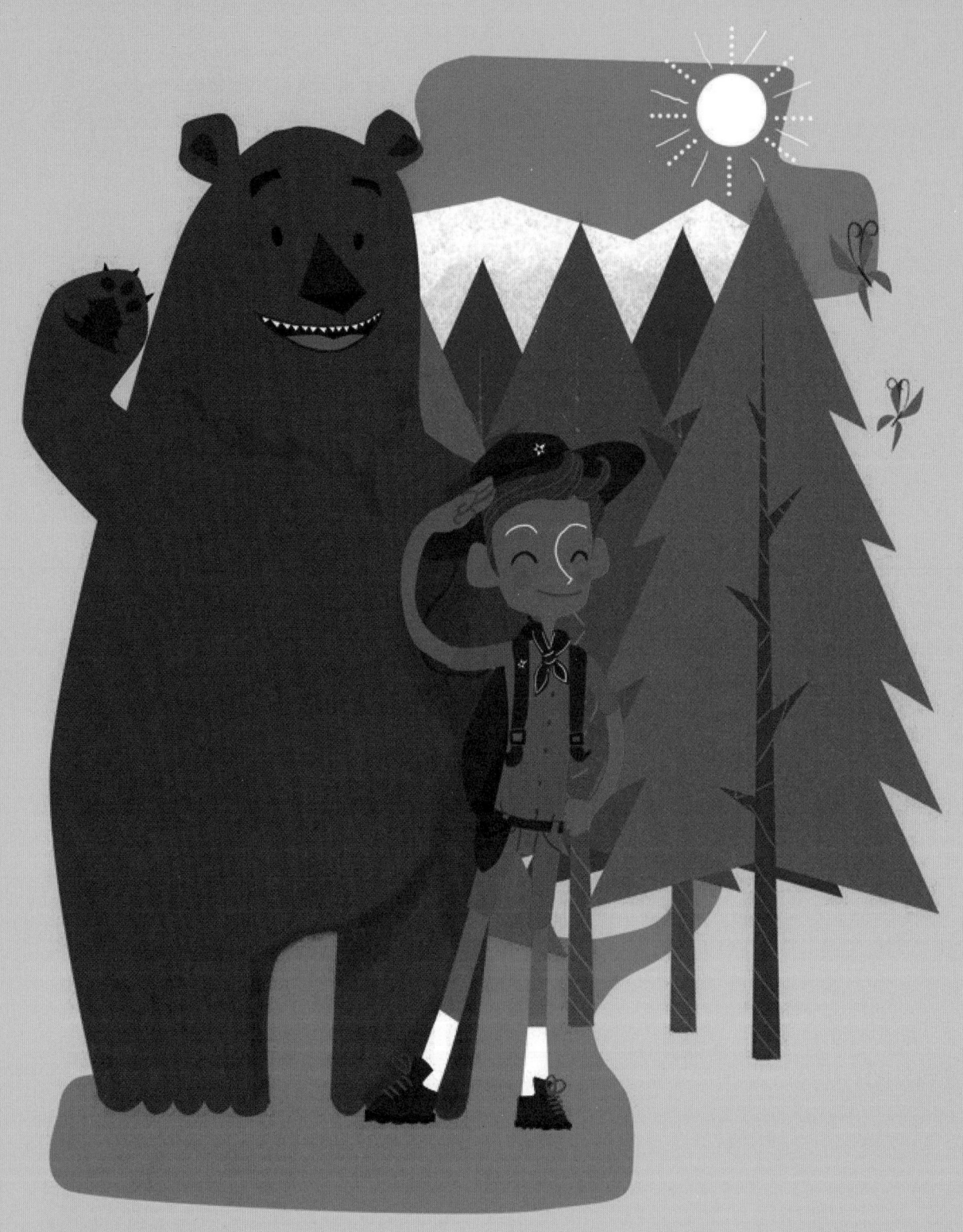

CREATIVE STORY

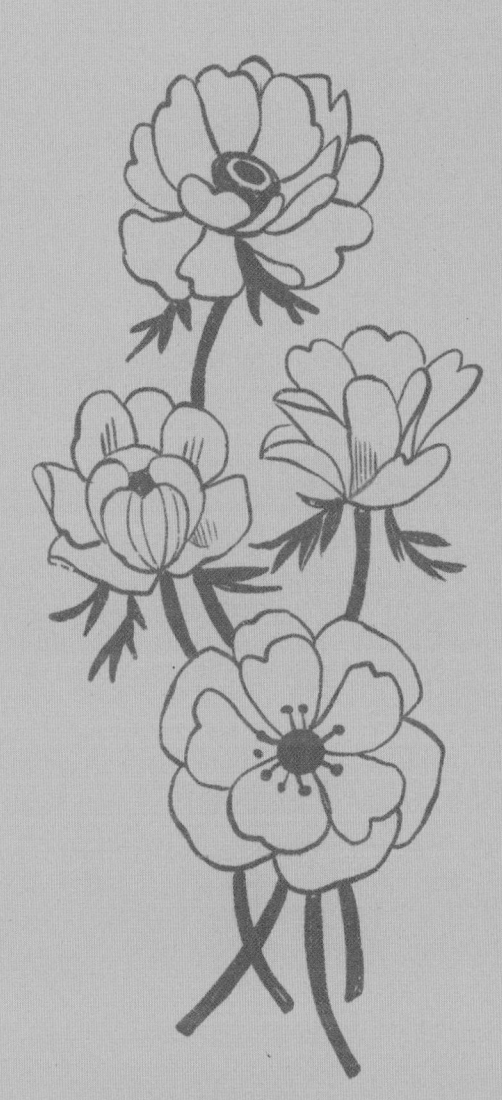

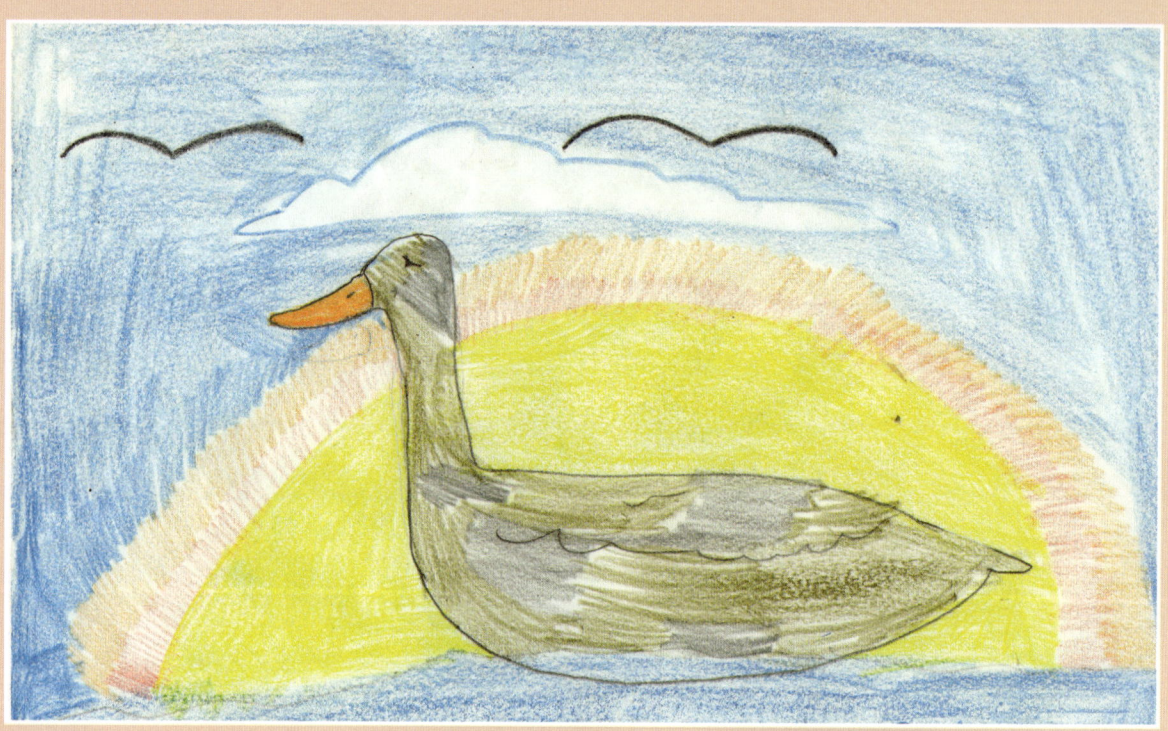

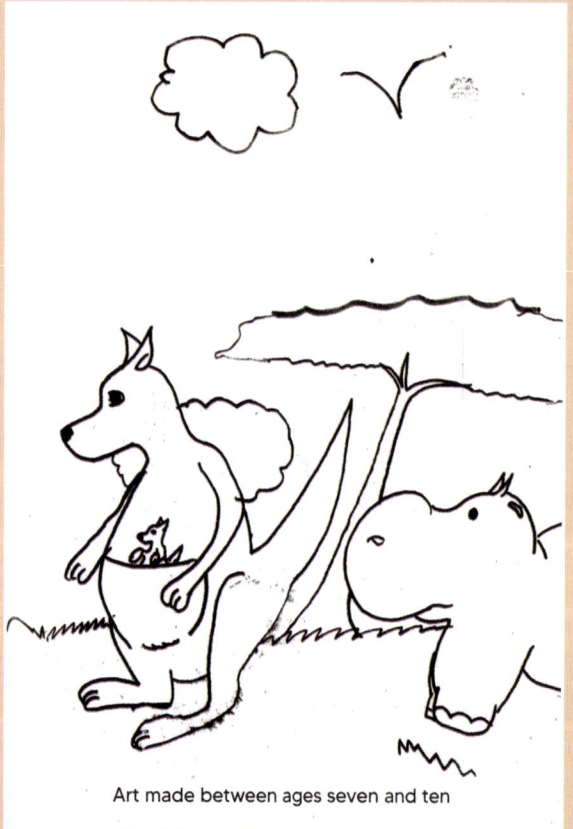

Art made between ages seven and ten

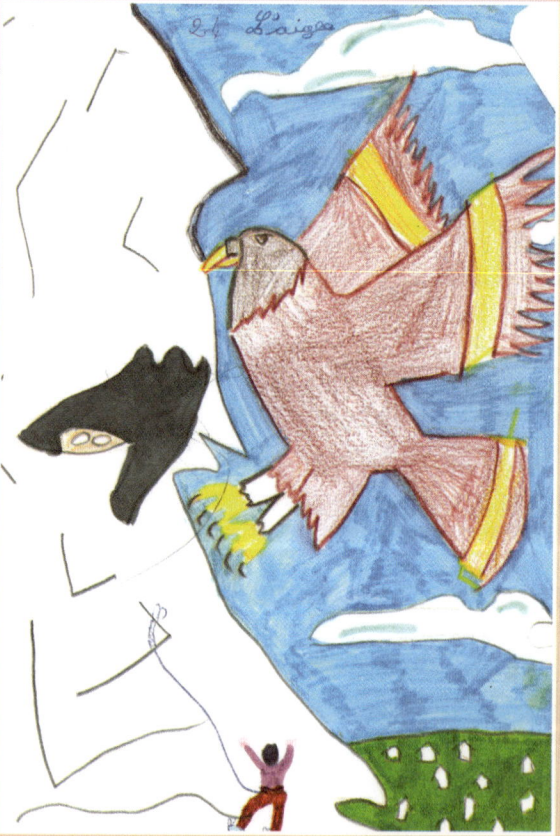

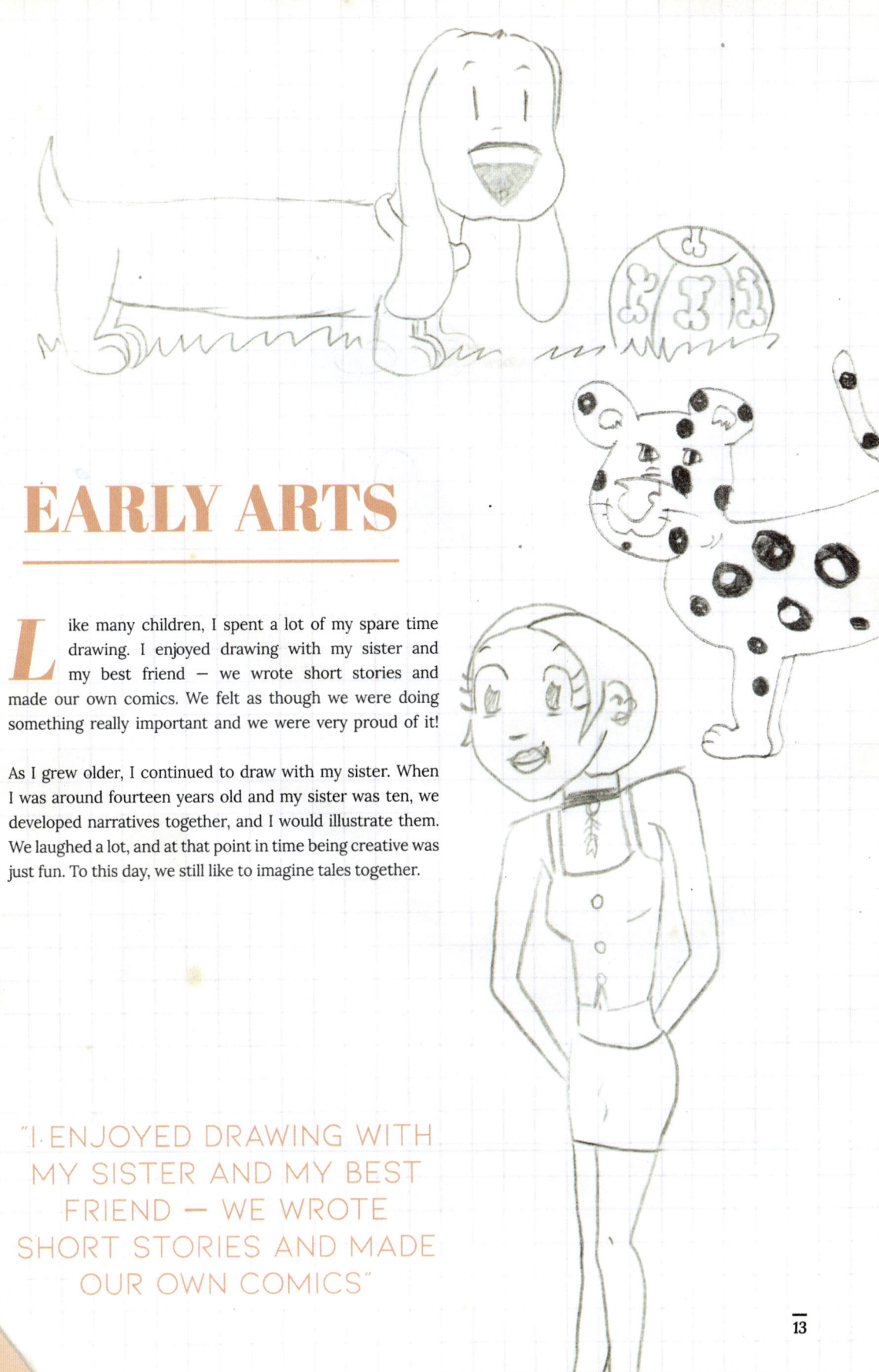

EARLY ARTS

L ike many children, I spent a lot of my spare time drawing. I enjoyed drawing with my sister and my best friend — we wrote short stories and made our own comics. We felt as though we were doing something really important and we were very proud of it!

As I grew older, I continued to draw with my sister. When I was around fourteen years old and my sister was ten, we developed narratives together, and I would illustrate them. We laughed a lot, and at that point in time being creative was just fun. To this day, we still like to imagine tales together.

"I ENJOYED DRAWING WITH MY SISTER AND MY BEST FRIEND — WE WROTE SHORT STORIES AND MADE OUR OWN COMICS"

AMBITION & OVERCOMING ADVERSITY

I knew from an early age that all I wanted to do was draw. I didn't like school in general, and I just wanted to launch straight into becoming a professional artist. I found transitioning from a small school of just 200 students to a high school of 2,000 students overwhelming. I didn't enjoy my classes and had to repeat my first year, which was discouraging and difficult, but what I struggled with the most was a feeling of disconnect from my fellow students. I felt that I couldn't relate to my peers who wanted to grow up too fast, and I didn't recognize myself in that lifestyle — I didn't smoke, I didn't drink, I didn't go to parties. Although I had friends and got along with everyone in my classes, I felt uncomfortable and out of place.

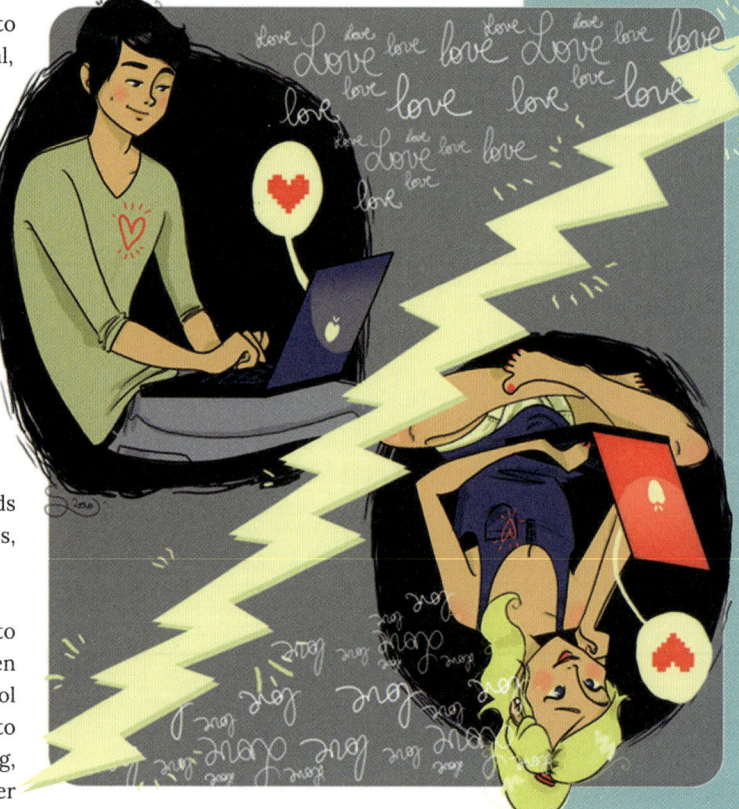

My family has always encouraged me to continue in the artistic field. However, when I asked my parents if I could quit school and start working instead, they asked me to graduate high school first. It was challenging, but the thought of working as an artist after graduating was a powerful motivator. I am happy to have been able to prove to my parents, and to myself, that I was able to finish high school with a diploma, especially as I struggled with adversity.

Despite boring classes, difficult teachers, and endless homework, a lot can be learned about yourself during this strange part of adolescence. My advice to those who are struggling is to just try to show up, take on your responsibilities as a student, and throw yourself into meeting new people and making new friends. Trying your best is all you can ever do.

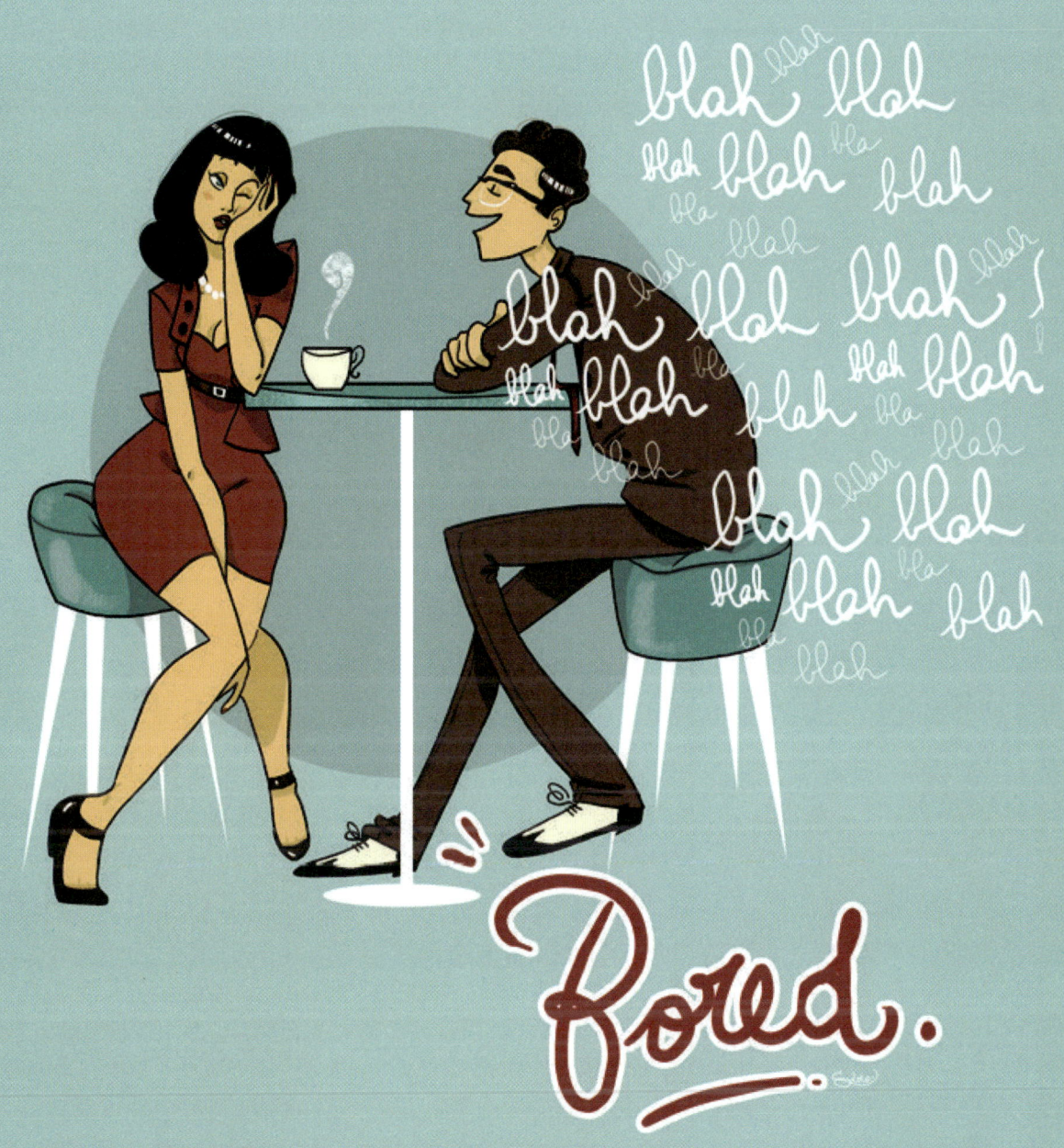

Art created at nineteen years old

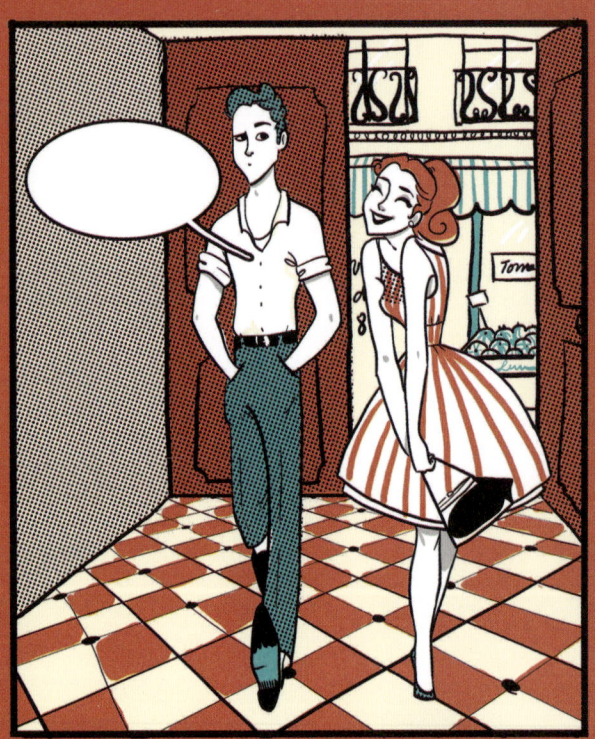
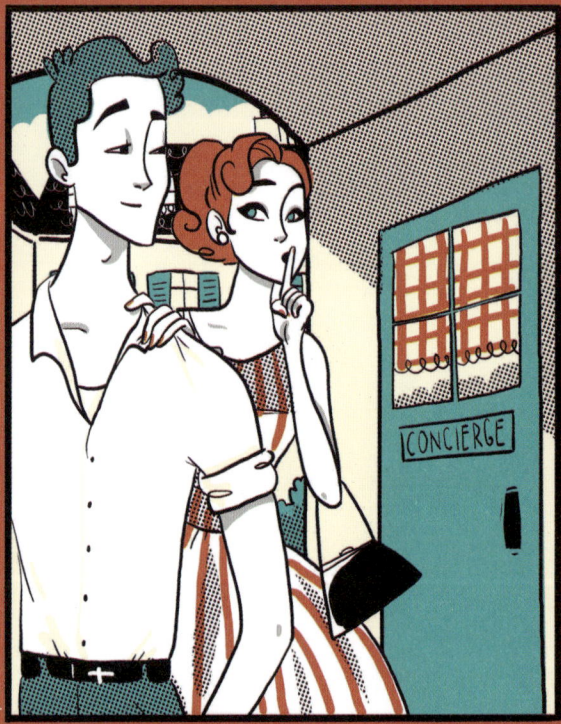
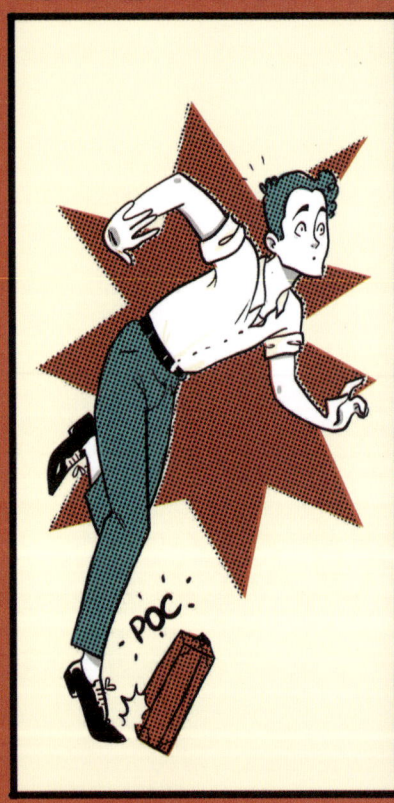
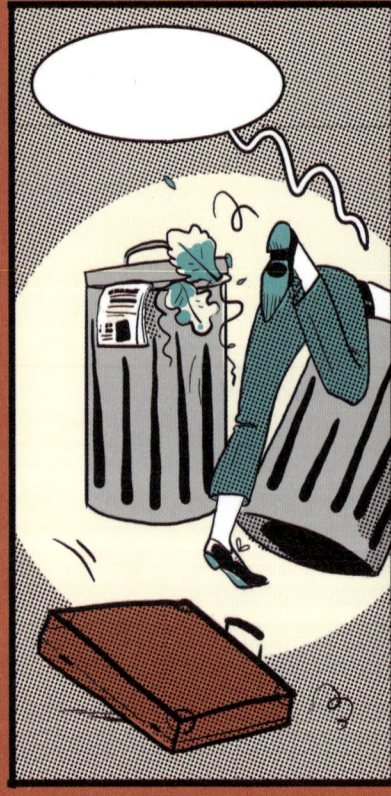
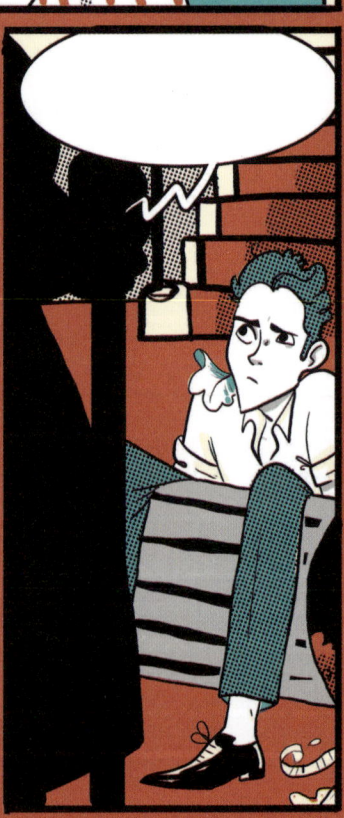

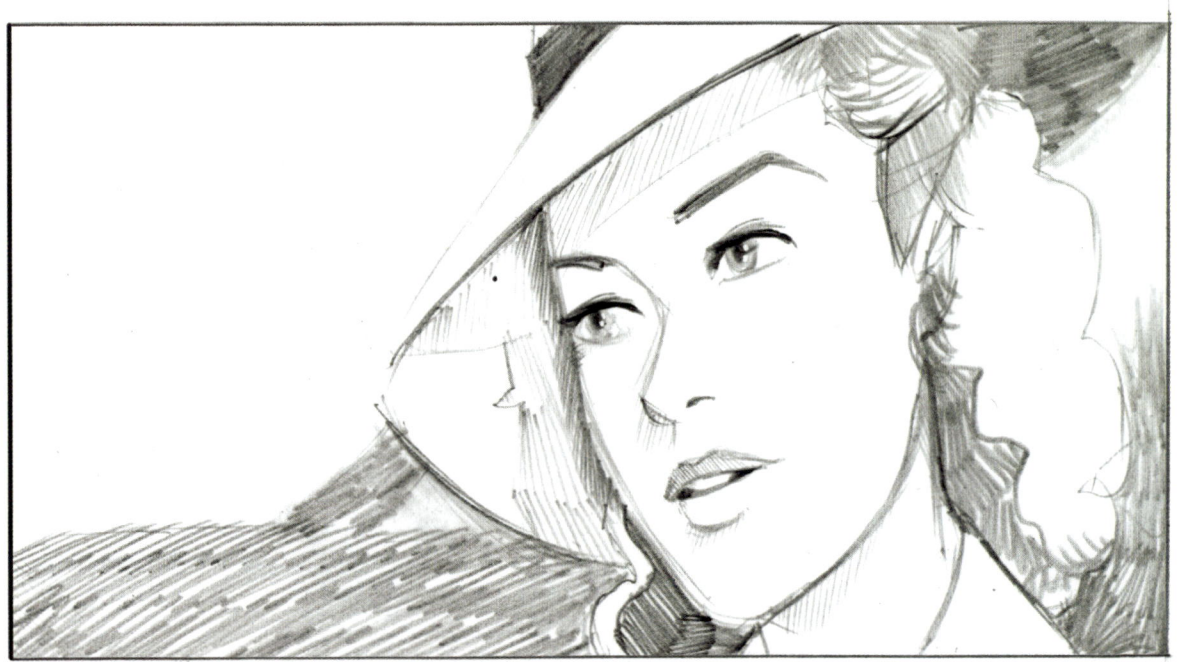

FUELING THE CREATIVE FIRE

Reading comics when I was a child gave me the initial motivation to become an artist. Thanks to my dad, I was lucky enough to visit many comic book conventions and meet authors. The encounter that made the biggest impact on me was with the comic author, Boulet. I asked him to look at my comic pages when I was thirteen years old, and he really took the time to sit down with me to tell me what was wrong, but also what was interesting about my project. I will remember that moment forever, because something changed in me: I understood that I was right in my desire to be an artist, that what I was doing might have potential, and that I had to continue in this direction.

I grew up knowing that being an artist is complicated but not impossible. That's why I never questioned my aspiration to become an illustrator, even though I didn't know for sure I would succeed.

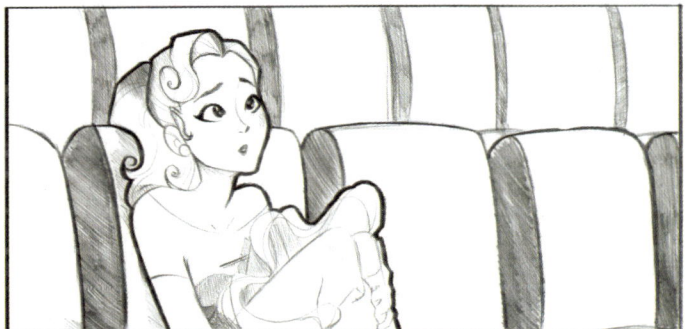

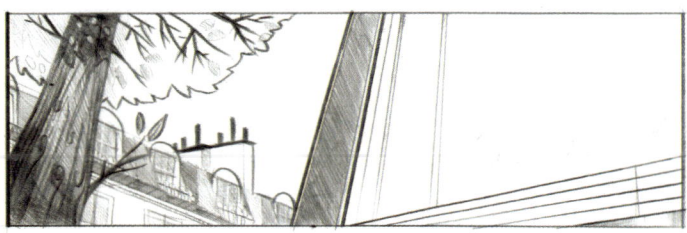

Comic designs created at around nineteen years old

BUILDING A PRACTICE

I was nineteen years old when I started working as an illustrator and I spent a lot of time improving my portfolio and meeting professionals at events. I was determined and very motivated, although it took a little while to find work and to be published in books and magazines. I thought networking and developing a portfolio would be enough to find a job, but no one ever called me back. In hindsight, I understand why I was unsuccessful, as I was not experienced or confident enough. Finding a style and finding yourself personally, too, takes time. It was when I felt good about what I was doing that people started offering me jobs.

Drawing has now become my main full-time job. Alongside exhibitions, commissions, and collaborations, I sell prints and other products in my online store. But what requires most of my working time is Patreon. I put a lot into this platform because my patrons and I have built a wonderful community. Their opinions mean a lot to me, and I have a relationship with them that motivates me, and gives me a sense of freedom to create whatever I feel inspired to create.

I'm very lucky to have a large supportive following, and people who trust me enough to invite me to work on projects with them. When I created my Instagram account in 2012, I used to post pictures of my daily life, just like everyone else, and then naturally I started sharing drawings because that's what I did all day. I hadn't expected Instagram to become such a huge platform years later and I certainly never expected to find an audience for my art. Gradually, I stopped sharing moments of my life with my followers and focused on just sharing my drawings. The more people enjoyed my work, the more my following grew, and that was how I was able to find my first real contracts. In 2013, I was contacted by BOOM! Studios, who asked me to illustrate a *Garfield* comic book. I was very happy, and it seemed totally unreal that they would ask me! Subsequently, I was able to work with other publishers such as Valiant Entertainment, and companies including Netflix, Microsoft, and Warner Bros.

However, the biggest milestone of my career to date was being asked by Gallery Nucleus to participate in an exhibition with Heikala and Meyoco in their gallery in Los Angeles in 2019. I took the opportunity to travel to the United States, meet Heikala and the lovely people at the gallery, and spend time with some of my followers during the opening.

I signed books and received gifts, and found that people were very nice and respectful. As an illustrator, I spend most of my time alone, working in my home office, so it can be difficult to fully understand that behind an Instagram comment is a real authentic person. Meeting my followers in real life for the first time is an experience that I will never forget.

Self-portrait, digital, 2014

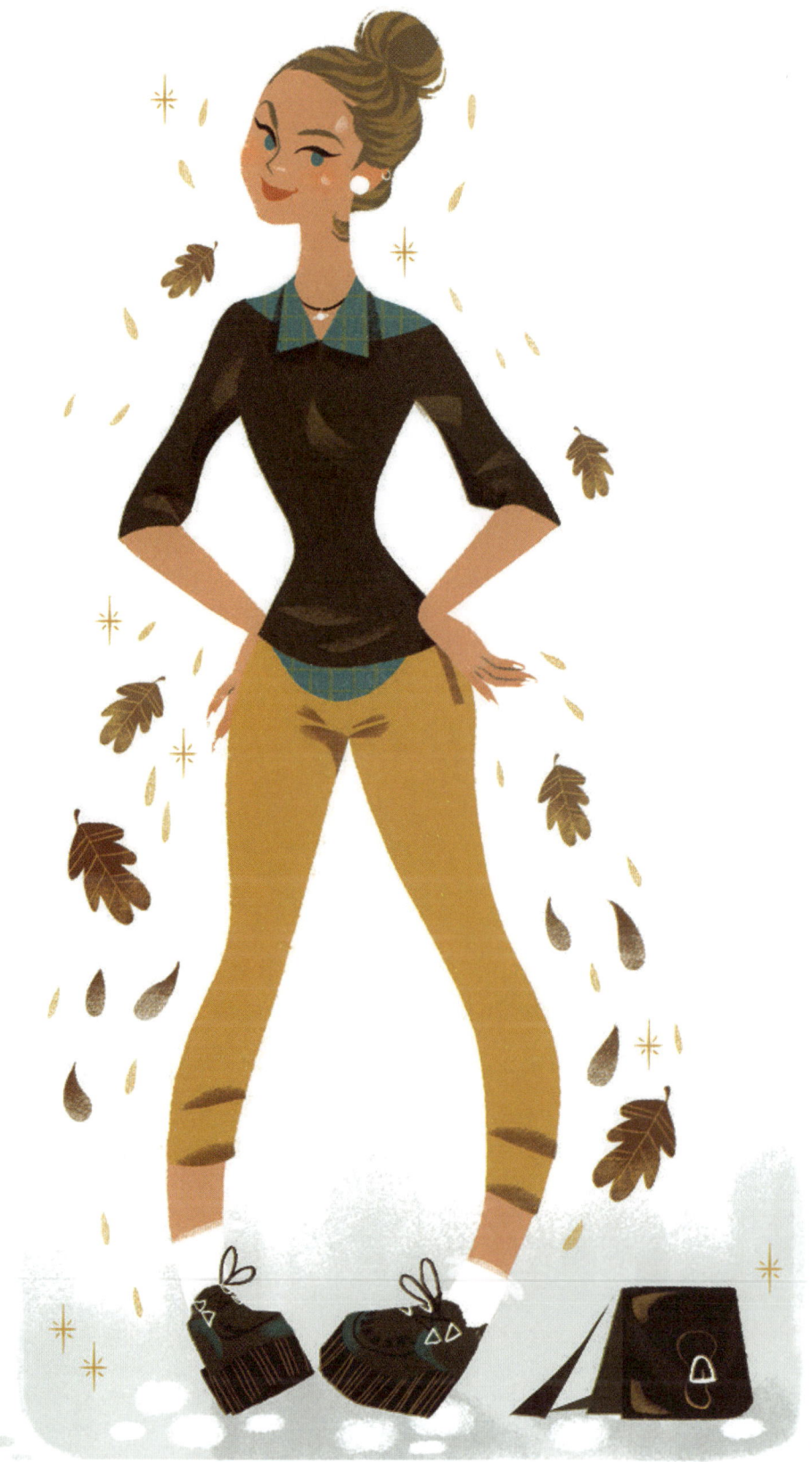

"THE BIGGEST MILESTONE OF MY CAREER TO DATE WAS BEING ASKED BY GALLERY NUCLEUS TO PARTICIPATE IN AN EXHIBITION WITH HEIKALA AND MEYOCO"

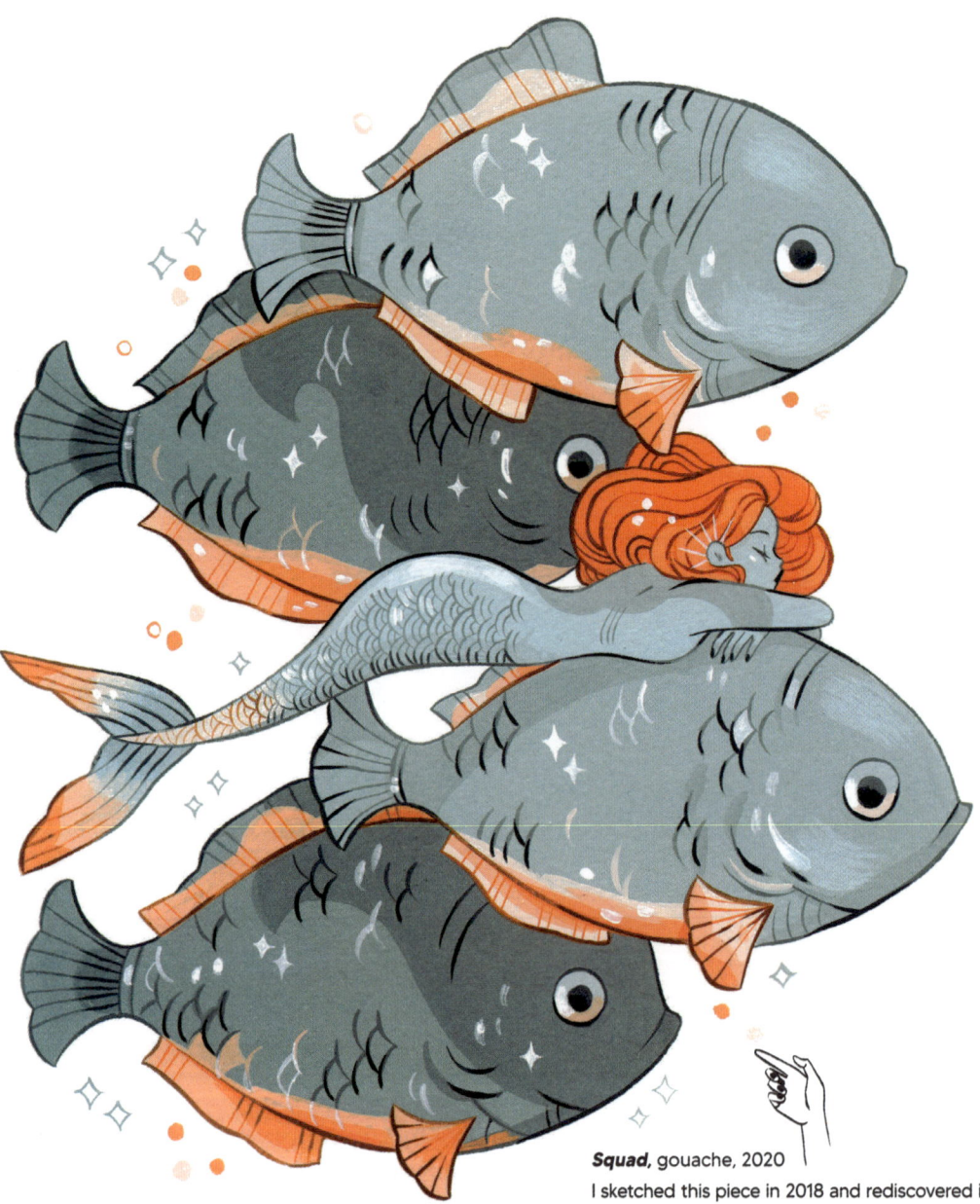

Squad, gouache, 2020

I sketched this piece in 2018 and rediscovered it on my iPad when I was looking for new ideas for paintings for the Gallery Nucleus exhibition. I love that the mermaid isn't the main focus of this piece. She blends into the crowd and highlights what I wanted to create: a piece that focuses on similarities (colors and theme) and differences (humans and animals). I like the idea of them being best friends, which is why I called this piece *Squad*.

20

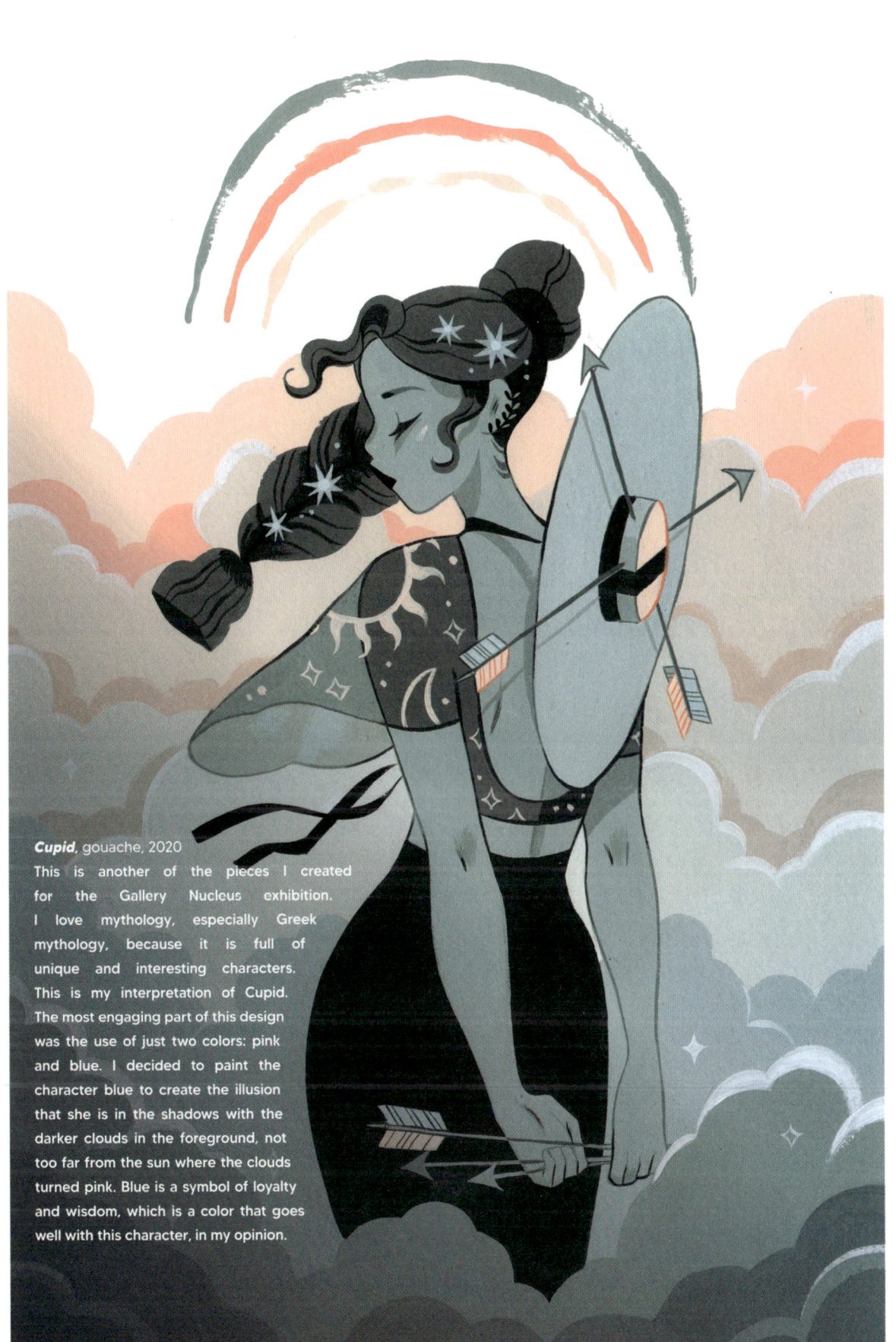

Cupid, gouache, 2020

This is another of the pieces I created for the Gallery Nucleus exhibition. I love mythology, especially Greek mythology, because it is full of unique and interesting characters. This is my interpretation of Cupid. The most engaging part of this design was the use of just two colors: pink and blue. I decided to paint the character blue to create the illusion that she is in the shadows with the darker clouds in the foreground, not too far from the sun where the clouds turned pink. Blue is a symbol of loyalty and wisdom, which is a color that goes well with this character, in my opinion.

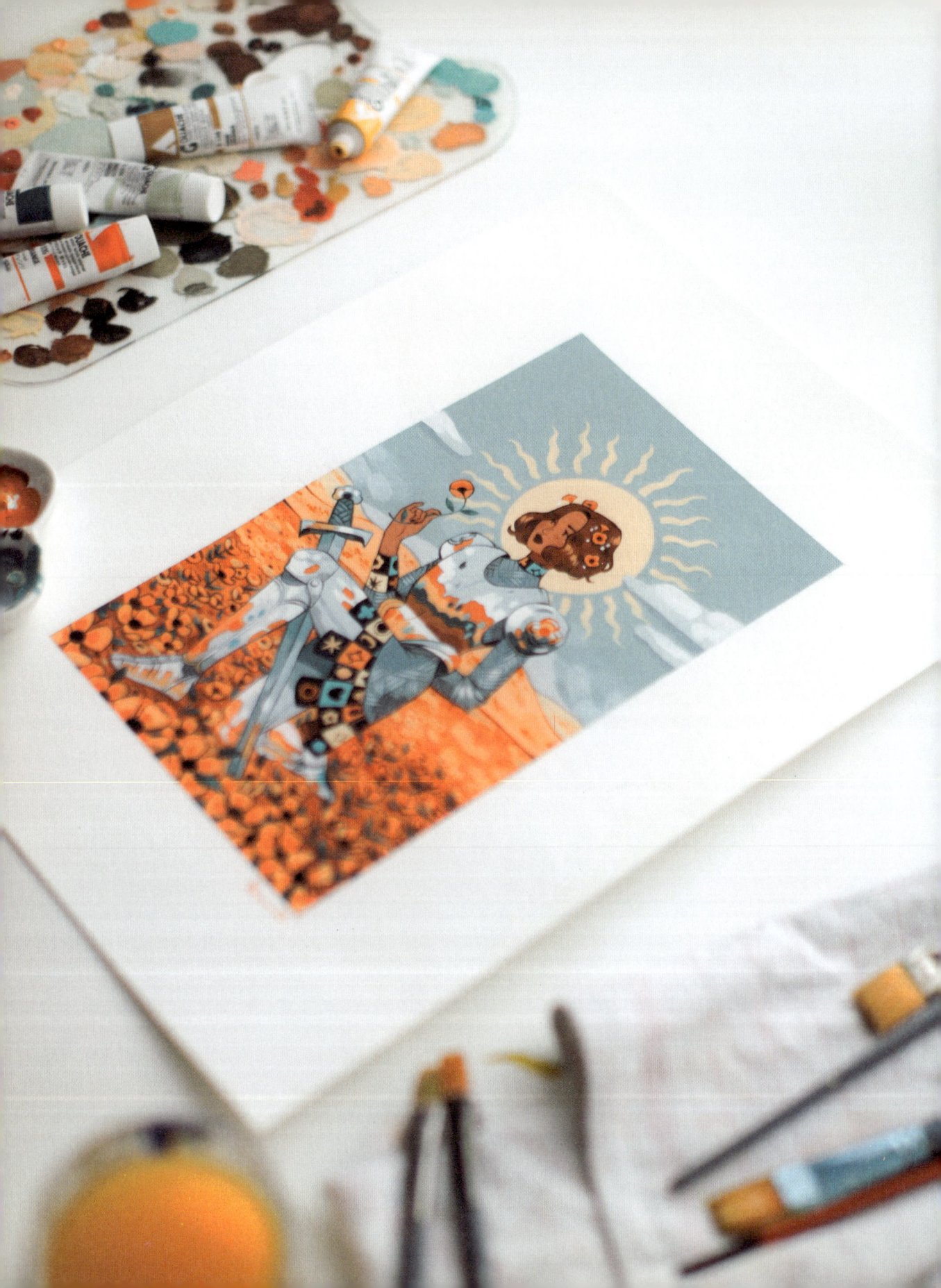

WORKSPACE

WORKSPACE

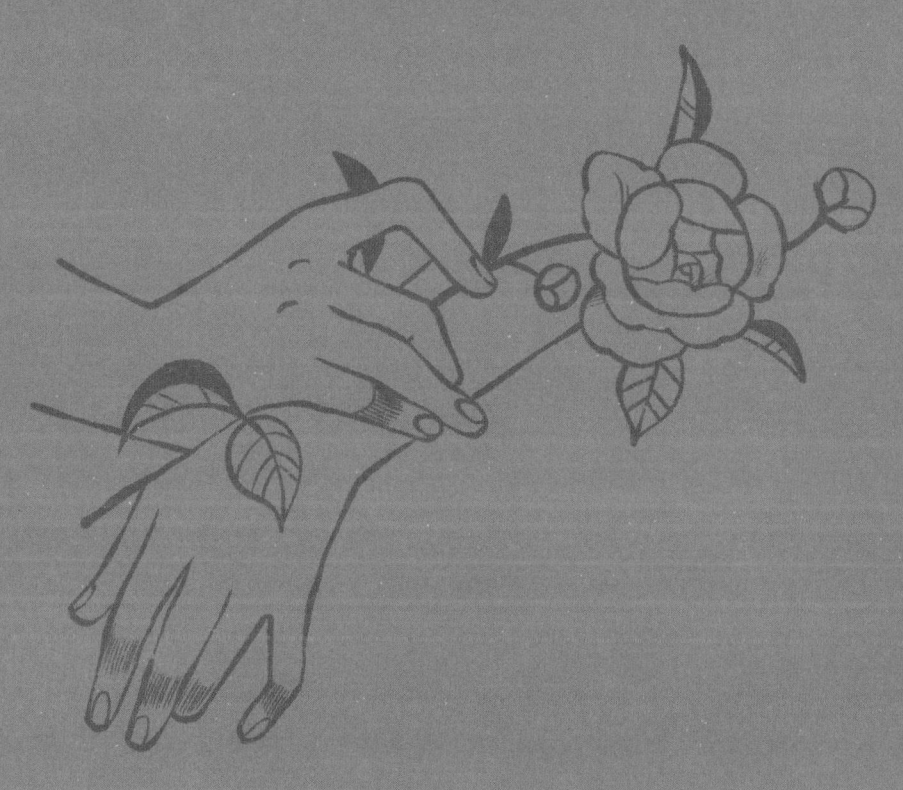

FLEXIBLE HOME WORKING

My desk is positioned under a window. As I work traditionally, natural light is very important. I paint in the morning and afternoon in order to make the most of the best light of the day and produce more accurate color rendering. When the light is too bright, I draw my curtains. They are white and transparent and help the light spread evenly throughout the room.

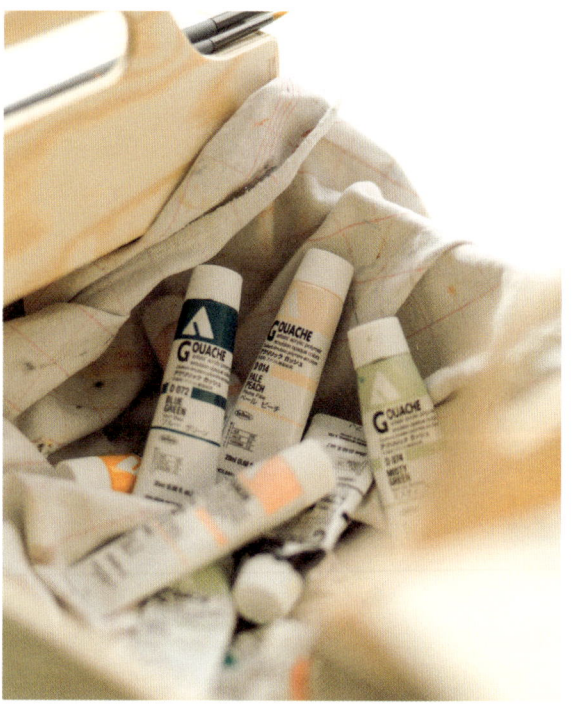

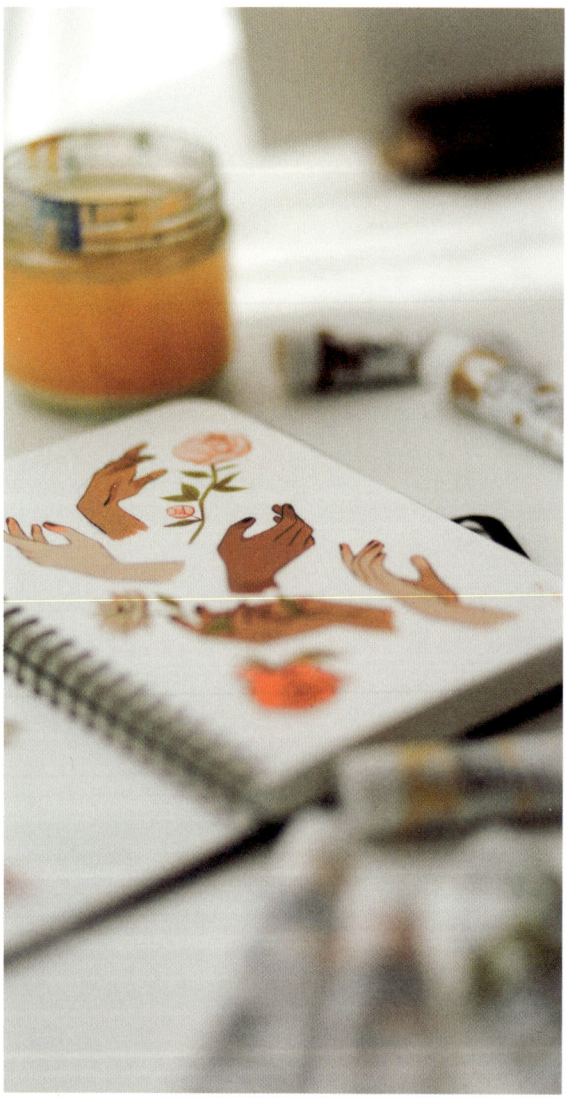

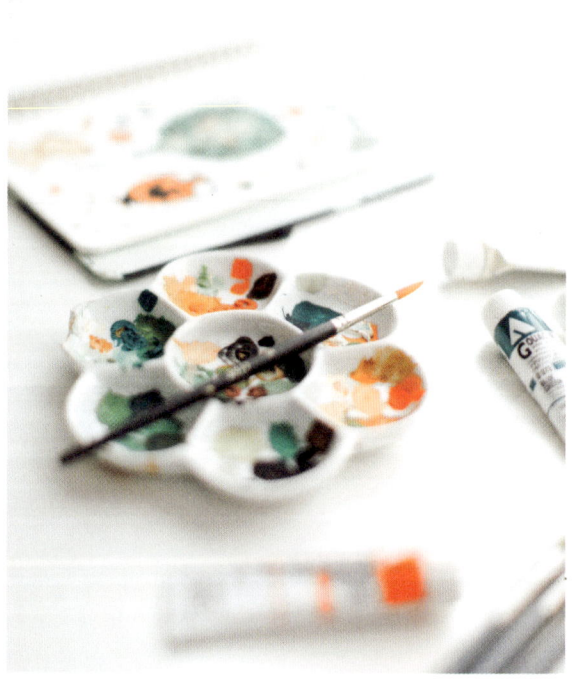

Photography by Benjamin Favrat, 2021

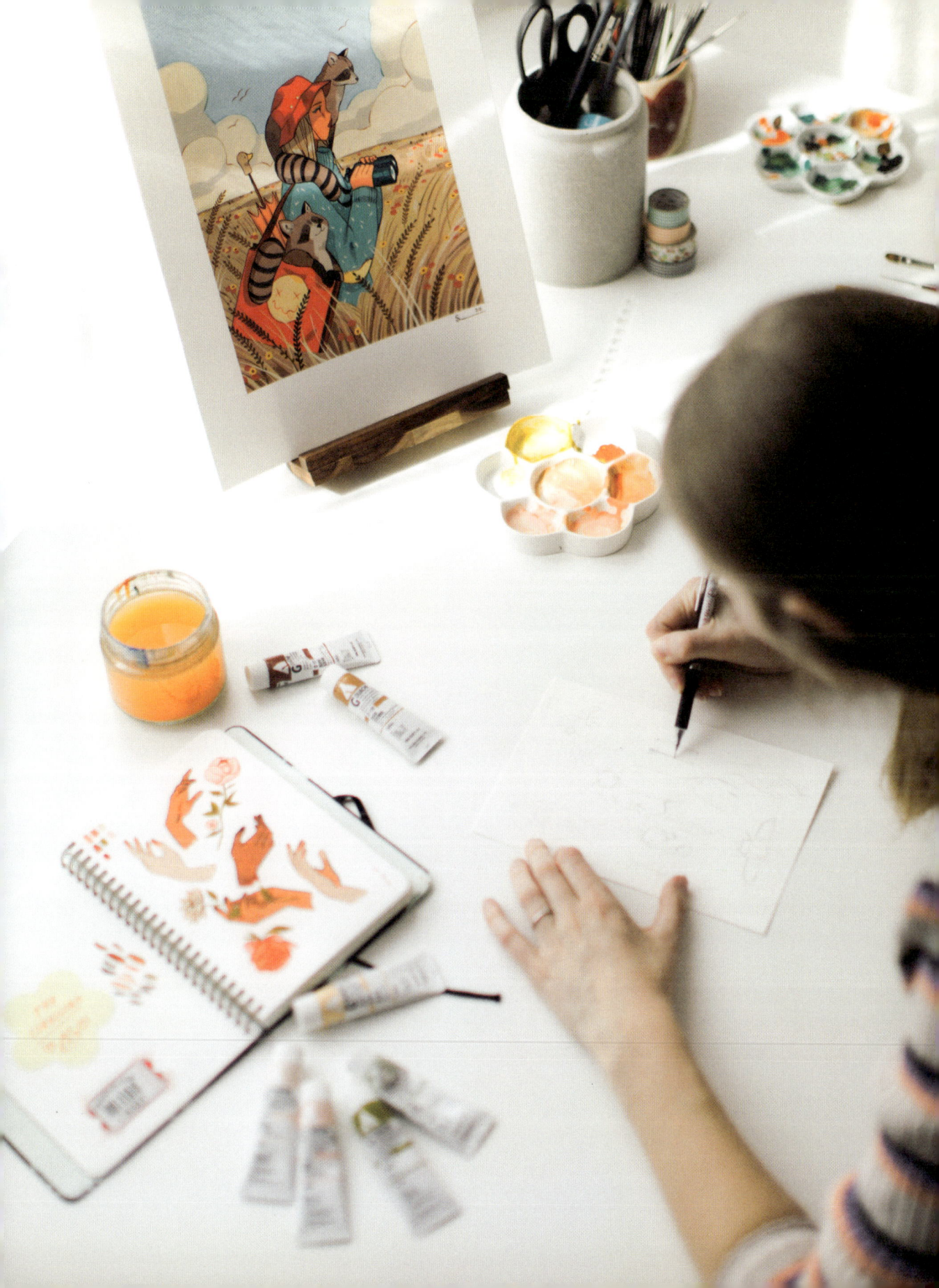

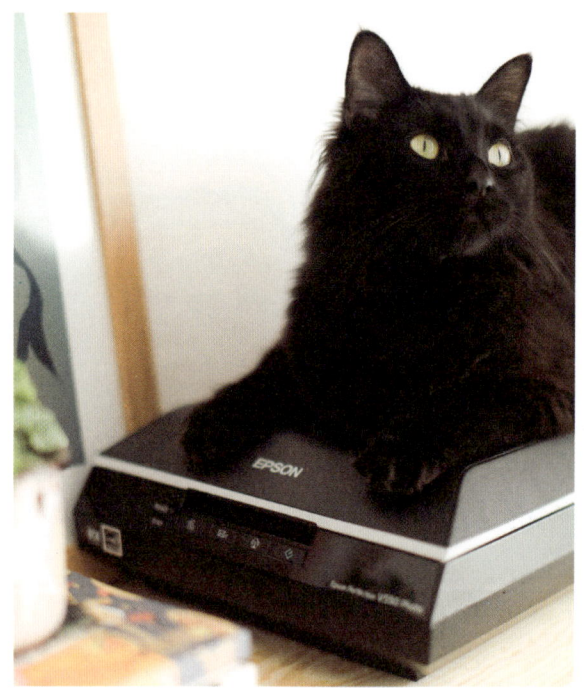

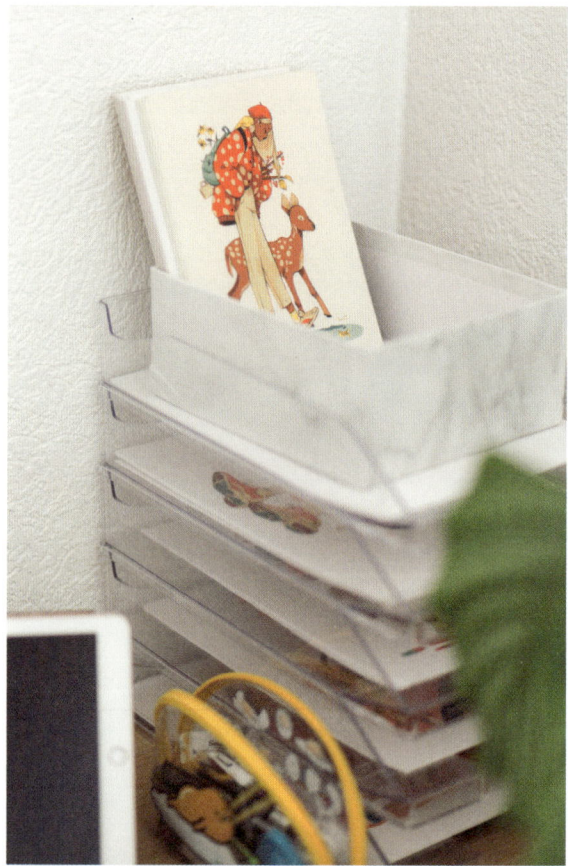

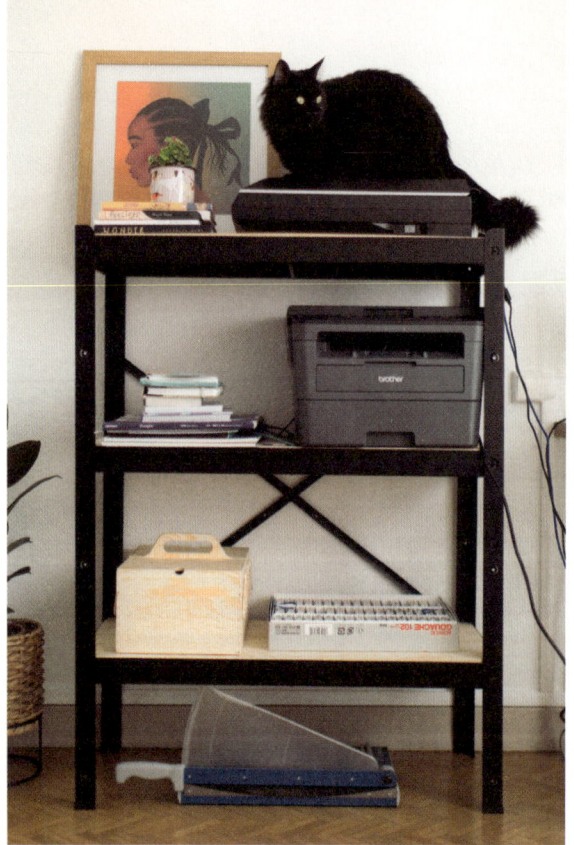

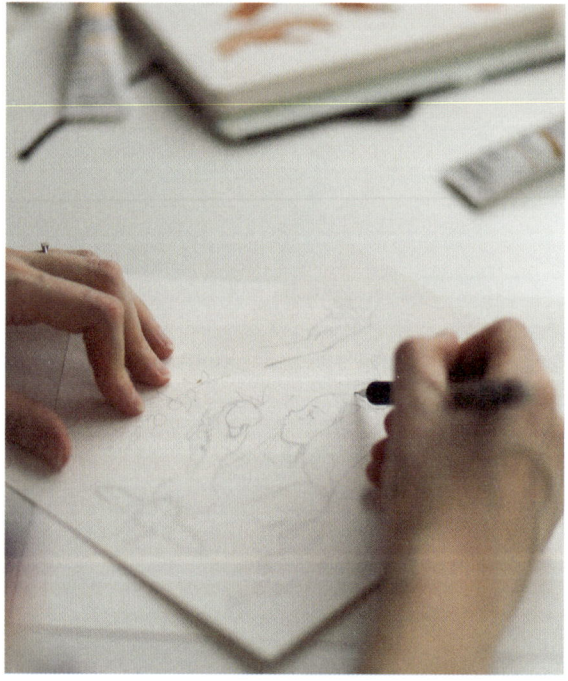

Having enough space is essential. As well as painting, I utilize my workspace to work on my computer, pack orders for my online shop, and undertake administrative tasks. I have to be organized to make my office multifunctional. After some adaptation, the space fulfills my needs; for example, I added a table with casters that I can move around to pack orders, take pictures, or work at if I want to work in the living room. It's very convenient!

In my office, everything has its own place: paints, brushes, paper, my original drawings, products for my store, even the envelopes! After spending a day at work, I like to tidy my space before leaving the room, to find it clean and tidy the next day.

Photography by Benjamin Favrat, 2021

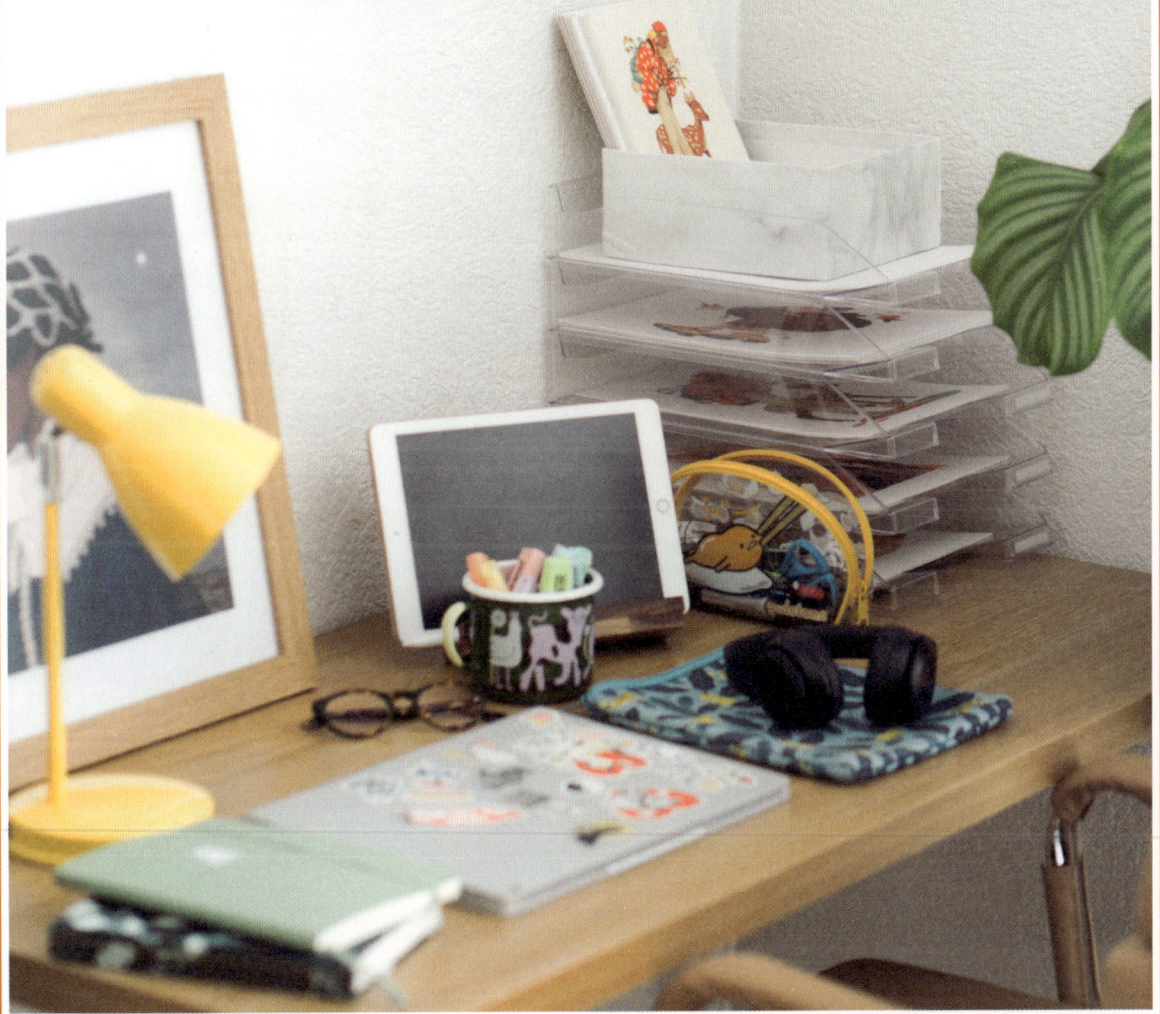

TOOLS & MATERIALS

PAINT

● **Holbein Acryla gouache and Winsor & Newton gouache sets**

Gouache is a water-based paint that is similar to watercolor paint but more opaque. Even once dry, standard gouache can be reused when mixed with water. Acryla gouache is a mixture of gouache and acrylic paint, which contains plastic. Once the paint has dried, it cannot be revived with water because the plastic it contains has hardened. I prefer to use Acryla gouache because I find it easier to work with and the colors are brighter than regular gouache. When using Acryla gouache I'm careful with the quantities I use to avoid waste, because it can't be reused once dry.

PENCIL

● **Pentel Orenz 0.5 mm mechanical pencil with 2H leads**

I mainly use this pencil to trace my illustrations on a light table. The leads it uses are the best I have found yet — they are not too thick and soft, which work perfectly with the subtly grainy paper I usually use (Canson XL Watercolor paper). I prefer to use pencil leads that don't smudge and soften the sketch when I lean over it with my hand while drawing.

BRUSHES

● **Arteza small liner brushes and Princeton Filbert Velvetouch brushes**

I use a few different synthetic brushes. I like to use Arteza liner brushes (sizes 4/0, 0, and 1) to outline my illustrations, but the Princeton Filbert Velvetouch size 8 brush is my favorite! I use it to paint larger areas. I also enjoy using the Princeton Round Velvetouch size 0 brush when painting little details or filling smaller spaces that the bigger brush is too large for.

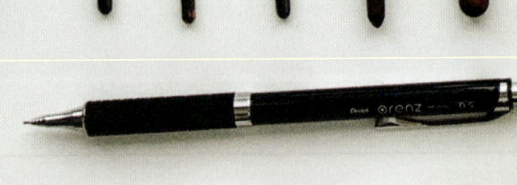

ERASER

● **Staedtler Mars plastic eraser**

I have always used this eraser, since I was at school! I choose to use it because I am used to it, but it also works very well with the pencils and paper I use. What I like about this particular eraser is the softness of it; some erasers can be too aggressive and start to remove the surface of the paper, which I aim to avoid.

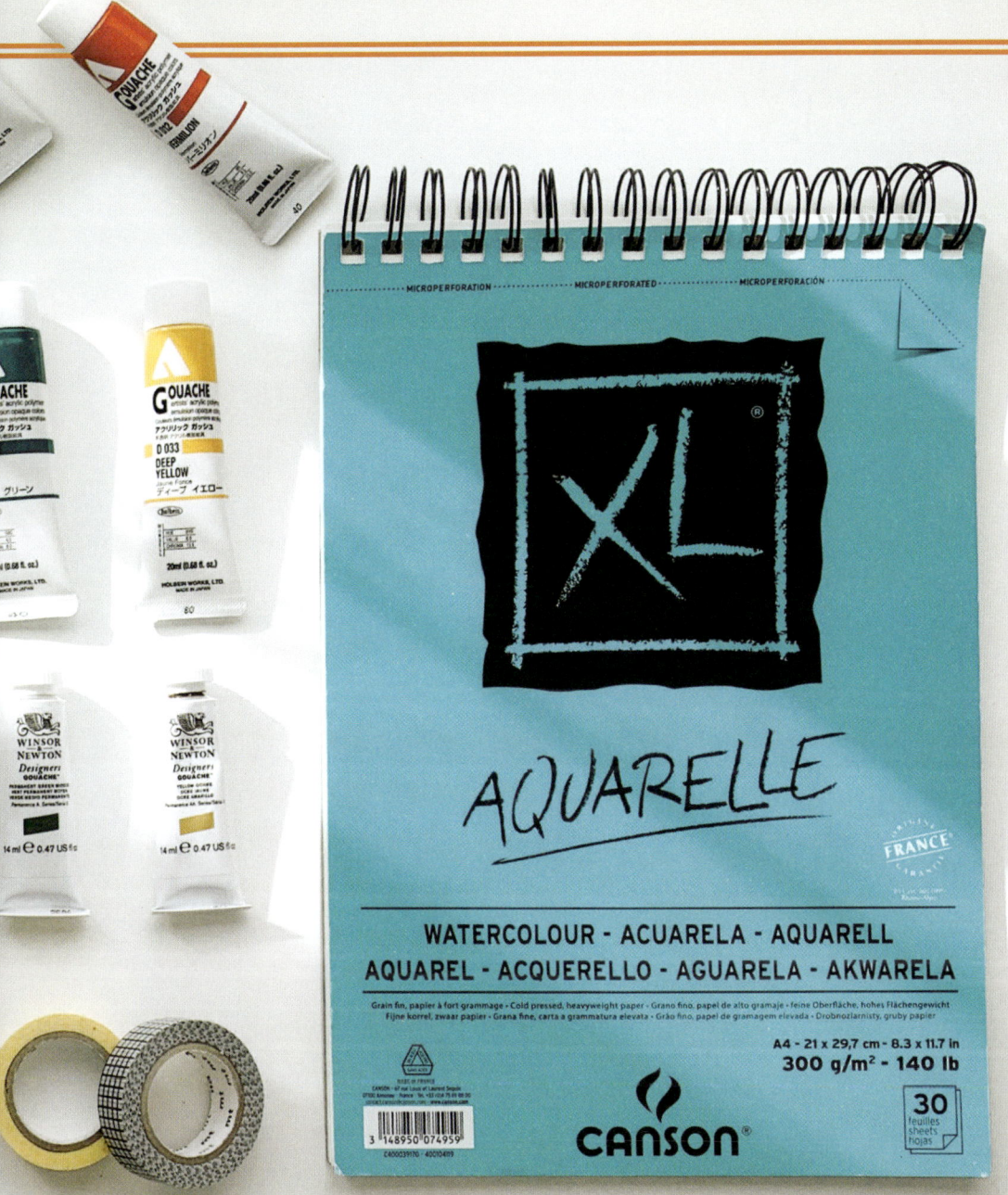

MASKING TAPE

I use masking tape when I want to create a precise frame for an illustration. The result is clean and the tape is easy to peel off the paper I use. Unfortunately, it doesn't peel away cleanly from every type of paper.

PAPER

● **Canson XL Watercolor paper, 300 gsm**

I usually trace A4-sized illustrations and use the A3 paper pad when I want a little more space to work.

SKETCHBOOKS

I have two sketchbooks that I use in different ways.

One is an inexpensive sketchbook that I bought in a set of three from the art store, Cass Art in London (shown bottom right). Inside, I draw with a black pen without making any sketches or plans in advance. It's small with few pages, but perfect for what I make of it. It's full of spontaneous sketches and errors. It teaches me to see my mistakes and acknowledge my weaknesses. When a drawing goes wrong, I start again, which is very useful for improving.

The second sketchbook is a Mossery Watercolor sketchbook (shown bottom left). It's a little more expensive, has a beautiful quality, and the paper is thick. Its paper is also very versatile, so it is perfect for painting with watercolor, gouache, and mixed media in general. In this sketchbook, I like to take my time and paint with gouache. It's much cleaner than the first sketchbook! Pages are never lost or wasted, as when I make a mistake, or don't like a page, I work over it with gouache — its opacity covers everything, like magic!

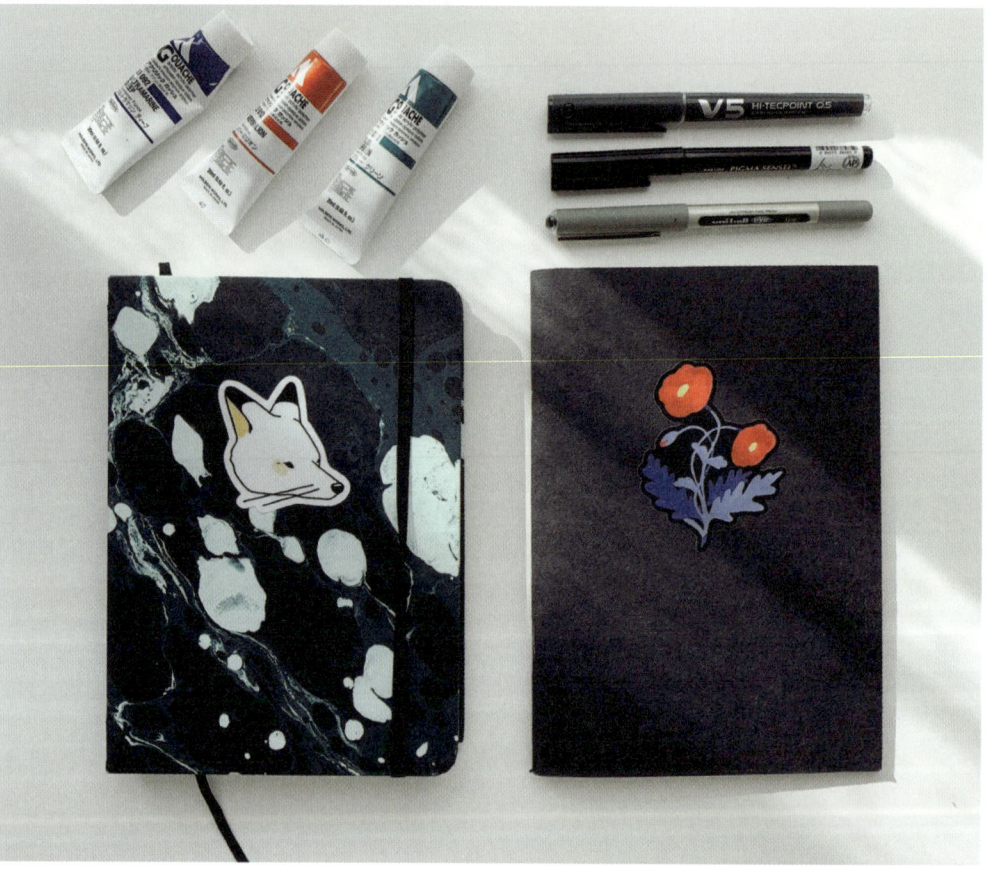

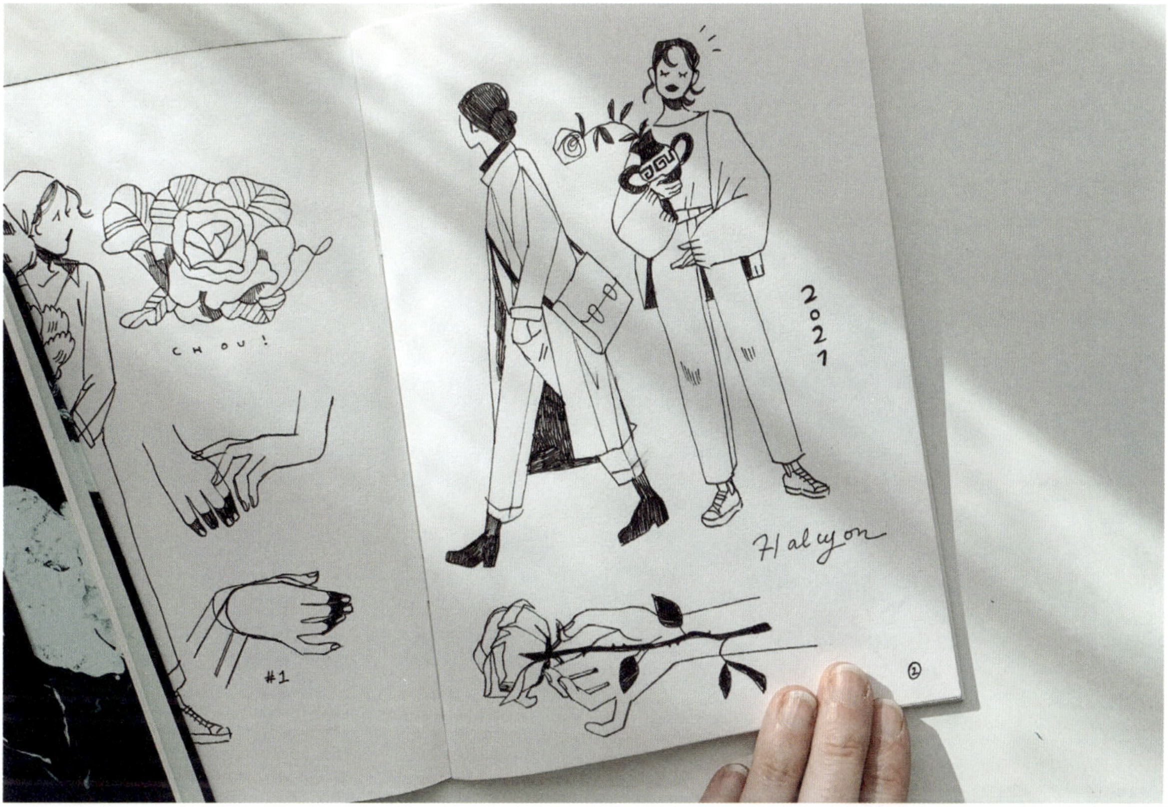

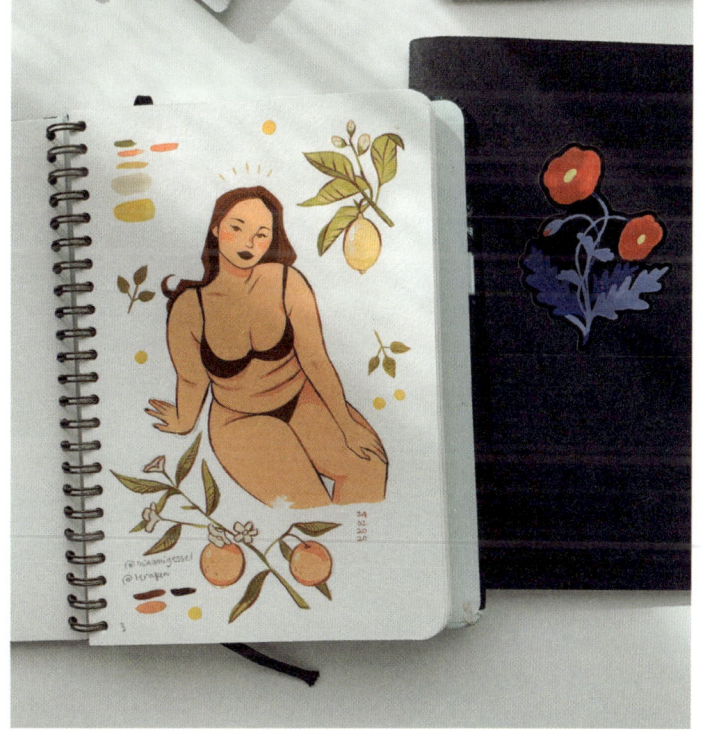

PENS

Black Pilot Hi-Tecpoint V5 roller-ball pens, Sakura Pigma Sensei pens, and Mitsubishi pens are my favorite pens to use when working in my "secret" practice sketchbook.

Above some of the black ink sketches within my practice sketchbook can be seen, whereas the right image shows a clean gouache page from the second, more refined sketchbook

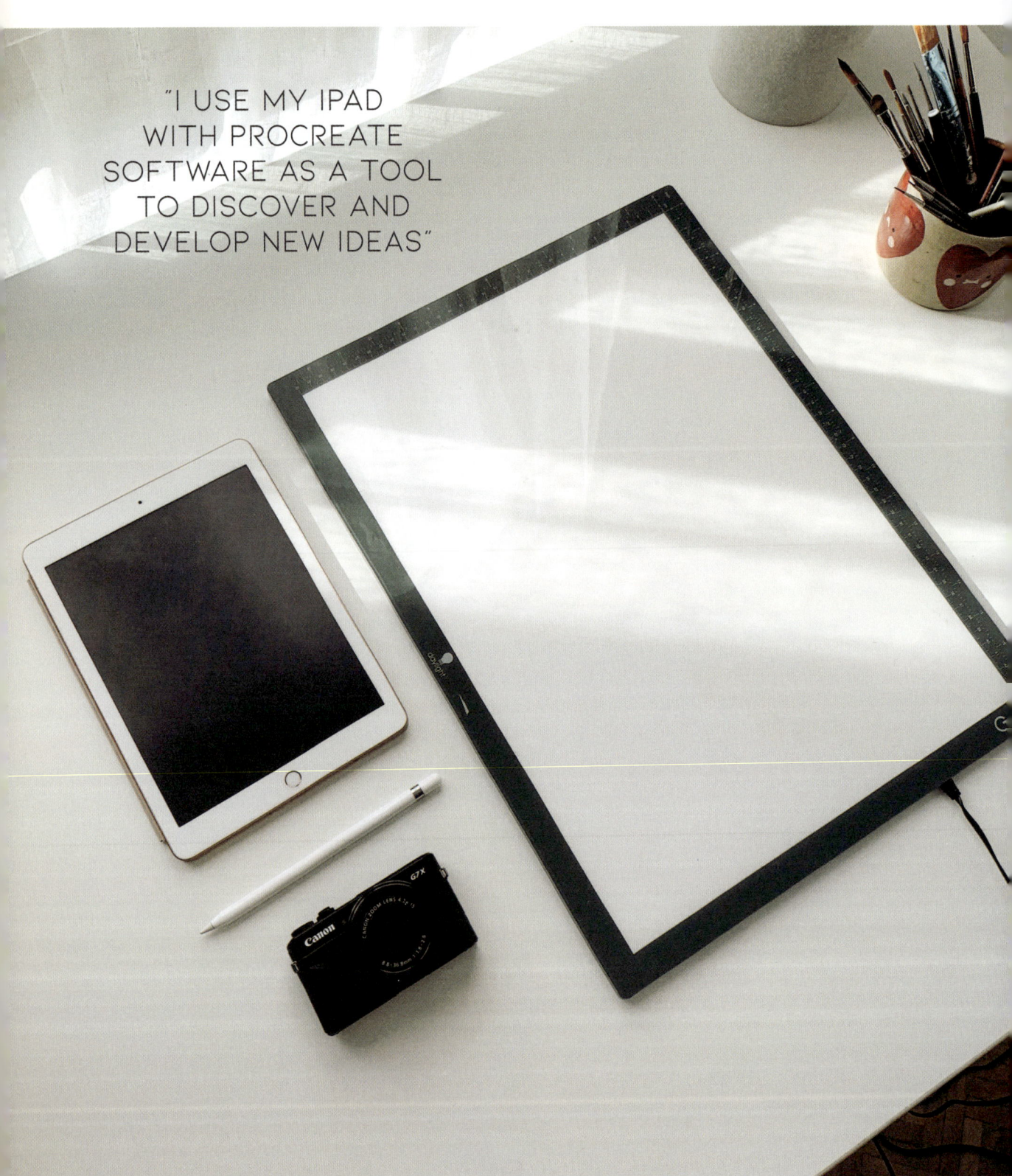

"I USE MY IPAD
WITH PROCREATE
SOFTWARE AS A TOOL
TO DISCOVER AND
DEVELOP NEW IDEAS"

DIGITAL TOOLS

CAMERA

● **iPhone XR and Canon G7X digital camera**

I use my iPhone to take pictures and my Canon G7X to record videos. Taking pictures with my phone for social media is so convenient. I just have to set up my layout, snap a few pictures, and edit them directly in my favorite editing app, VSCO: Photo and Video Editor. The app has many lovely filters and the possibilities are endless. I use my Canon G7X to record process videos that I then upload to my YouTube channel. This camera is small, light, and compact, and the image quality is impeccable, so it's just what I need!

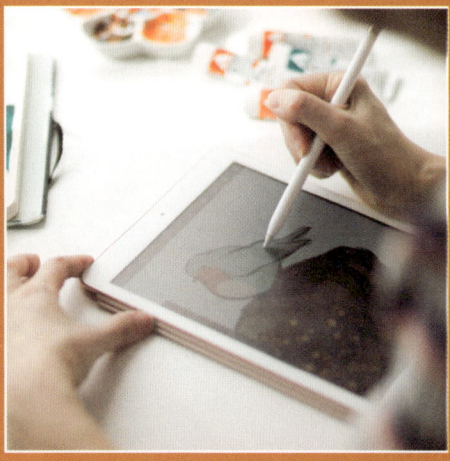

LIGHT BOX

● **Daylight A3 Lightbox**

With this product, I can choose the intensity of the light, which is very convenient when I can't use it in complete darkness.

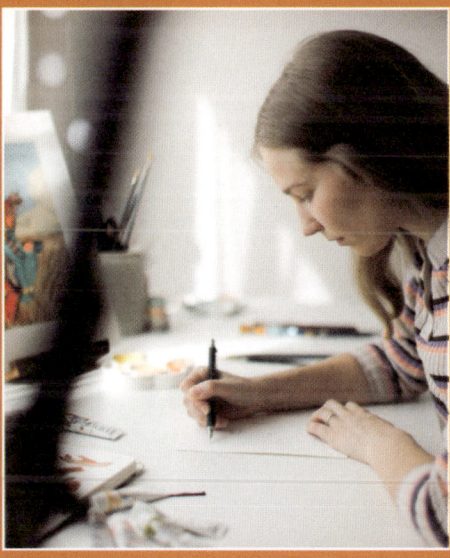

Photography on this page by Benjamin Favrat, 2021

TABLET

● **iPad and Procreate**

I use my iPad with Procreate software as a tool to discover and develop new ideas. I create sketches, and when I really enjoy a particular idea, I work closely to alter and perfect it. I then choose my color palette, trying several palettes to achieve different moods.

Since buying an iPad, the way I work has totally changed. I find that I can plan further ahead, completely change the composition of a drawing, and work on it until I'm satisfied. I also save precious time by choosing colors in advance. When I like a design, I print out the sketch in black and white and then trace it onto a sheet of Canson XL Watercolor paper using my light table. I can then start painting, referring to the refined color palette I developed on the iPad.

Thanks to this tool and the software, I am more confident and prouder of the result of my drawings on paper.

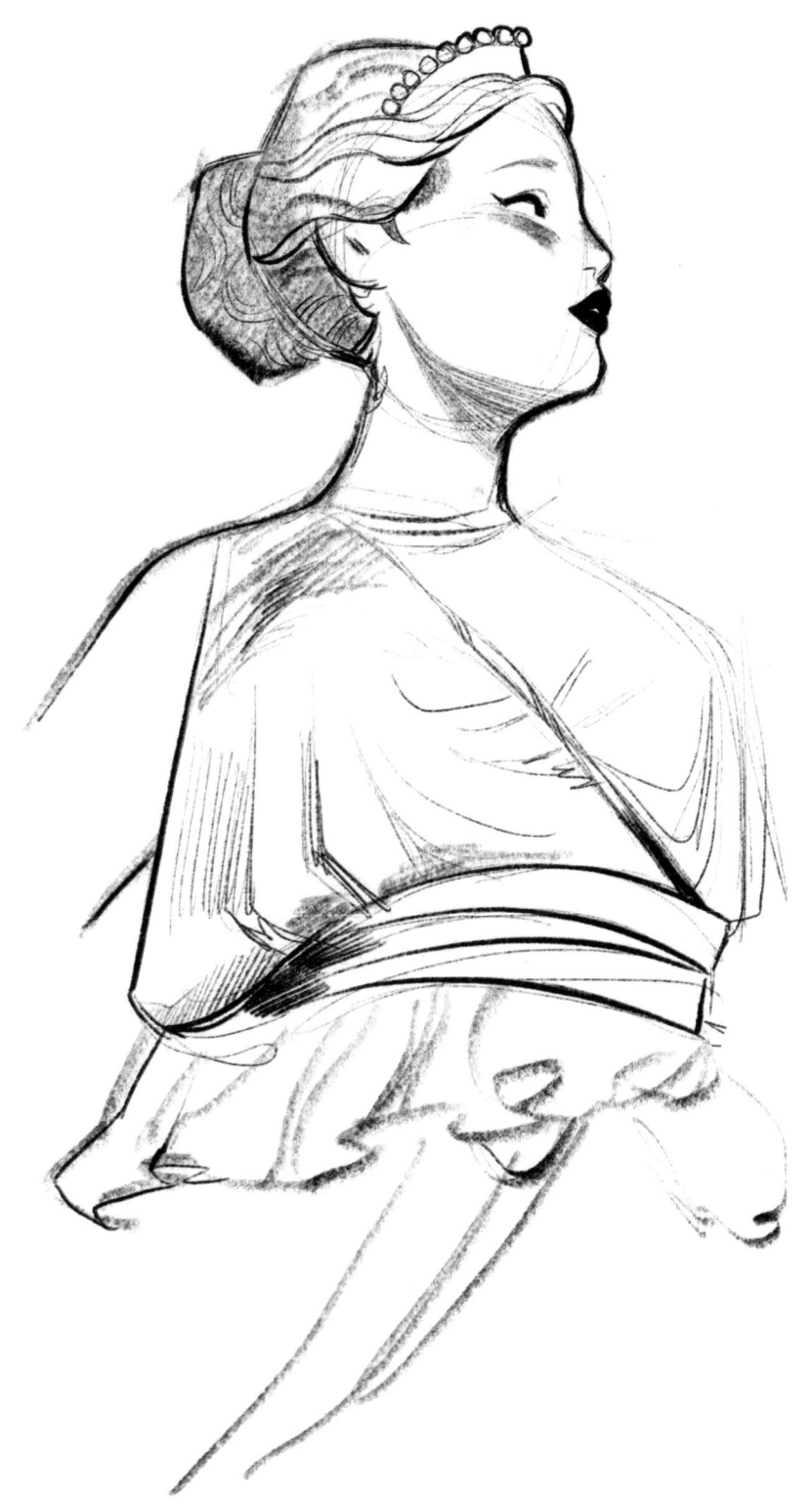

INSPIRATIONS

INSPIRATIONS

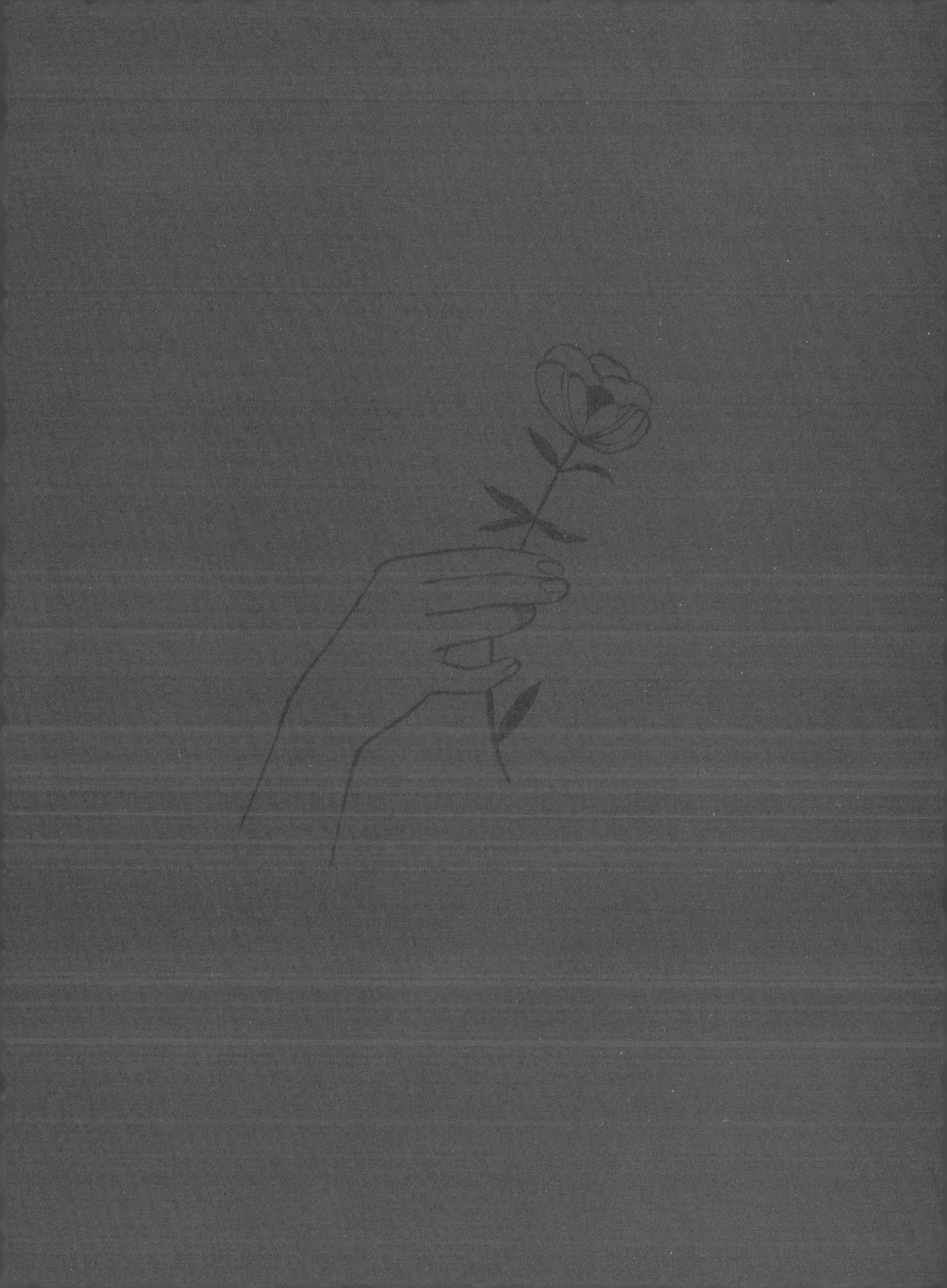

ARTIST & INSPIRATION

WHAT DOES INSPIRATION MEAN?

D*efinition: the process of being mentally stimulated to do something creative. The stimulant needed to animate artists and researchers.*

As it is so deeply personal, feeling inspired is a concept that can be difficult to explain. But, ultimately, I believe we have to follow what we are instinctively inspired and driven by. I tend to discover the most potent inspiration when I least expect it, but the truth is that most of the time I actively look for it. I need to keep creating to be able to find an interesting idea — a little detail that will brighten a piece.

I believe that we are all inspired by our everyday lives. Inspiration could appear in the form of a color, a melody, a word, or a person. Inspiration and creativity are specific to each of us — it's a very personal journey. The themes of solitude, tranquility, reflection, and inner journey inspire me, most probably because I am myself a solitary and pensive person. Nature and animals bring light, warmth, and another perspective to my illustrations, just as in my everyday life, and I always like to add a touch of adventure and magic to my pieces to make their stories a little more fantastic.

What lies beneath my illustrations is also a sense of nostalgia for my childhood — everything is magical through the eyes of a child! The Middle Ages, Ancient Greece, Ancient Egypt, flora and fauna, and astronomy are all subjects that fascinated me as a child, and these are themes that stand out today because my inner child will always be with me.

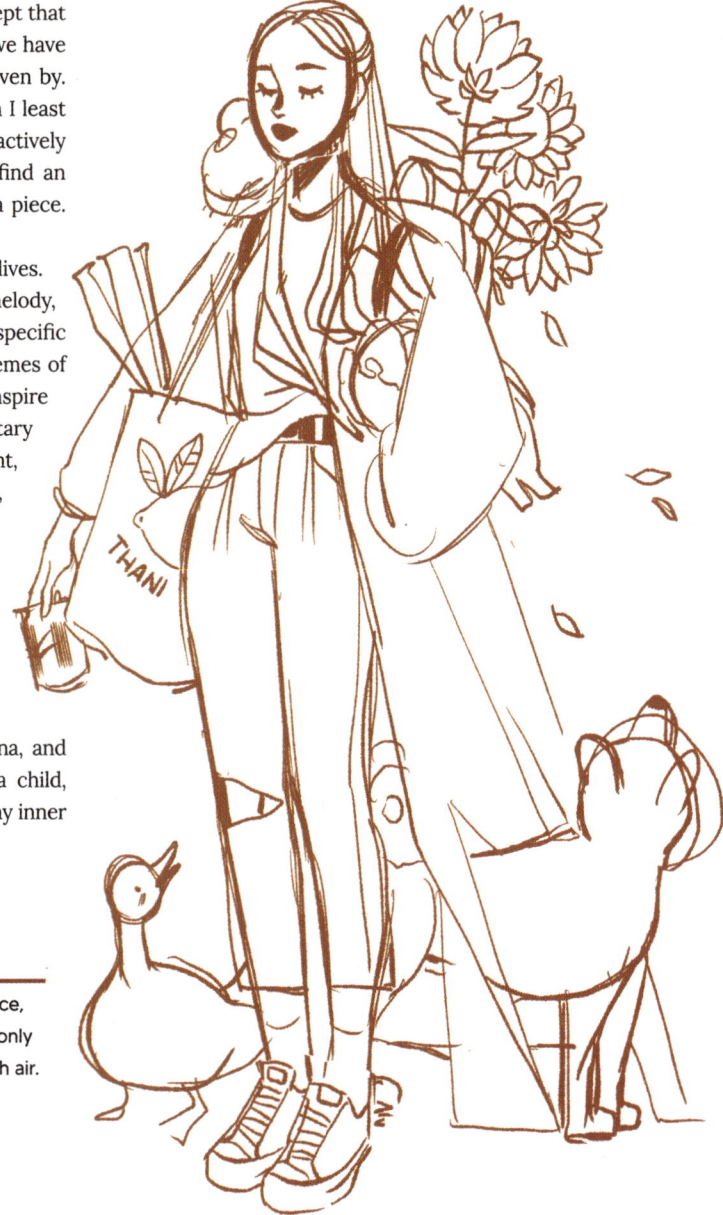

An illustration I created during the first lockdown in France, April 2020. At the time, going out for groceries was the only thing we could do to get out of the house for some fresh air. This image is inspired by that experience.

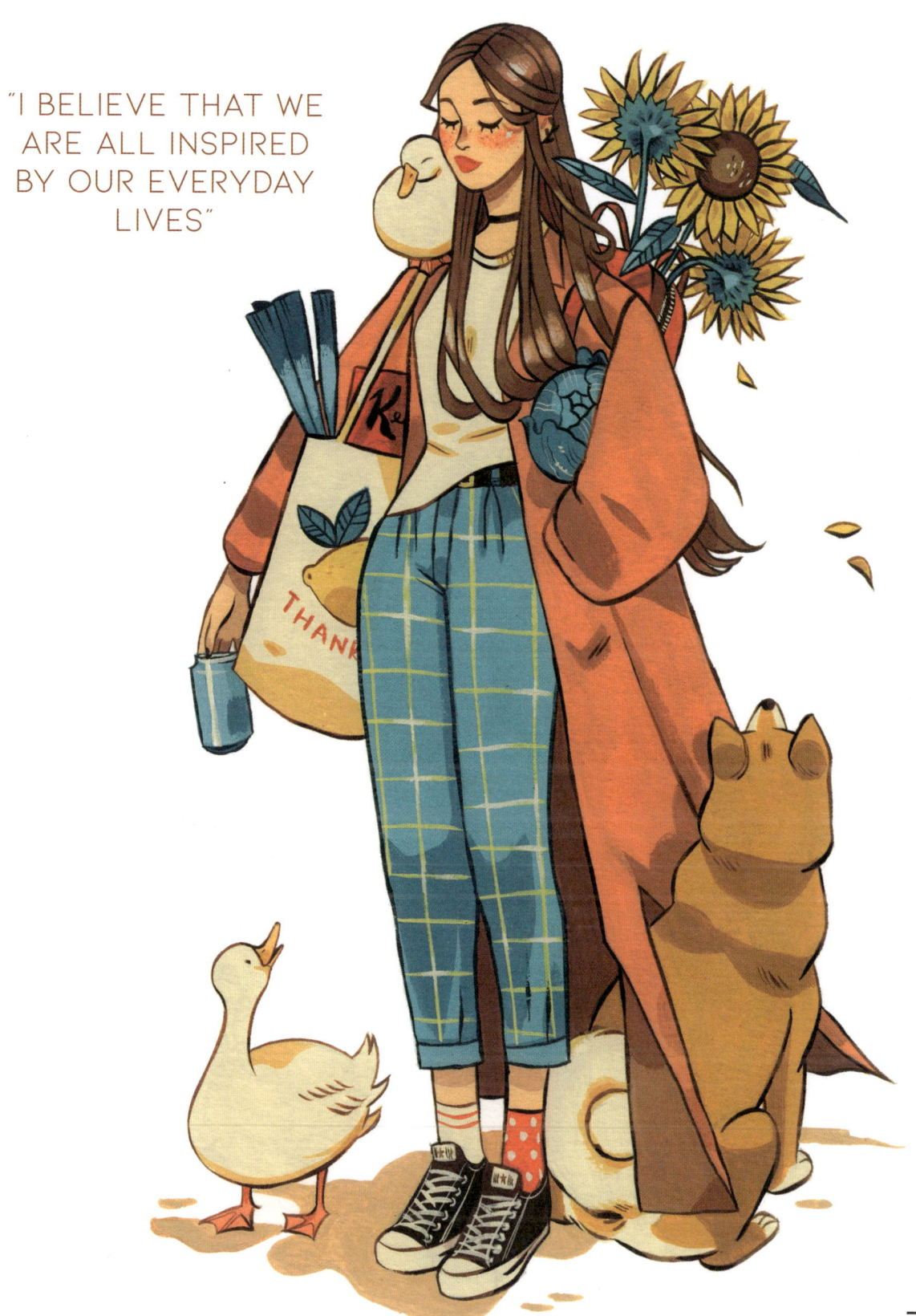

"I BELIEVE THAT WE ARE ALL INSPIRED BY OUR EVERYDAY LIVES"

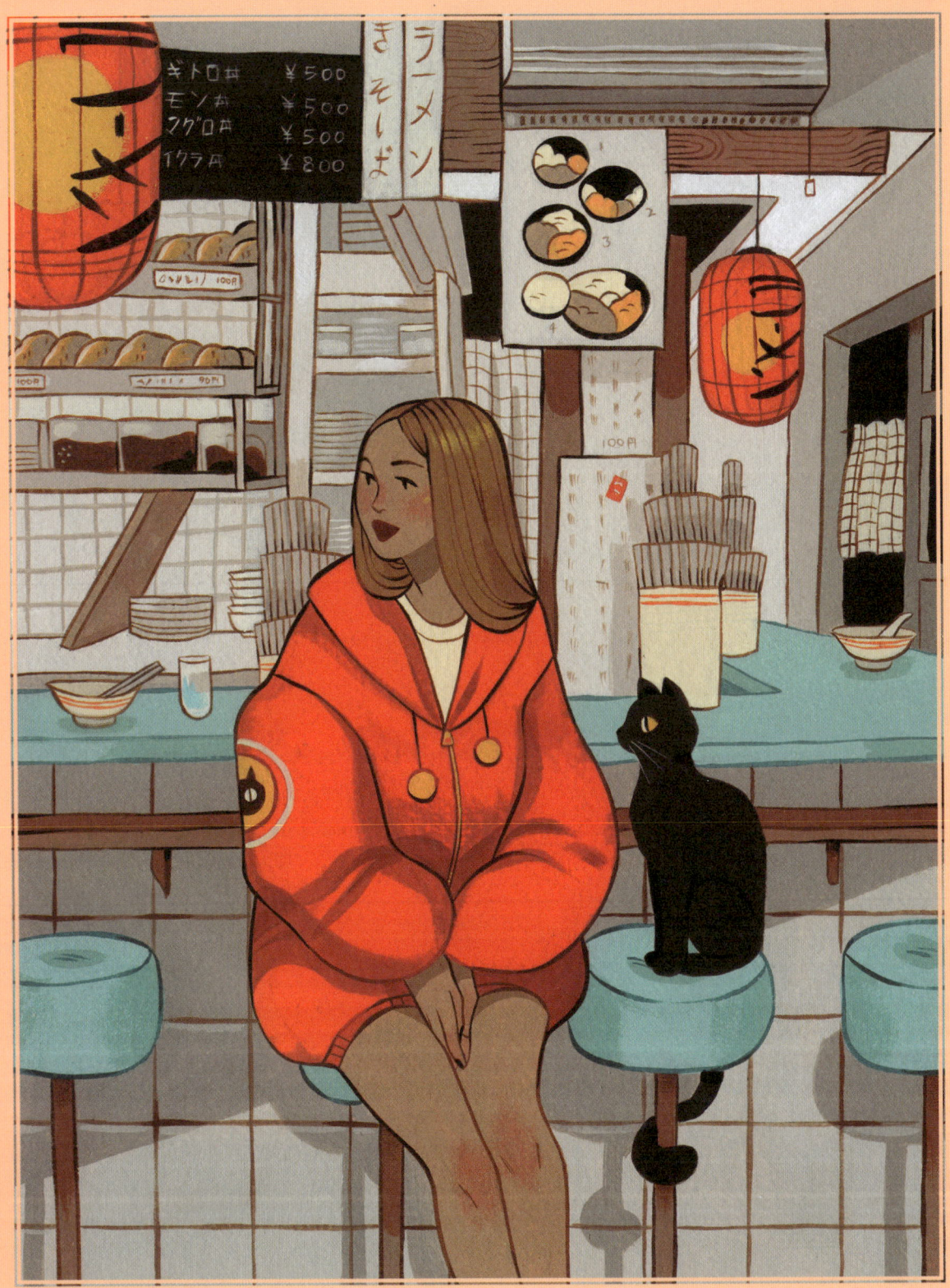

THE SEARCH FOR
INSPIRATION

Nowadays, everything is accessible, thanks to the internet. The whole world's resources are at the end of our fingertips. But does this mean inspiration has become more accessible too? I find that the time spent with my loved ones often sparks new, more personal ideas. Talking, laughing, eating, going on a walk with my dog; these simple things can awaken my creativity. Sometimes, it only takes a moment.

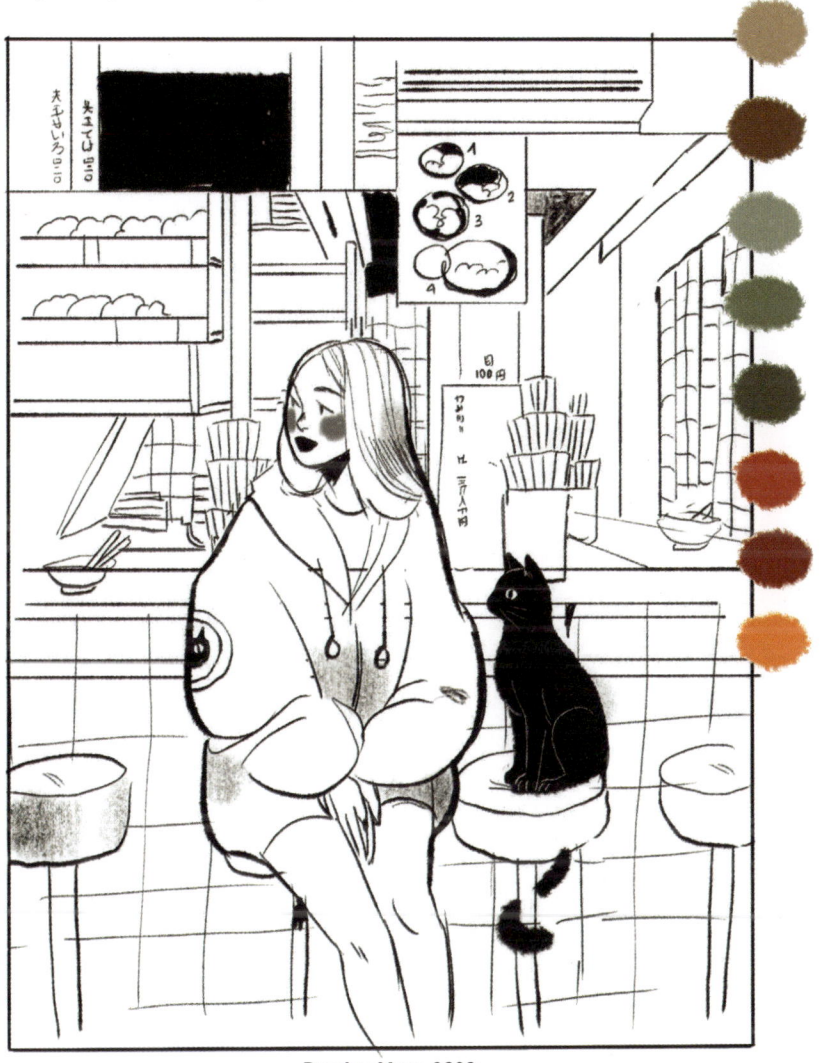

Rendez-Vous, 2020
This design was inspired by a photograph by Natacha Birds

INSPIRATIONAL DISCOVERIES

When looking for new ideas for my illustrations, I spend hours sketching. If I don't know what to draw, I take a look at my saved images on Pinterest or Instagram. Sometimes, I go back to basics and look at the great painters and classical paintings. I like to take time to closely study my reference images, or even sometimes focus on certain elements that interest me. I take a step back from my work to simply observe and paint.

With a little distance from a piece, I usually discover a specific element I want to highlight, such as an object, an animal, or a color. From there, I build a composition and tell a story by drawing that single element. I often challenge myself in this way and embrace the potential of a seemingly basic concept.

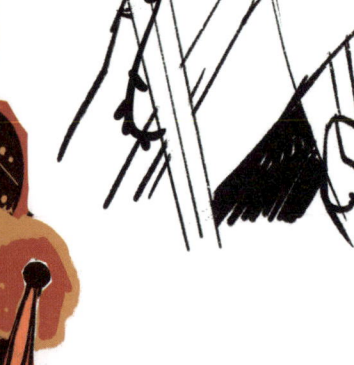

Dark Knight, **digital sketches (this page), gouache (opposite)**
The elements that inspired me to draw this image were a skeleton and a human heart. I knew I wanted to draw cool, dark armor and bones. I wanted the heart to stand out, so I drew it in the center of the chest plate, on top of the skeleton, to create a contrast. Once partially drawn, the calmness of the woman inspired me to add dramatic flames everywhere.

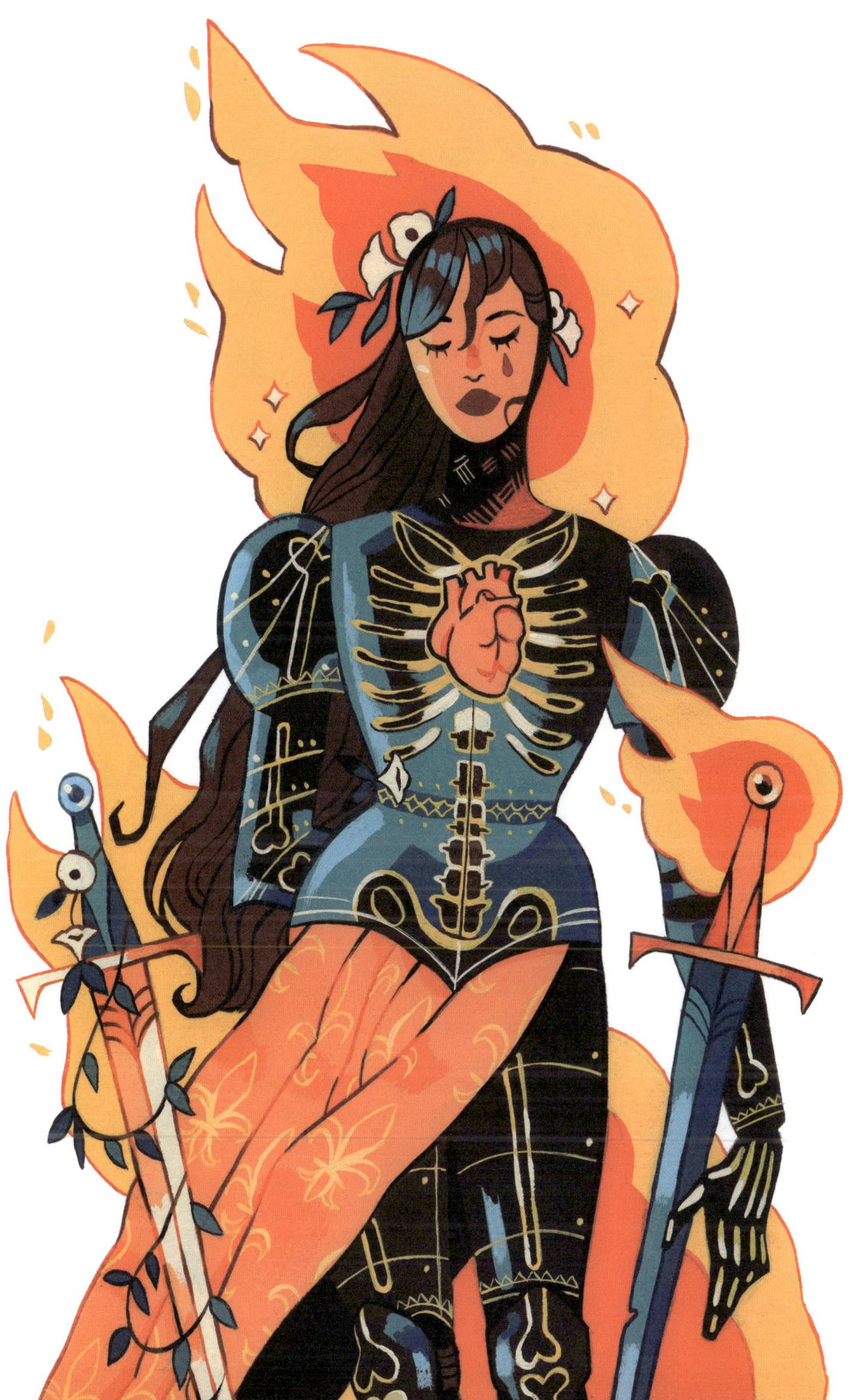

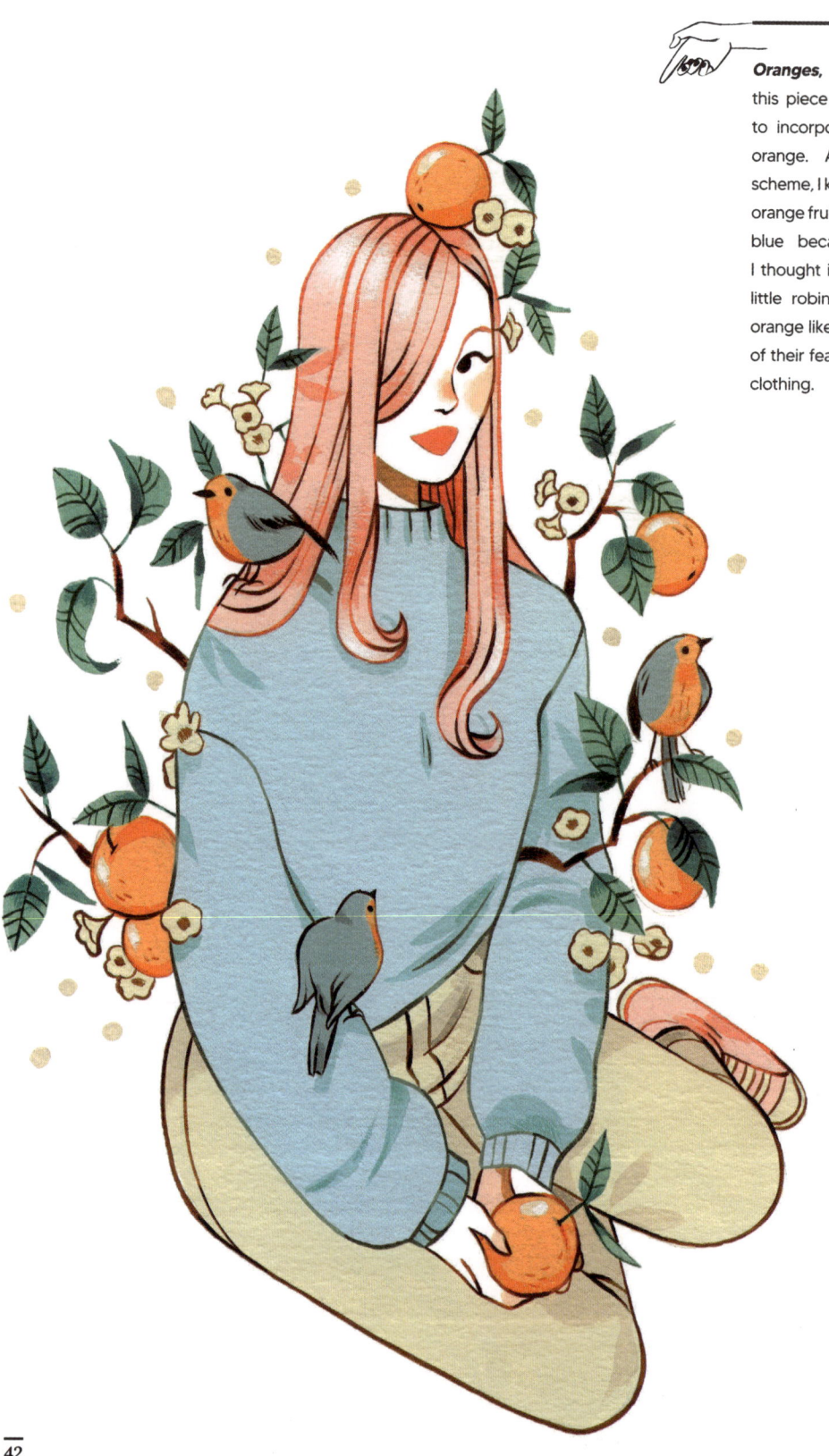

Oranges, gouache The concept for this piece originated from the desire to incorporate two colors: blue and orange. After deciding the color scheme, I knew I also wanted to include orange fruit. As I developed the design, blue became the dominant color. I thought it would also be fun to add little robins, as they are round and orange like the fruit and the blue-gray of their feathers tones in with the blue clothing.

STORIES TO TELL

My work is also inspired by the stories I wish to tell. Escape, dreams, calmness, delicacy, and the time we spend with ourselves are themes that I love to draw. The characters that feature in my work are often accompanied by animals that reflect and act as an extension of them and their stories. I really enjoy combining characters and their animal companions with minimal backgrounds to build a sense of intrigue and offer a blank canvas for the viewer's imagination to build upon. Viewers can then create their own story with what I offer them.

My illustrations represent moments, memories, and wishes for the future. I want people to feel good when they look at my designs. I simply want to convey a positive feeling, and evoke a calm and peaceful atmosphere. This is also what I personally look for in the art of other artists. The message I would like to spread through my work is to keep dreaming, telling stories, and sharing positivity. Anything is possible if we give ourselves the means to do so.

As mentioned, themes in my illustrations are often centered around spending time alone. Although many people associate being by themselves with loneliness, I believe being alone can be a positive experience. Sometimes it is enjoyable and empowering to take time to discover more about yourself. I try to never be bored and revel in moments where I do nothing. In my work I want to highlight these moments of calm reflection and appreciation of well-being. Being happy with yourself is very important.

"IT IS ENJOYABLE AND EMPOWERING TO TAKE TIME TO DISCOVER MORE ABOUT YOURSELF"

MOTIVATION

To me, inspiration is closely connected to motivation. When I am demotivated, no matter how hard I try, I cannot find original ideas. However, when I am highly motivated to create something new, my ideas flow and I feel more creative. Positive attracts positive!

Staying motivated all the time is difficult. I believe rest is an important part of the creative process. Taking time to step back and try new things while stimulating your creativity is important. I find working on an idea and maturing it through thought for a few hours, or even a few days, can be a good way to motivate myself. I think it's important to create an urge to manufacture with my own hands, whether that is painting, writing, or drawing. With a fully formed idea in mind, I then just have to sit at my desk and commit what I have created in my mind to paper or screen.

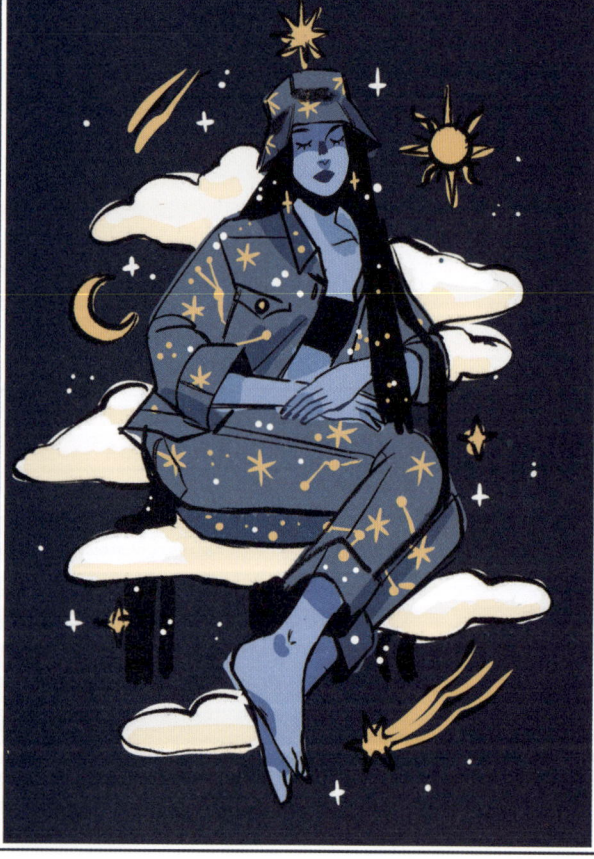

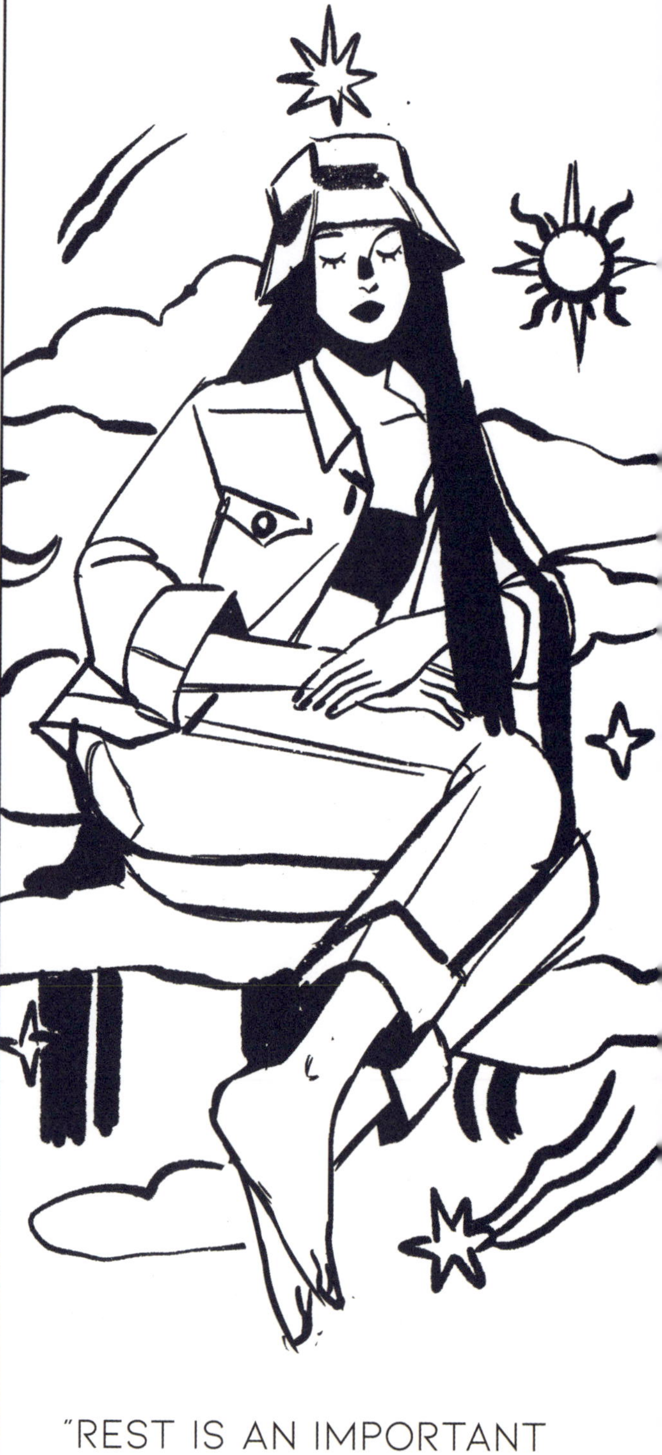

"REST IS AN IMPORTANT PART OF THE CREATIVE PROCESS"

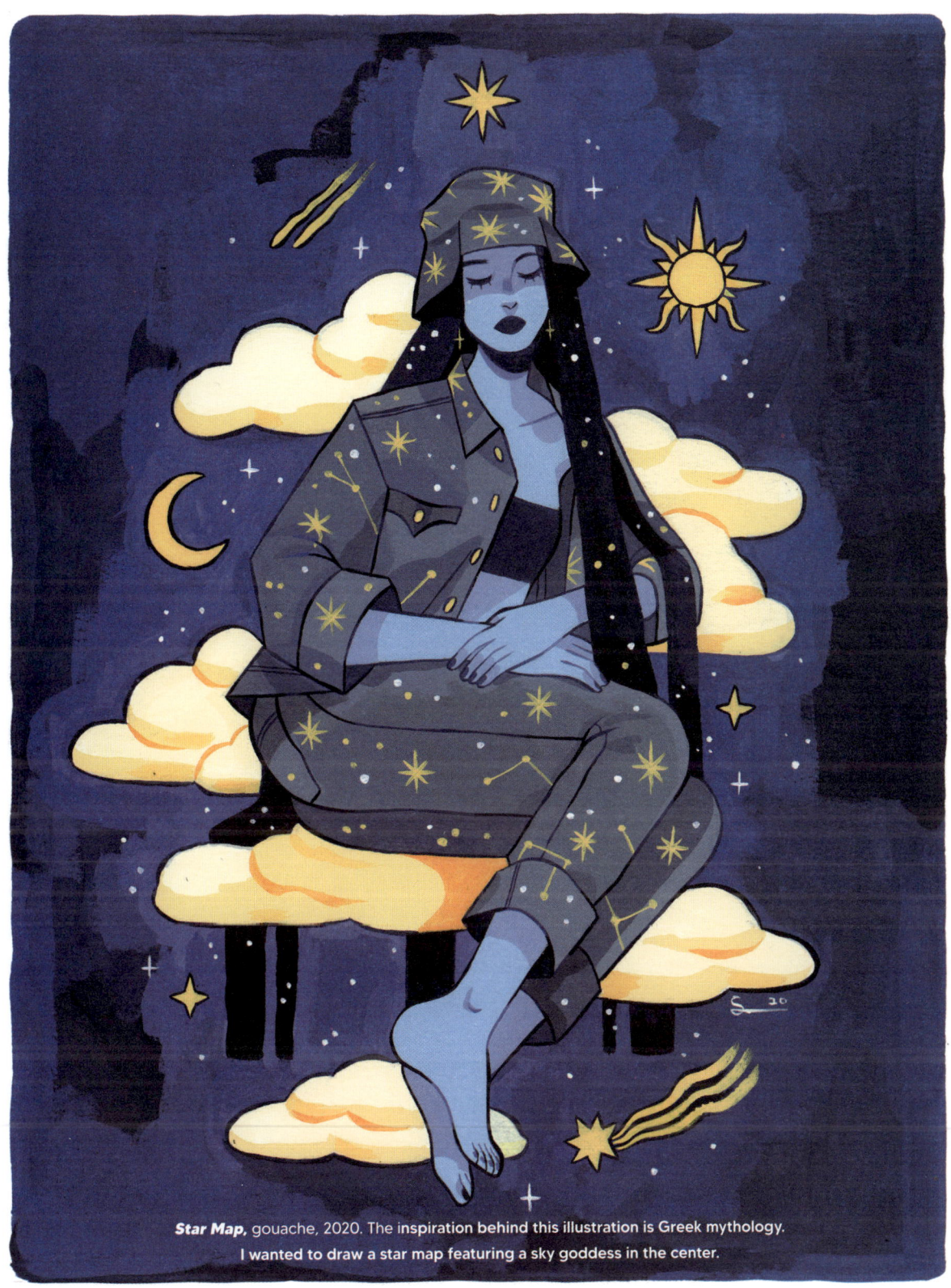

Star Map, gouache, 2020. The inspiration behind this illustration is Greek mythology.
I wanted to draw a star map featuring a sky goddess in the center.

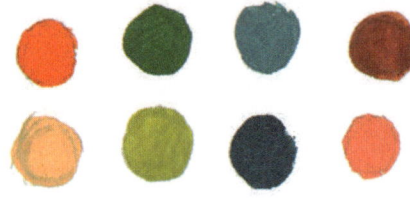

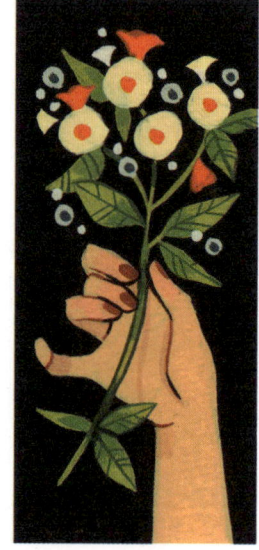

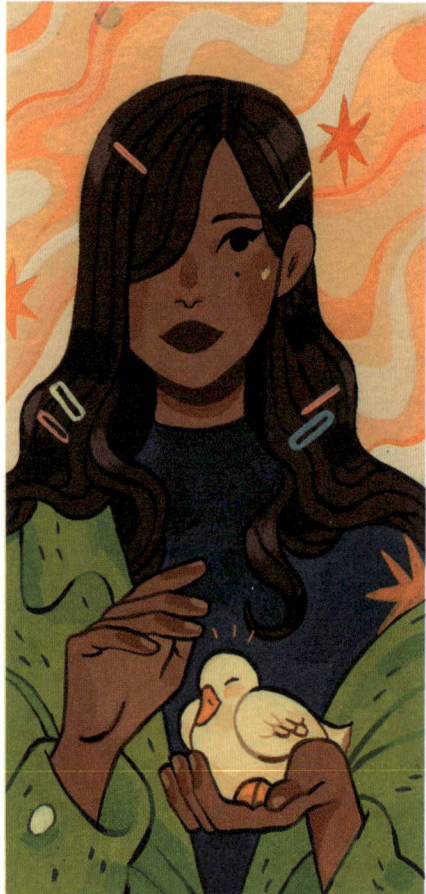

Orange mood board The colors I wanted to use here were orange and green. I chose olive green and peachy orange hues because I never usually combine these two colors together. Here I drew flowers and fruits, as well as a cup of tea to undertake some still life drawing practice. I had to add an extra color to the palette to increase the coloring possibilities, so I selected a light yellow.

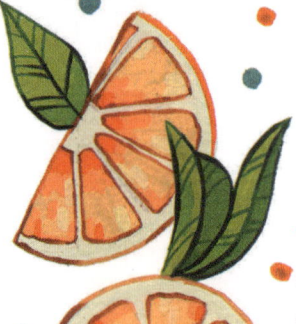

ART BLOCK

There are times when I want to create ten illustrations at the same time, study paintings, and explore new techniques, and then there are periods of self-doubt when I don't know which direction to take. Usually, when I can't draw, I don't force myself to create, I just take a break, go out, see friends and family, or spend some time with myself. I watch movies, take pictures, and draw whatever comes to mind in a sketchbook, as if writing my doubts and fears in a diary.

When I feel artistically blocked and lack inspiration and motivation, I like to create mood boards. Most of the time, I choose to build mood boards based on a color (which often perfectly reflects my mood at the time!). From there, I will compose my illustration with objects, animals, insects, and elements of the same color.

Keep the creative spark burning

To survive in the creative industry, it's important not to lose the fun side of creativity. Don't forget to create for yourself from time to time. Work is good, but art isn't about work. When you decide to make your passion a business or a profession, you have to know how to protect your creativity to avoid burnout. Creating for yourself or doing a completely different manual activity in your free time to clear your mind can be fun and effective solutions to not lose the spark.

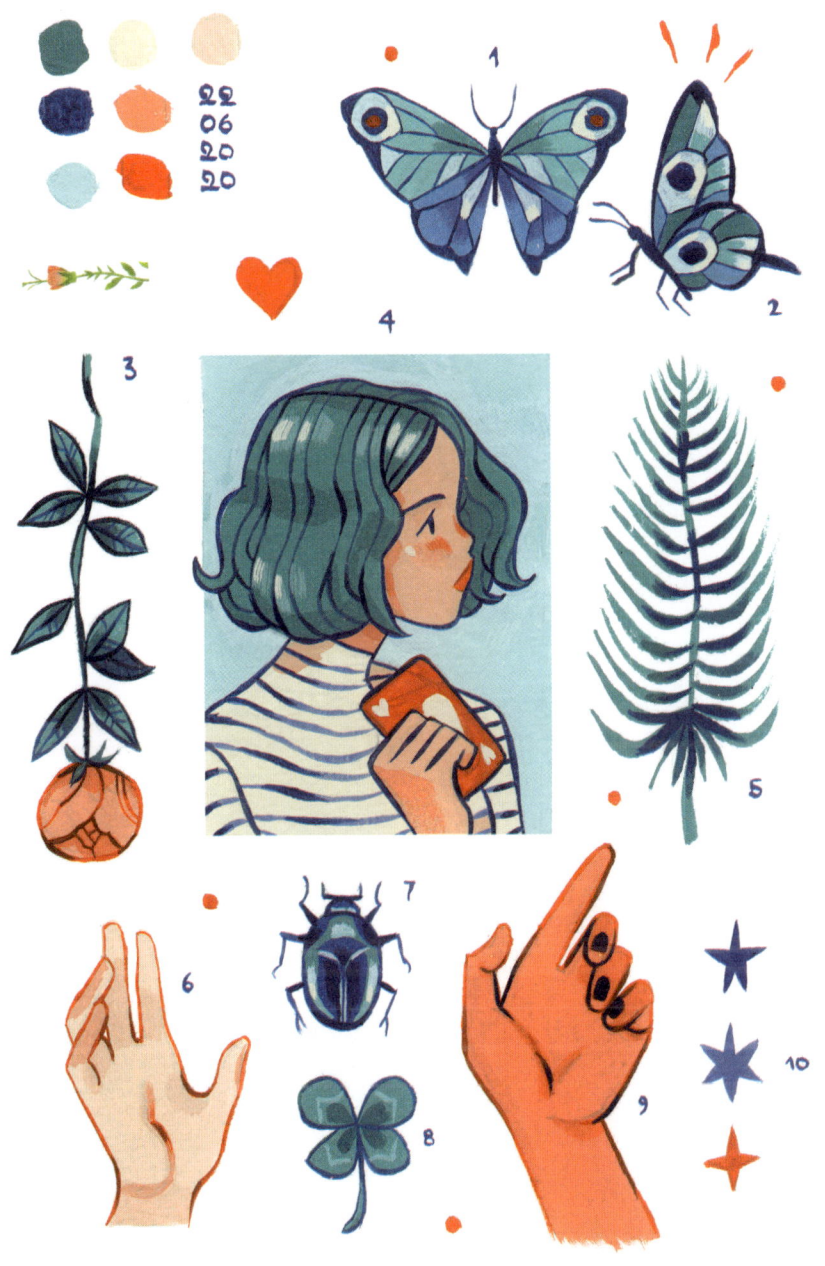

Blue mood board The day I created this mood board, I wanted to paint with teal. I found some elements that I could paint with this color; that is why a beetle, leaves, a flower, and butterflies all feature. I wanted to create a contrast across the board, so I introduced a few different elements in red tones that pop against the teal. I really enjoy the combination of ultramarine, teal, and red — I think they work so well together.

REFERENCES

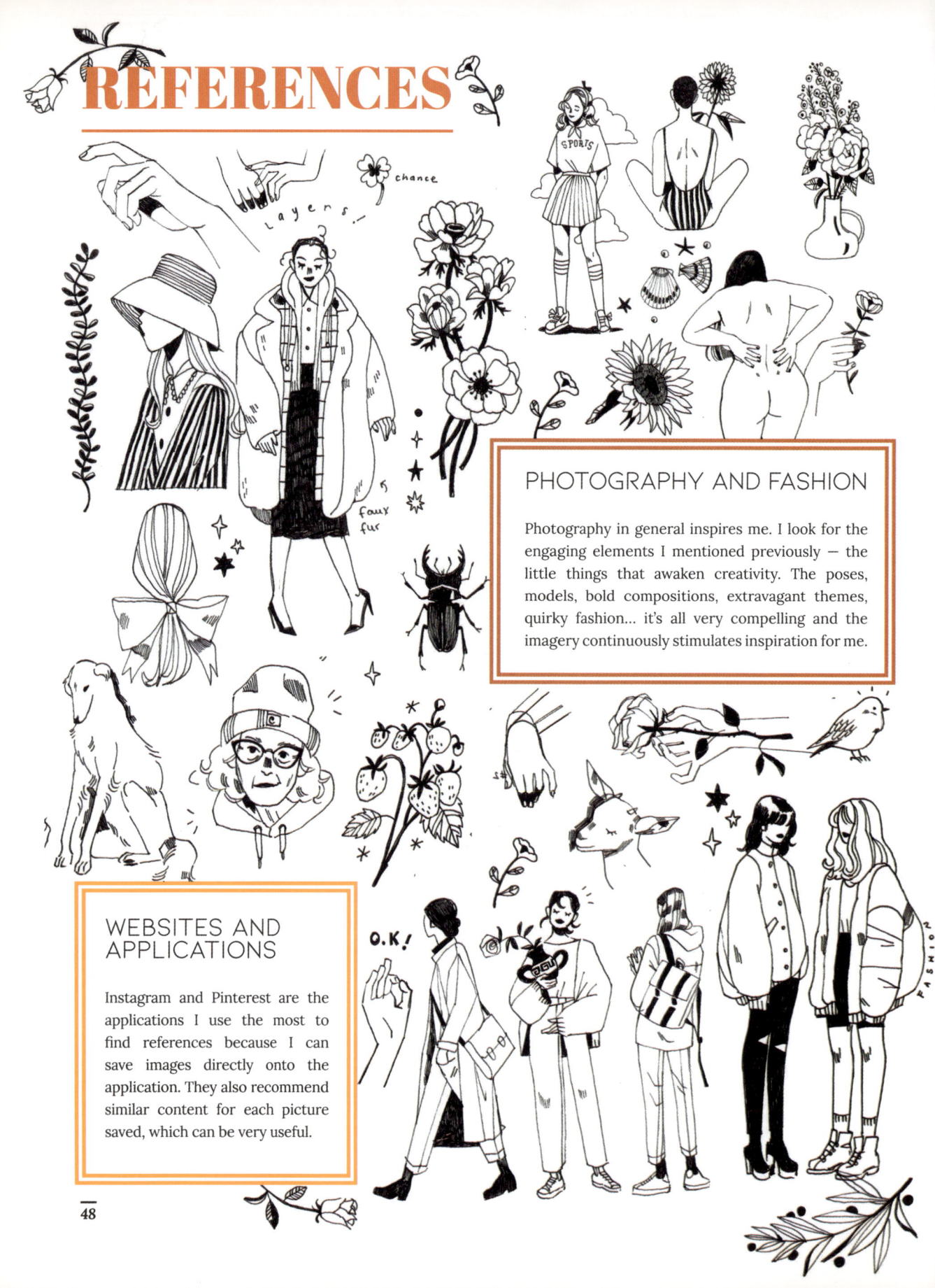

PHOTOGRAPHY AND FASHION

Photography in general inspires me. I look for the engaging elements I mentioned previously — the little things that awaken creativity. The poses, models, bold compositions, extravagant themes, quirky fashion... it's all very compelling and the imagery continuously stimulates inspiration for me.

WEBSITES AND APPLICATIONS

Instagram and Pinterest are the applications I use the most to find references because I can save images directly onto the application. They also recommend similar content for each picture saved, which can be very useful.

NATURE

Nature offers such magnificent treasures. A rainbow, a bird sitting in a tree, a sunset. Everything around us, if we observe, can be used to tell a story. Nature is immense and gives us all kinds of references that we can simply watch and absorb through the window.

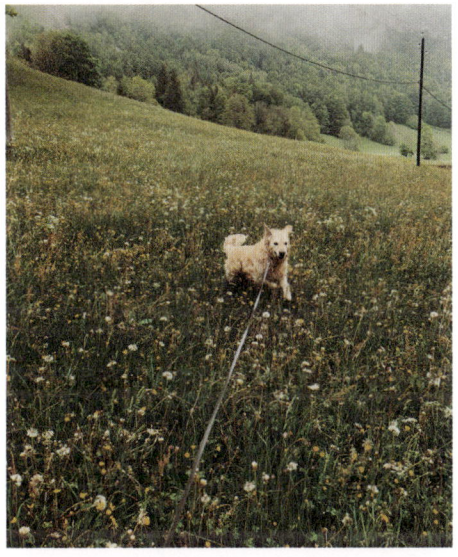

CLASSICAL PAINTINGS

In order to be fully appreciated, I believe classical paintings need to be admired and studied carefully. Focusing on an area or character of a painting and trying to understand how the artist worked to make the masterpiece iconic is essential to my own practice. Studying classical paintings closely helps to understand not only a great deal about art, but also yourself. When I used to live in Paris, I especially enjoyed visiting local museums and sketching statues from many angles.

FILMS

I love to paint movie scenes. It has taught me a lot about composition, color theory, ambience, lighting, and how to say something with just one image, one character, or one facial expression.

My go-to exercise when I don't know what to paint is to simply select a scene from a film that I love and paint it. The results are always fascinating, and never disappointing.

INFLUENCES

WHAT MADE ME WANT TO DRAW

I watched a lot of Disney movies growing up. According to my parents, when I was little my favorite was *Fantasia* (1940). I watched it again not long ago and understood why I draw today. I kept a magical memory of this film, which I'm sure led me to draw and tell stories through drawing.

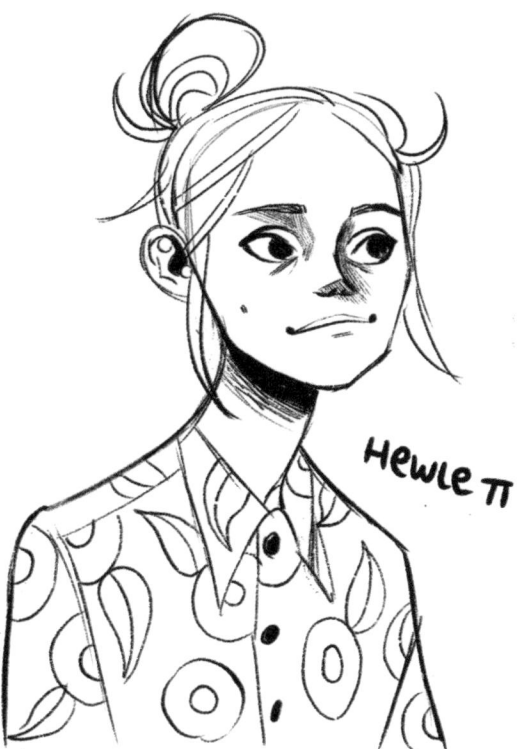

HEWLETT

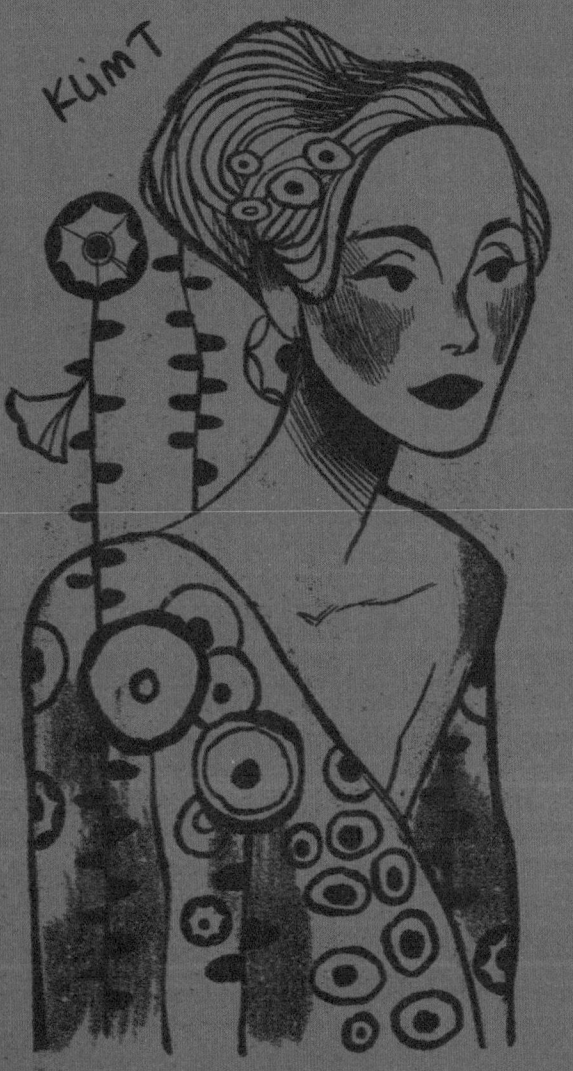

KLIMT

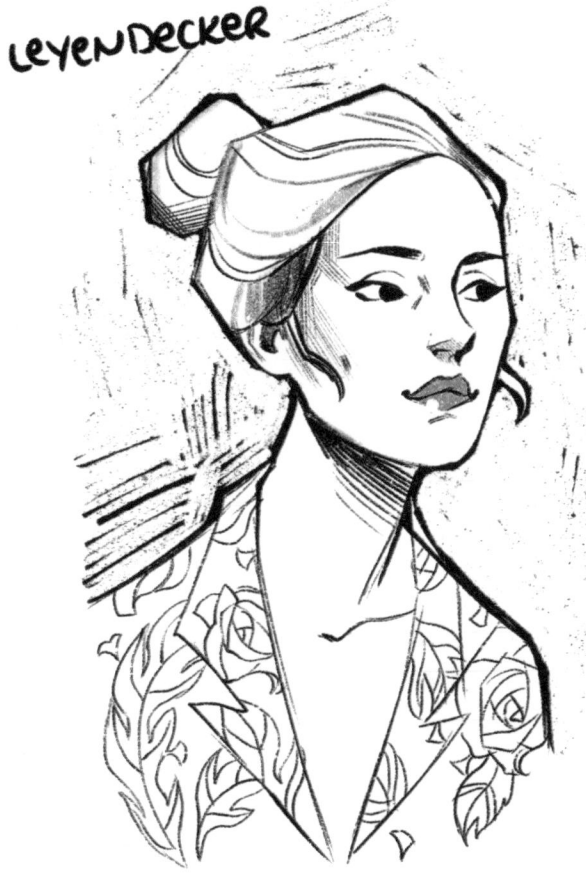

LEYENDECKER

Artists I admire

There are so many artists that I adore. I am often fascinated by art that looks nothing like mine. The artists that I have found to be most influential to my artistic development are:

GUSTAV KLIMT for his use of shapes and colors, and his ability to capture the essence of a woman and her body in all its shapes and sizes. His sketches tell so much with so few strokes.

JEAN-MICHEL BASQUIAT for his great creativity and desire to paint everywhere, all the time, his small meticulous sketches at the corner of a gigantic canvas, and being able, through his abstract art, to read his mind.

EDWARD HOPPER for building intriguing scenes with engaging atmosphere, the solitude of the characters, the large spaces, and the mystery behind every window he painted.

DREW STRUZAN for his one-of-a-kind, incredible style to which he knows how to add a touch of fantasy. For his perfect compositions and dynamic characters — every concept is creative and he knows how to capture the essence of each film he has worked on.

JAMIE HEWLETT for the iconic cartoon characters he created for the band, Gorillaz. The darkness mixed with a certain melancholy speaks to me. He proves that dark stories can be told with cartoon characters, which is powerful.

J.C. LEYENDECKER for his gorgeous color palettes, the details he puts into each of his pieces, and his capacity to create new paintings at a tight pace. A great tenderness shines through his work that touches my heart.

ANNETTE MARNAT for her use of shapes, incredible color palettes, and textures, as well as her original ideas. I feel nostalgia just looking at her illustrations.

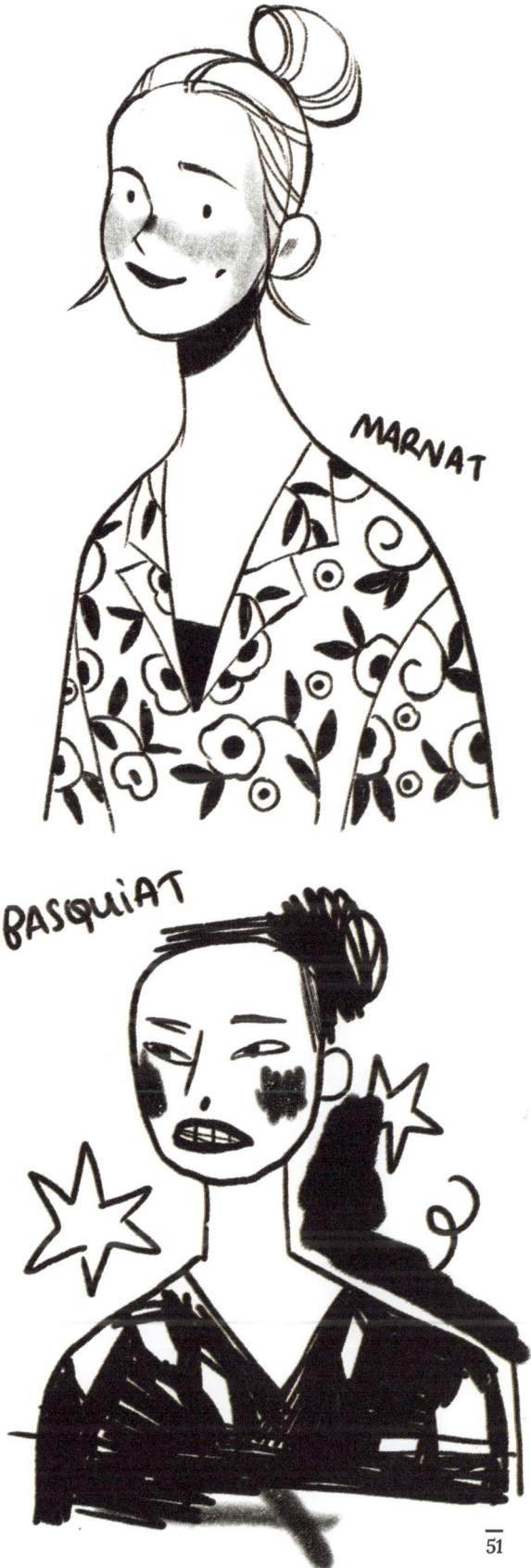

MARNAT

BASQUIAT

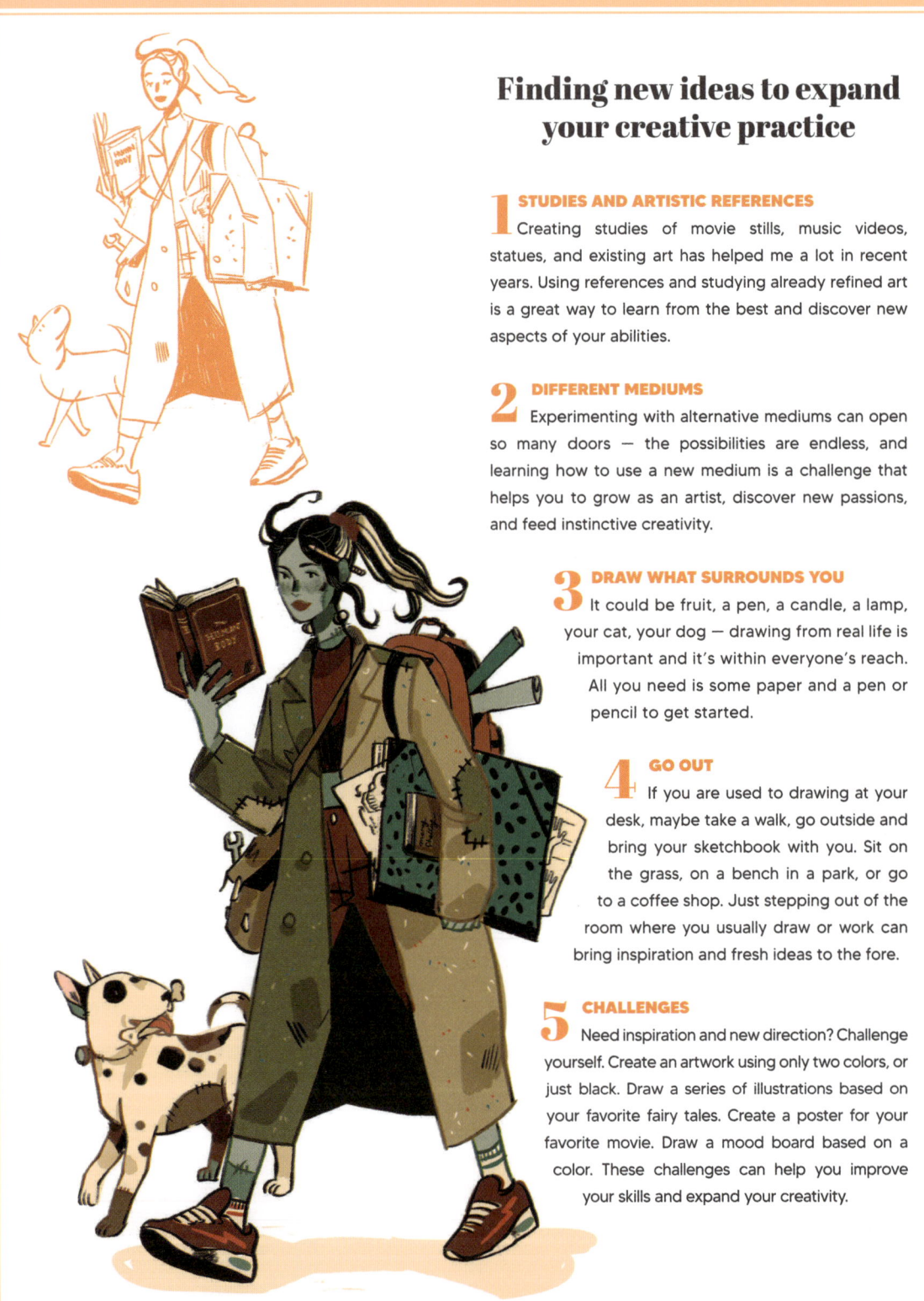

Finding new ideas to expand your creative practice

1 STUDIES AND ARTISTIC REFERENCES
Creating studies of movie stills, music videos, statues, and existing art has helped me a lot in recent years. Using references and studying already refined art is a great way to learn from the best and discover new aspects of your abilities.

2 DIFFERENT MEDIUMS
Experimenting with alternative mediums can open so many doors — the possibilities are endless, and learning how to use a new medium is a challenge that helps you to grow as an artist, discover new passions, and feed instinctive creativity.

3 DRAW WHAT SURROUNDS YOU
It could be fruit, a pen, a candle, a lamp, your cat, your dog — drawing from real life is important and it's within everyone's reach. All you need is some paper and a pen or pencil to get started.

4 GO OUT
If you are used to drawing at your desk, maybe take a walk, go outside and bring your sketchbook with you. Sit on the grass, on a bench in a park, or go to a coffee shop. Just stepping out of the room where you usually draw or work can bring inspiration and fresh ideas to the fore.

5 CHALLENGES
Need inspiration and new direction? Challenge yourself. Create an artwork using only two colors, or just black. Draw a series of illustrations based on your favorite fairy tales. Create a poster for your favorite movie. Draw a mood board based on a color. These challenges can help you improve your skills and expand your creativity.

Early concepts for an illustration of a modern take on the Bride of Frankenstein character. I thought the idea of her learning how to build another human could be fun! The sketches on these pages were created on my iPad using Procreate.

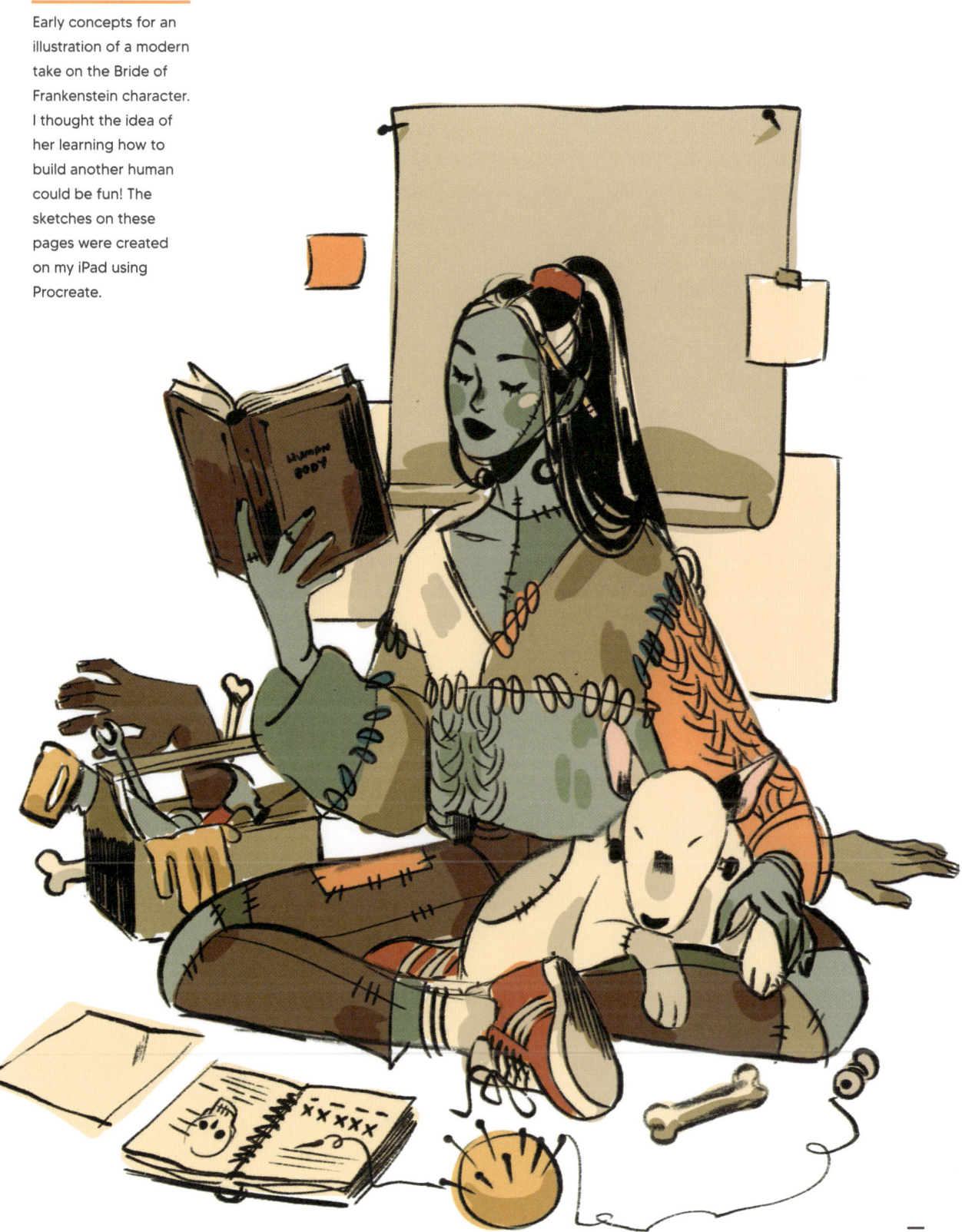

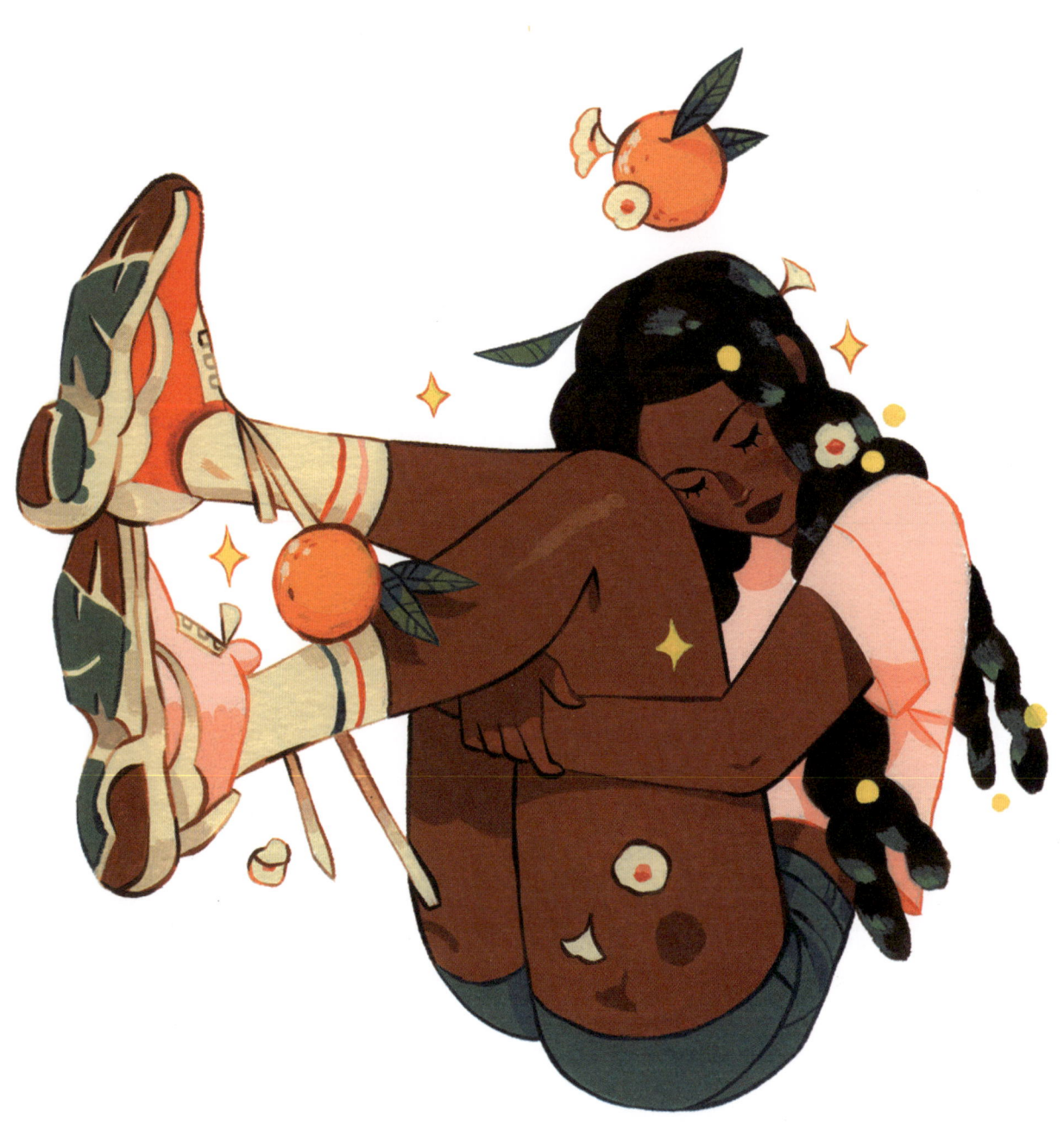

ILLUSTRATION

ILLUSTRATION

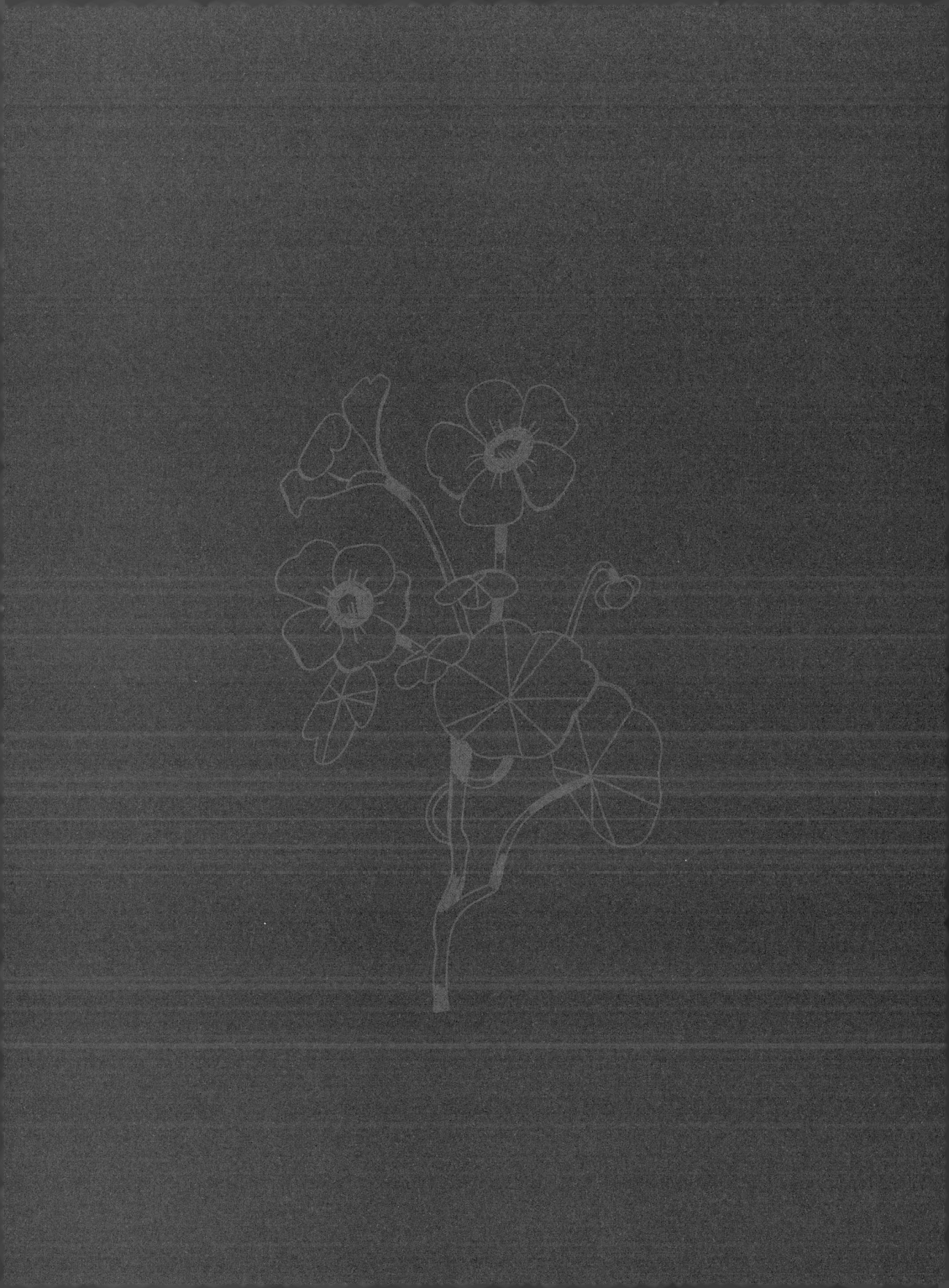

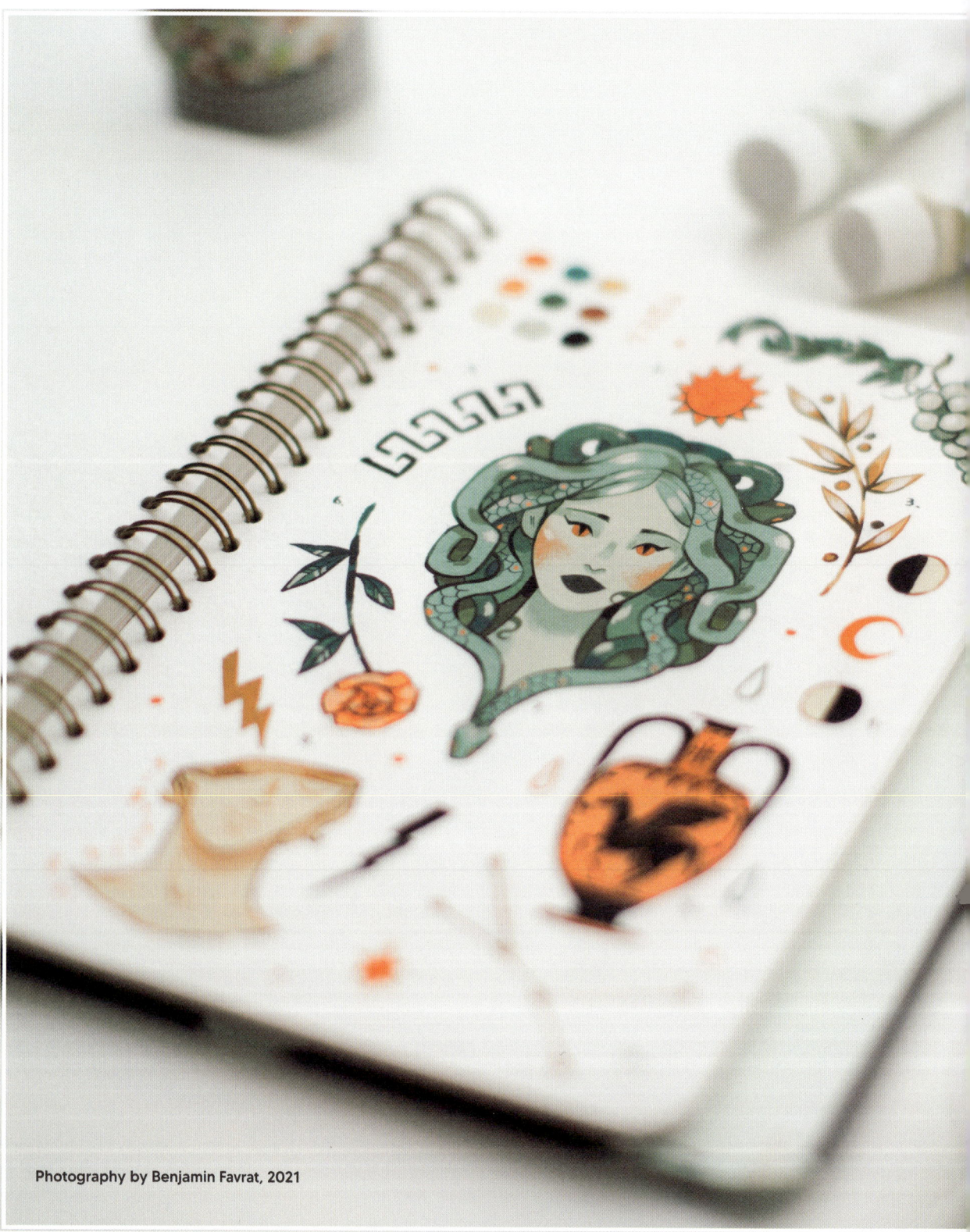

Photography by Benjamin Favrat, 2021

MY APPROACH

I have always drawn but I didn't formally study art. In this chapter, I share my understanding of illustration and the visual arts in general, as well as the methods I have developed over my creative practice. If you wish to delve into the theory behind illustration, I invite you to study this subject further by reading books, undertaking courses taught by professors, and watching specialized videos.

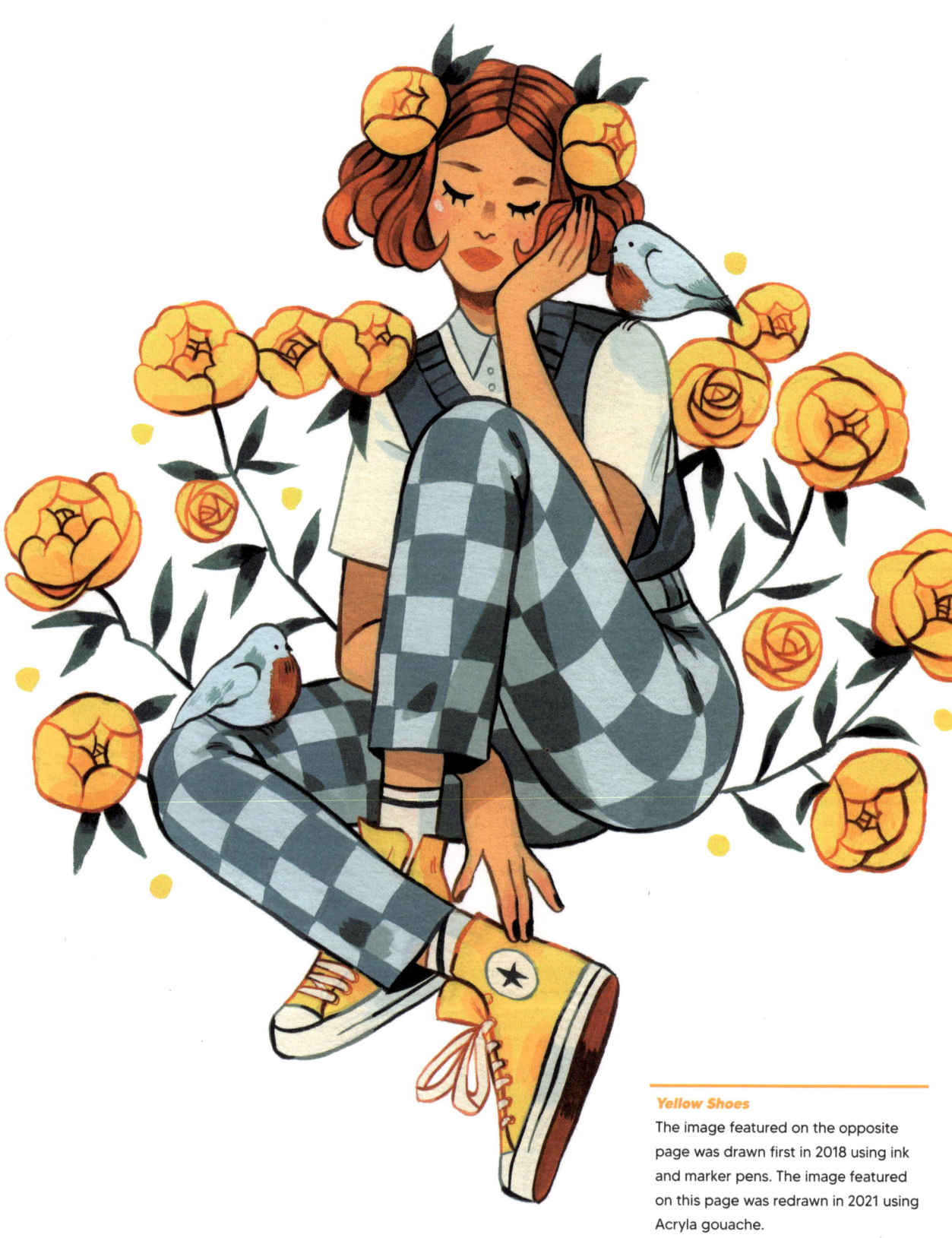

Yellow Shoes

The image featured on the opposite page was drawn first in 2018 using ink and marker pens. The image featured on this page was redrawn in 2021 using Acryla gouache.

STYLE

Developing a style takes time. I believe it's an adventure we embark upon alone because our style is influenced by our personal experiences — our perception of the world, what we have learned, what we want to learn, criticism from others as well as ourselves, and an inherent willingness to express something. Our style is also influenced by the art and creatives we love and connect to. The search for style is a deeply personal and unique experience.

What we create is a representation of ourselves. The influences and experiences of an artist's life can often be seen in their art — their chosen color palettes reveal their mood, and the story they tell is a fragment of their own. There is a reflection of themselves in every image they create.

The most important thing is to draw what you want and how you want. Create for yourself, without putting yourself under pressure. Everyone needs to be able to tell their story through art, without worrying about judgment.

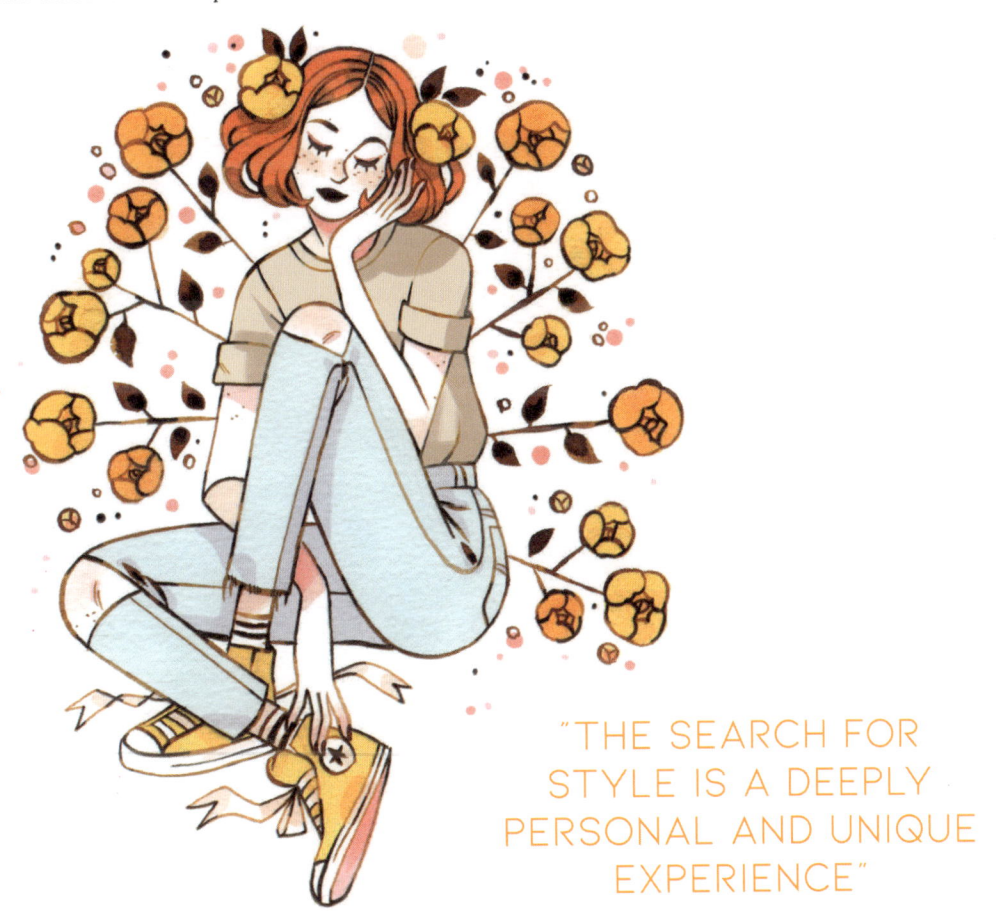

"THE SEARCH FOR STYLE IS A DEEPLY PERSONAL AND UNIQUE EXPERIENCE"

FINDING MY STYLE

When I was a teenager, I didn't have a strong urge to find my "style," I just wanted to have fun, so I experimented with many different creative avenues. After some creative play and artistic research, I started to take an interest in fashion illustrations of the 1950s and 1960s, specifically the elegance of illustrator René Gruau, and the sharp lines of his brush.

I was also fascinated by cartoons, especially those by Disney. I have always been in awe of the simple and effective graphics, magnificent scenery, and aesthetically pleasing characters of Disney films. Watching Disney films such as 101 *Dalmatians* and *Sleeping Beauty* as a child,

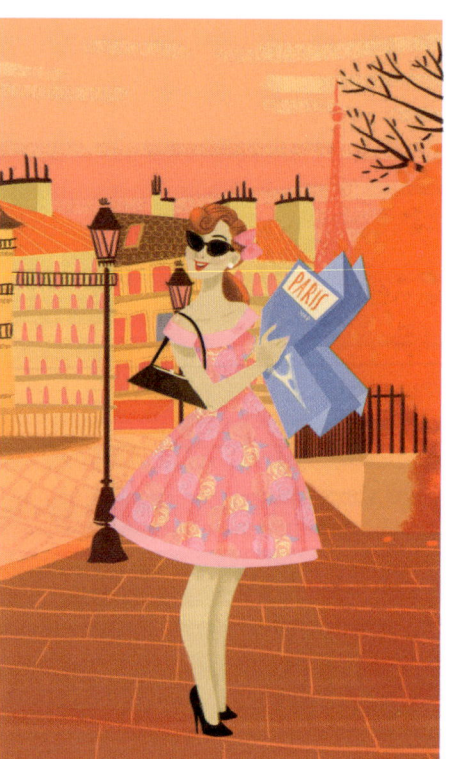

> "I KNEW I WANTED TO DRAW JUST LIKE THE DISNEY ANIMATORS, AND DEVELOP MY OWN SIGNATURE RETRO STYLE"

I knew I wanted to draw just like the Disney animators, and develop my own signature retro style. I then began to draw chic women in tulip dresses living in Parisian apartments or sitting on the terraces of bijou cafes.

I had a rather cartoonish style at the time, and over the years I have worked to make my style more solid, refined, and "mature." I drew mostly in Photoshop using a graphics tablet, then moved on to working with paper and pencil. I continued to draw constantly and my style evolved. I used new materials, and drew with ink and markers for a long time.

During my creative journey, I had a desire to paint with gouache, to create art similar to that of beautiful old movie posters from the 1960s. A fondness for Mary Blair's dreamy gouache illustrations and concepts for Disney inspired me to endeavor to paint just like her. I admired the medium so much that I became nervous to try it — it took me many years to build up the courage to get started with gouache! The new medium allowed me to explore new ideas, fueled my creativity, and offered artistic possibilities that I did not have with other mediums. Discovering gouache had a huge impact on my style: I finally found the tool that made me feel comfortable.

Visiting, digital sketch, 2011

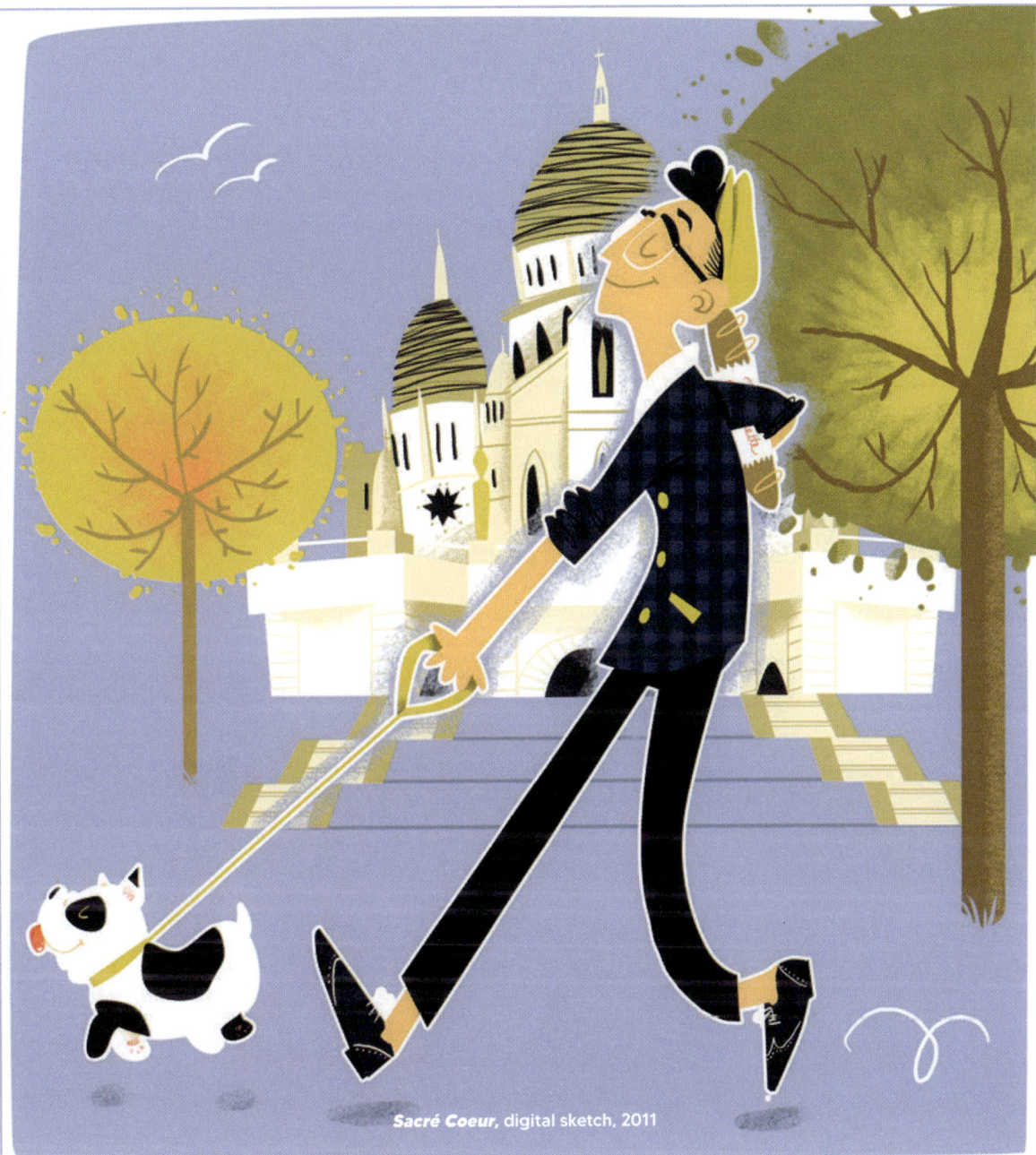

Sacré Coeur, digital sketch, 2011

Style evolution

Artistic style constantly evolves. Continuous creation accelerates progression as knowledge and experience builds and preferences are uncovered. I believe style grows and changes and is impacted by what is happening at the time. When I look at my old illustrations, even the ones from three months ago, I notice what is wrong, what I could have improved, and I know I would do it differently today. Everything that we learn in our lifetime will be reflected in what we create: I believe that's how style evolves and allows art to grow with the artist.

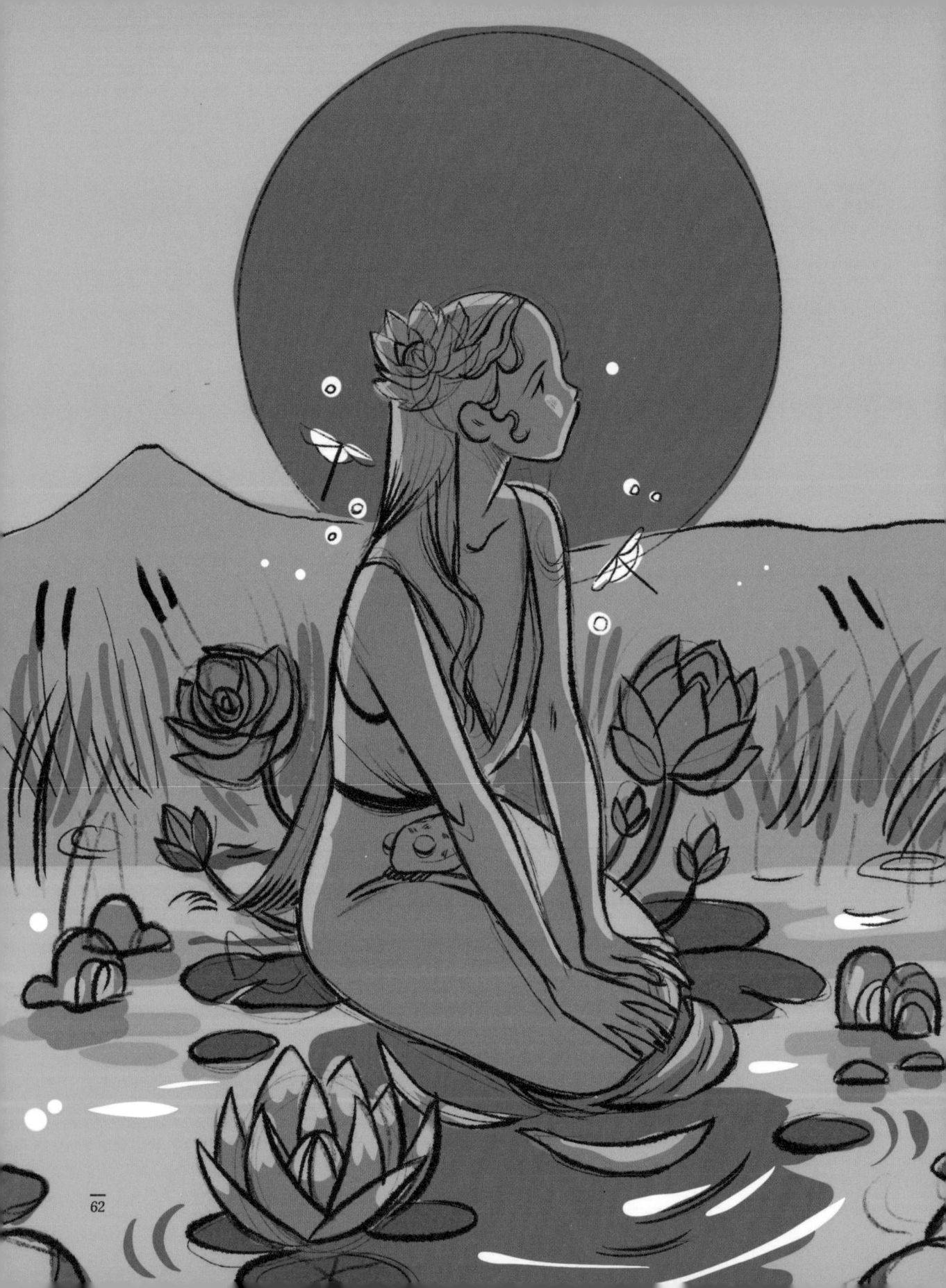

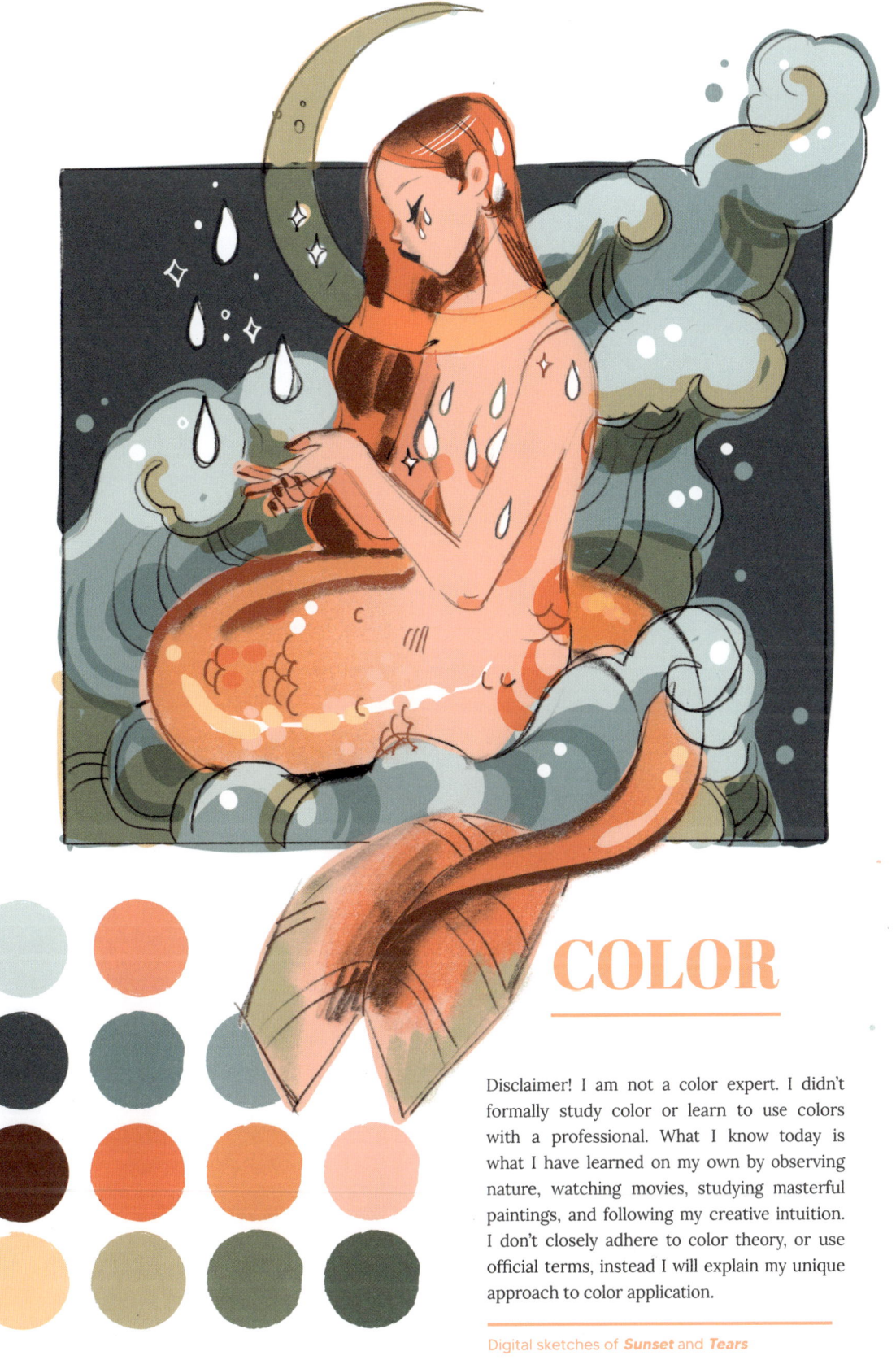

COLOR

Disclaimer! I am not a color expert. I didn't formally study color or learn to use colors with a professional. What I know today is what I have learned on my own by observing nature, watching movies, studying masterful paintings, and following my creative intuition. I don't closely adhere to color theory, or use official terms, instead I will explain my unique approach to color application.

Digital sketches of *Sunset* and *Tears*

BUILDING COLOR PALETTES

I allow my mood and intuition to guide my color choices; for example, sometimes I prefer to use bright colors and in other situations, I might incorporate lighter pastel tones. The directions I follow in my color schemes are also affected by the messages I want to convey to the viewer, or the atmosphere I want to create in the scene. I often work in phases; sometimes I'll use the same color scheme for months, then when I want to use a fresh color combination, I look for a new palette.

My preferred color palette contains a mixture of warm and cool colors. Turquoise, duck egg blue, and mint green are my favorite cold tones, while bright red, orange, and mustard yellow are often my warm colors of choice to complement the cool tones.

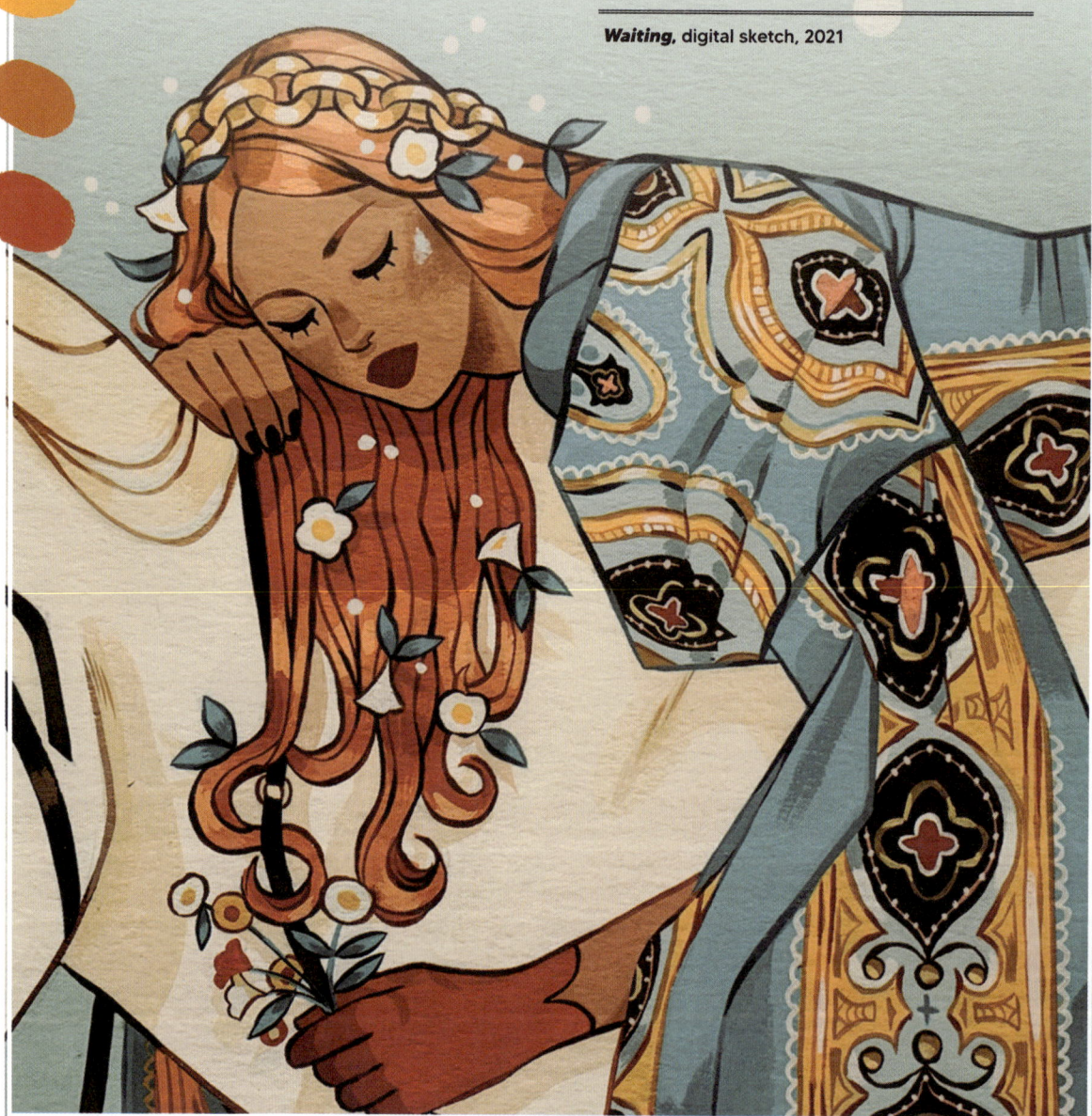

Waiting, digital sketch, 2021

"MY PREFERRED COLOR PALETTE CONTAINS A MIXTURE OF WARM AND COOL COLORS"

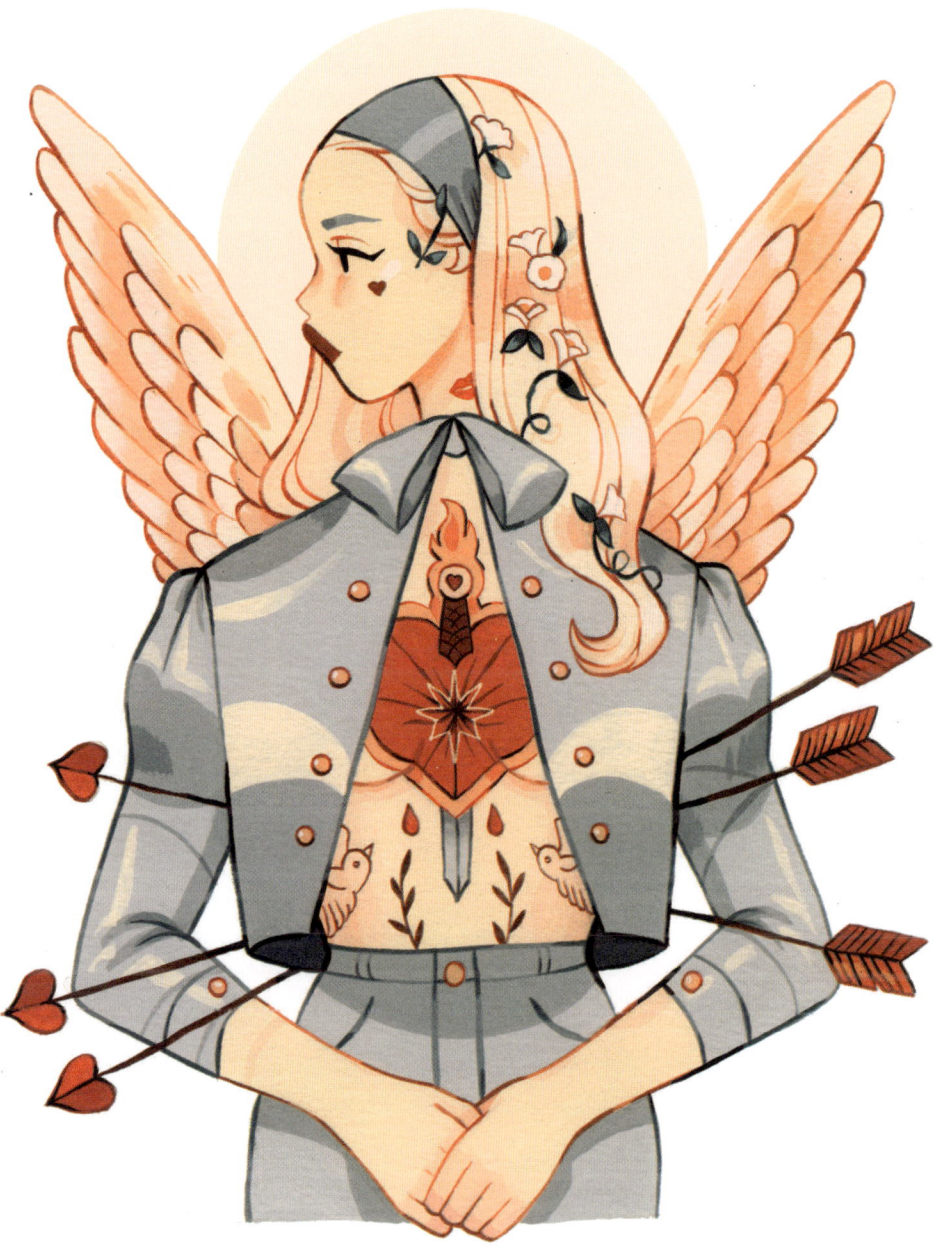

Valentine's, gouache, 2021. I wanted to give this piece a pastel look, to make it appear almost translucent. The girl's skin, hair, and wings are the same color, as well as the flowers in her hair and the halo around her head. I chose a light blue to make her clothes pop a bit. Here, the heart tattoo on her chest and arrows are highlighted by bright red, to create a contrast. I wanted these elements, mostly heart shapes, to be the main focus so the viewer understands at a glance that she is Cupid.

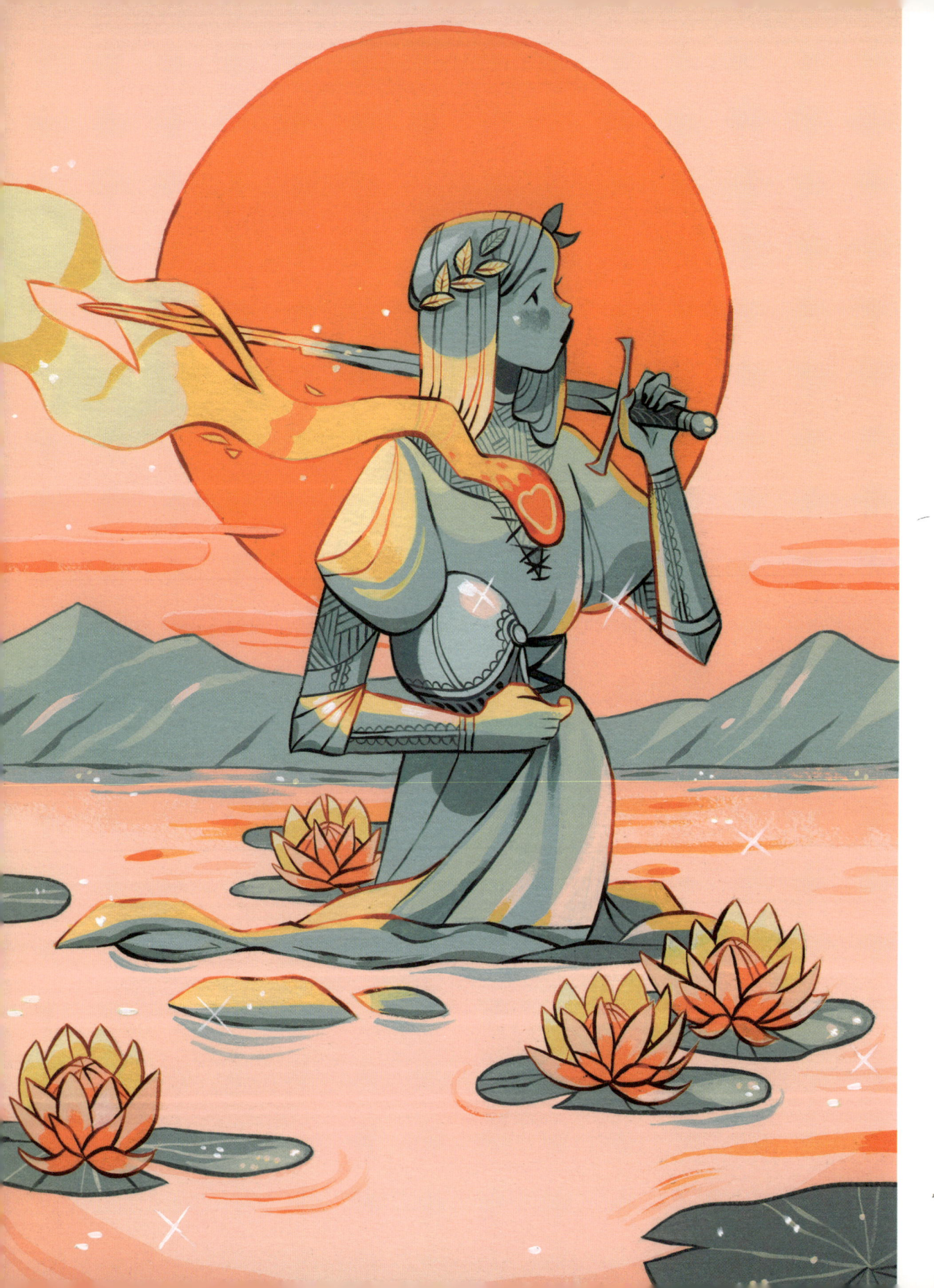

Brave Heart,
gouache, 2020

In this piece, warm colors take more space than cold colors. I chose this palette because I wanted to create a sunset vibe, and sense that the night is on its way. I wanted to use a dreamy palette to create a contrast between the colors and the subject of this illustration — a brave warrior ready to fight; a burning heart giving her best on her quest to reach her goal.

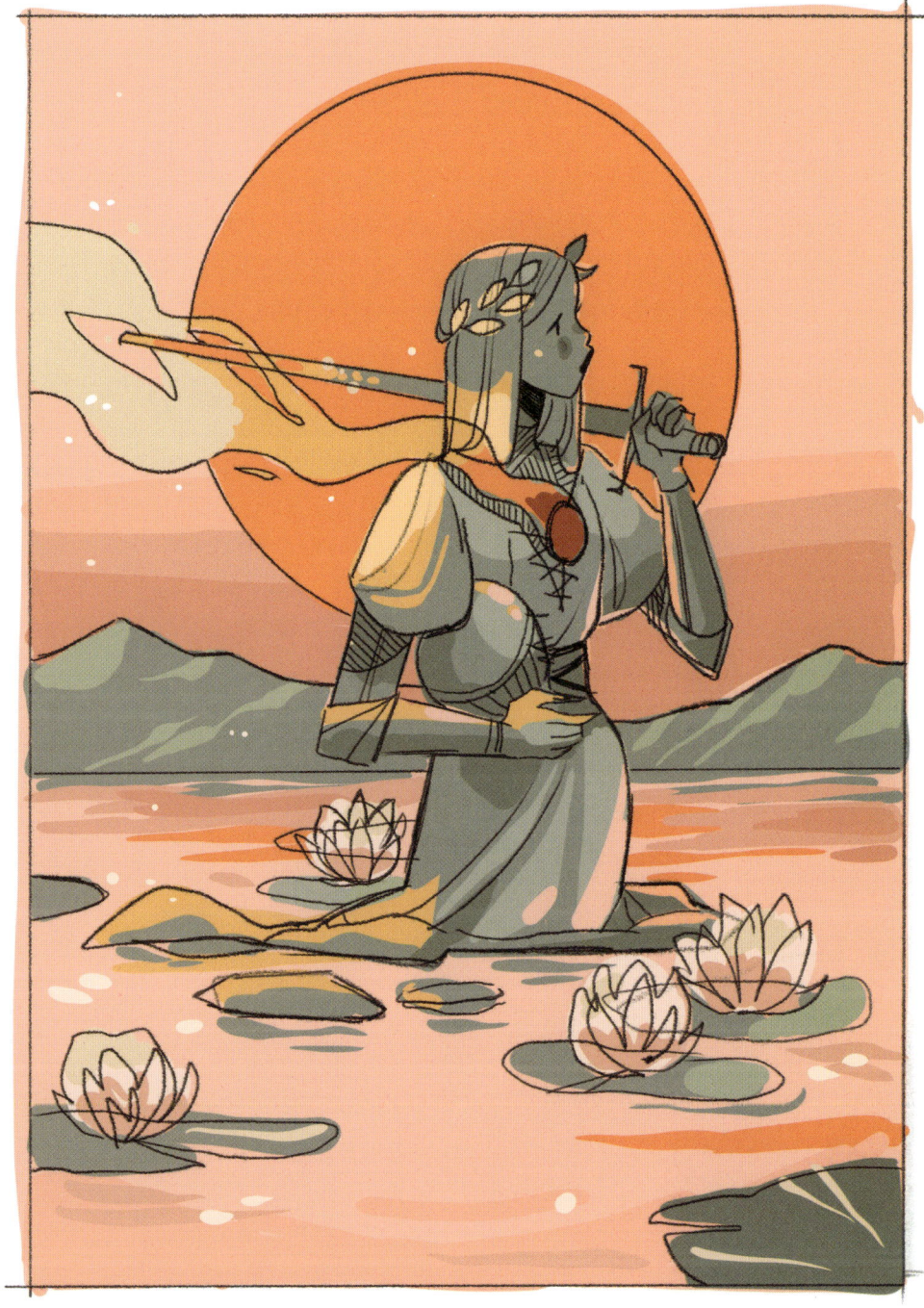

CONTRASTING COLORS

When building a color palette, I often consider contrast. For example, if I want an illustration to have a mostly warm palette, I will add a cool color to the scheme, to be used on small details across the design. Conversely, if the tones are mostly cool, I will add a touch of red to create a balance of cool and warm tones and add an interesting accent to the painting. The sudden change in color temperature creates an attention-grabbing contrast that pops off the piece and catches the eye of the viewer.

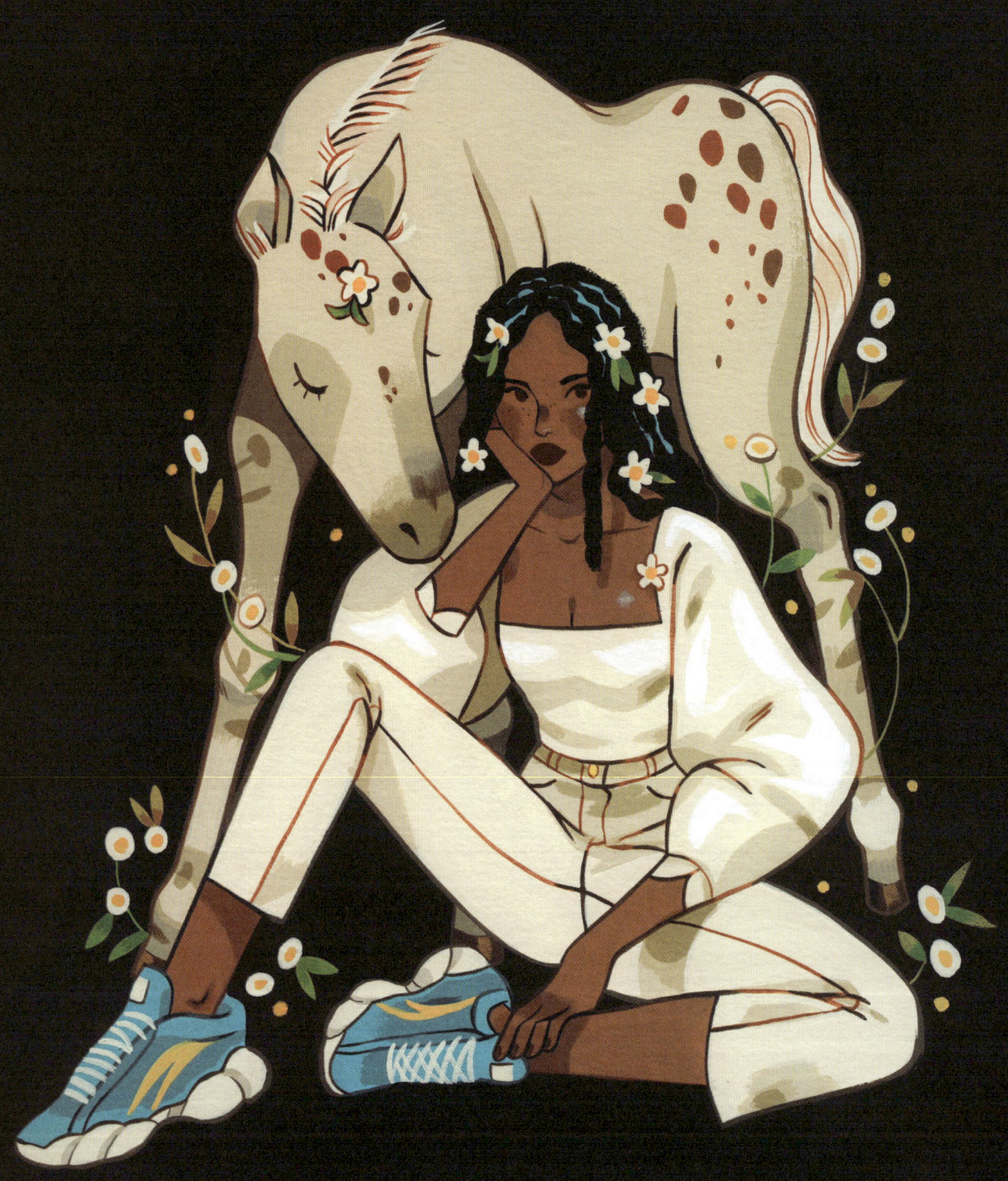

Daisies, Acryla gouache, 2020

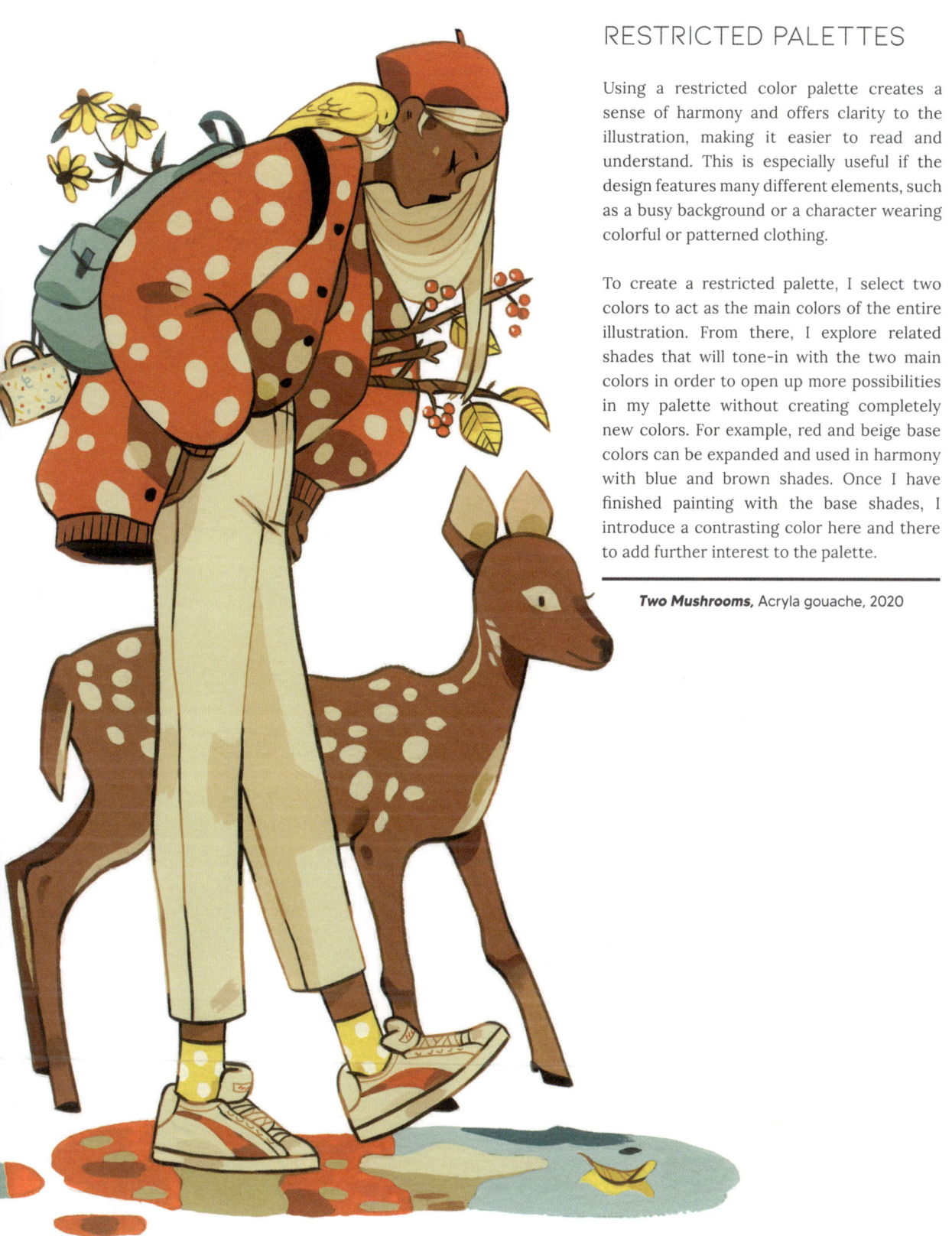

RESTRICTED PALETTES

Using a restricted color palette creates a sense of harmony and offers clarity to the illustration, making it easier to read and understand. This is especially useful if the design features many different elements, such as a busy background or a character wearing colorful or patterned clothing.

To create a restricted palette, I select two colors to act as the main colors of the entire illustration. From there, I explore related shades that will tone-in with the two main colors in order to open up more possibilities in my palette without creating completely new colors. For example, red and beige base colors can be expanded and used in harmony with blue and brown shades. Once I have finished painting with the base shades, I introduce a contrasting color here and there to add further interest to the palette.

Two Mushrooms, Acryla gouache, 2020

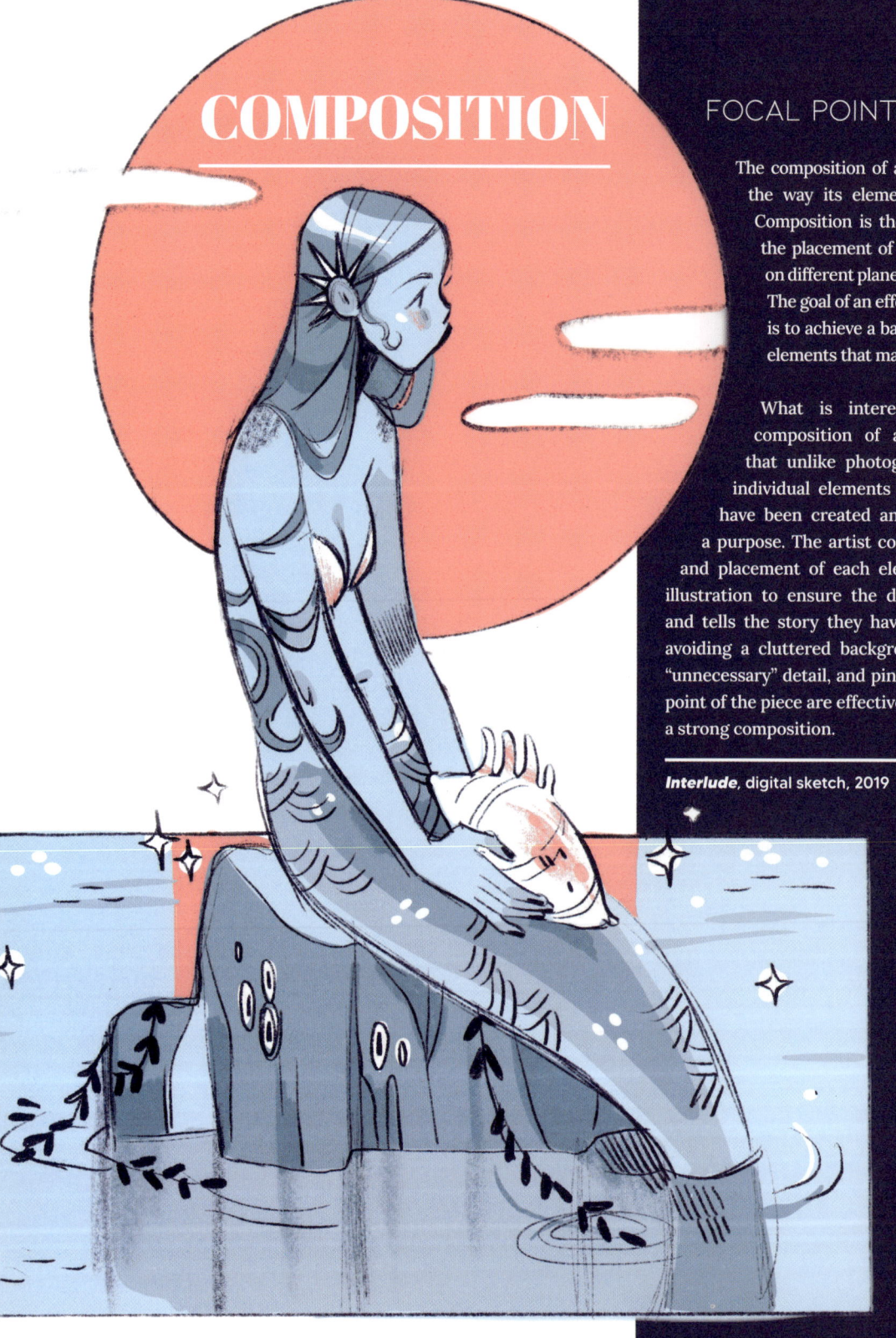

COMPOSITION

FOCAL POINTS

The composition of an image refers to the way its elements are arranged. Composition is the consideration of the placement of colors and shapes on different planes within the frame. The goal of an effective composition is to achieve a balance between the elements that make up that image.

What is interesting about the composition of an illustration is that unlike photography, all of the individual elements in an illustration have been created and therefore have a purpose. The artist considers the detail and placement of each element within the illustration to ensure the design is readable and tells the story they have in mind. I find avoiding a cluttered background, eliminating "unnecessary" detail, and pinpointing the focal point of the piece are effective ways to produce a strong composition.

Interlude, digital sketch, 2019

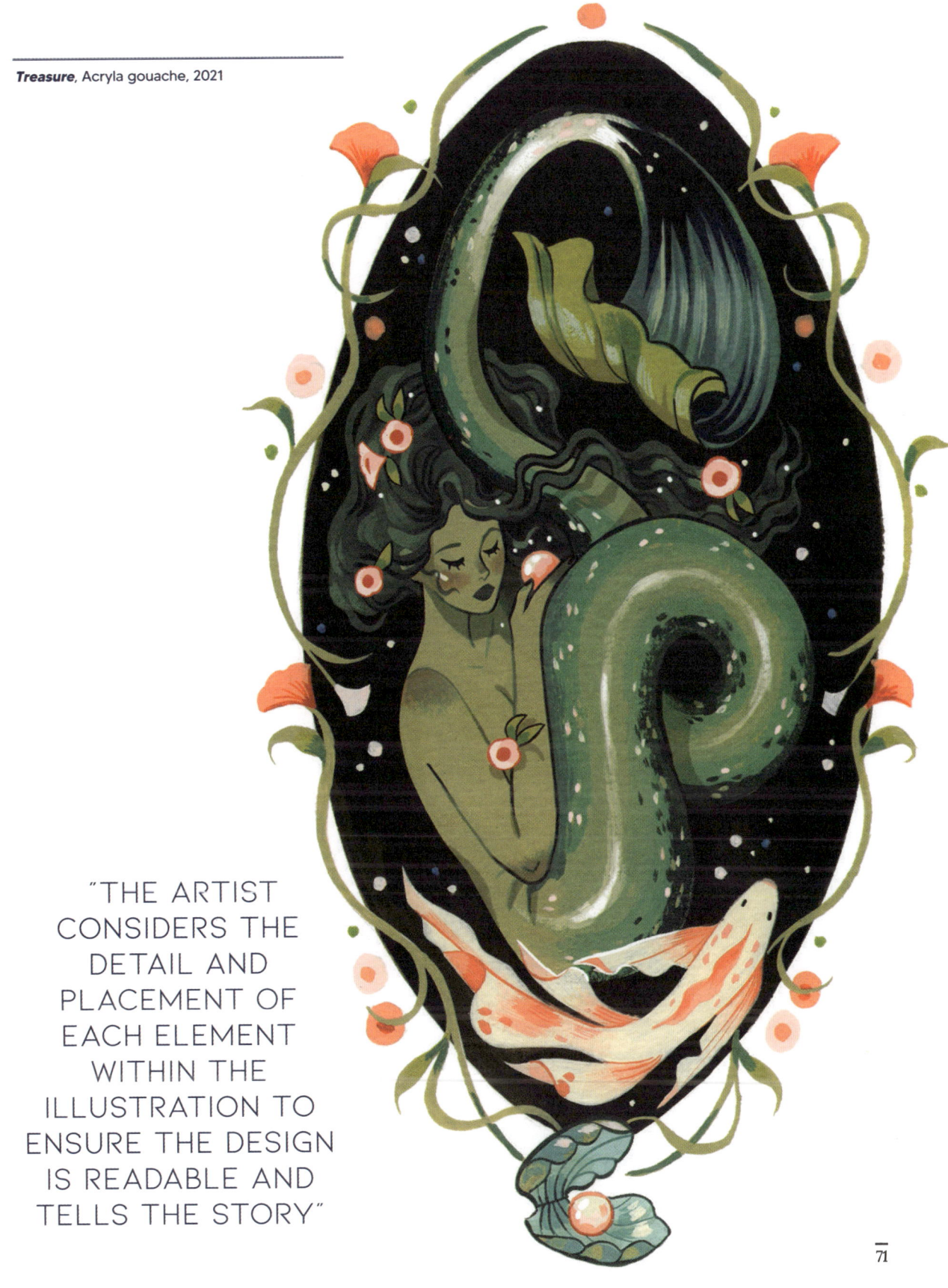

"THE ARTIST CONSIDERS THE DETAIL AND PLACEMENT OF EACH ELEMENT WITHIN THE ILLUSTRATION TO ENSURE THE DESIGN IS READABLE AND TELLS THE STORY"

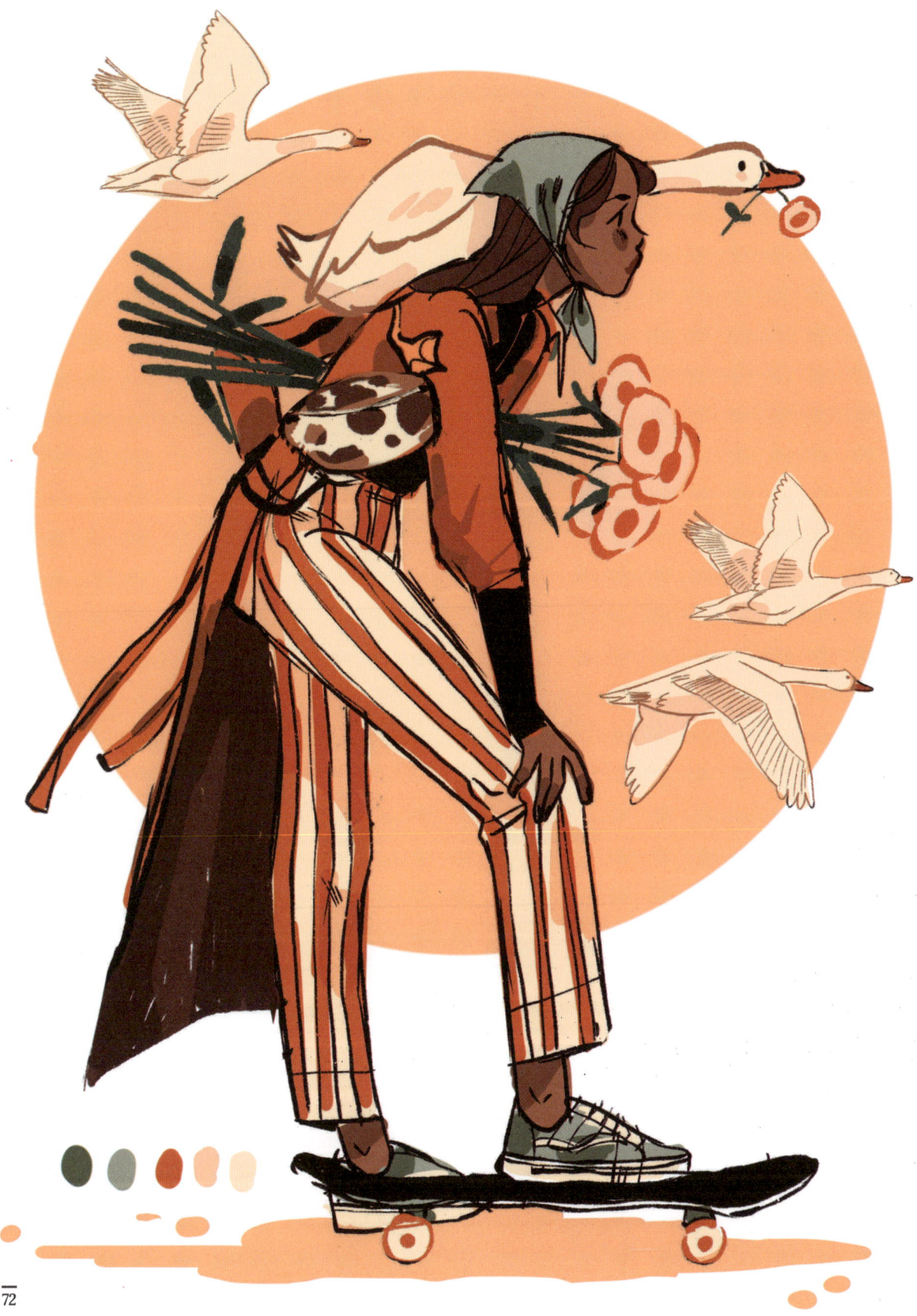

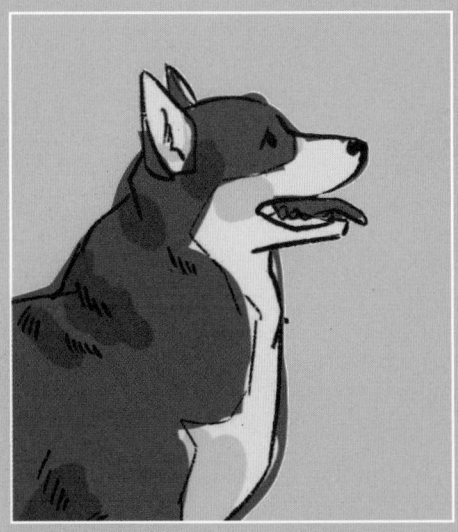

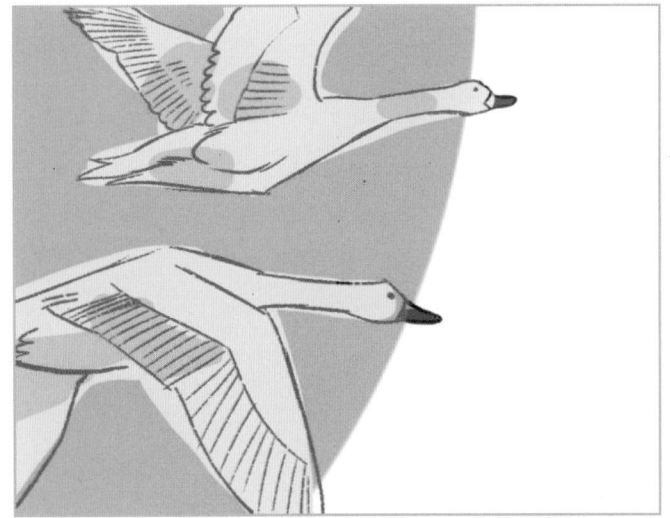

BALANCE

To create visually harmonious illustrations, I try to create a balance between the key elements of the piece, such as the characters and the decorative details, to enhance the drawing. My starting point for a design is often a character posing. From there, I like to add objects and smaller elements that will give life and personality to the character. In many of my designs, the character is accompanied by an animal friend or pet.

I initially incorporated a dog in this drawing (image shown on right). I enjoyed the addition of the cute dog, but unfortunately it disturbed the balance of the illustration and confused the focal point a little. So, I move the girl's skateboard to the left, remove the dog, and add birds in the distance to create a more comfortable balance of elements.

The girl and the goose on her shoulder are leaning and looking toward the right side of the image, so it is important to balance the heavily right-side-weighted composition with an element on the left. In this case, I add a flying goose in the top left and pull the viewer's gaze to the center of the image using the colored circle in the background.

***New Horizon**, digital sketch, 2021*

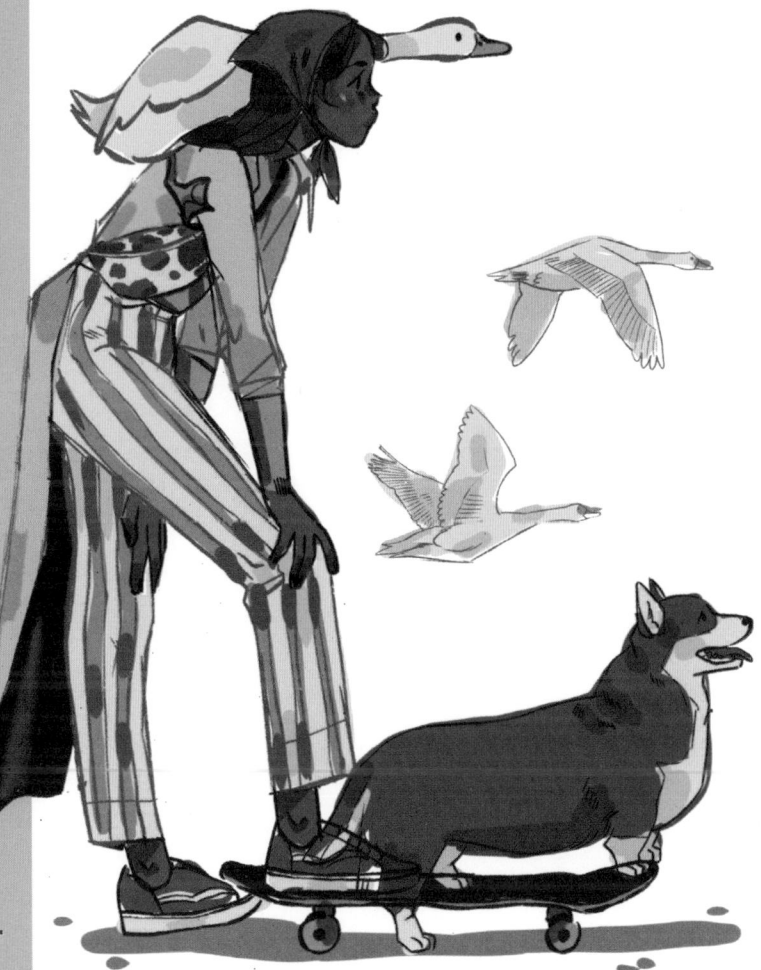

READING DIRECTION

When considering the reading direction of a design, you need to ask yourself the following questions: what do you want the viewer to see when they look at your drawing? And how should their eye travel across the image?

Reading direction is an interesting subject that can be applied to all visual art forms, especially paintings, illustration, film, and photography. The direction of reading gives an order to the identification of the elements in an image. Not only does it guide the path of the viewer's eye,

it also directs the reading of the story within the artwork. Classical paintings often have very intentional reading directions that have been considered to optimize the viewing experience. Often, the first element to draw attention will be either a color that denotes the entire work, a character almost filling the entire frame, an area that feels emptier than the rest of the work, a homogeneous shape, or text written among drawn elements.

Foxes, Acryla gouache, 2020

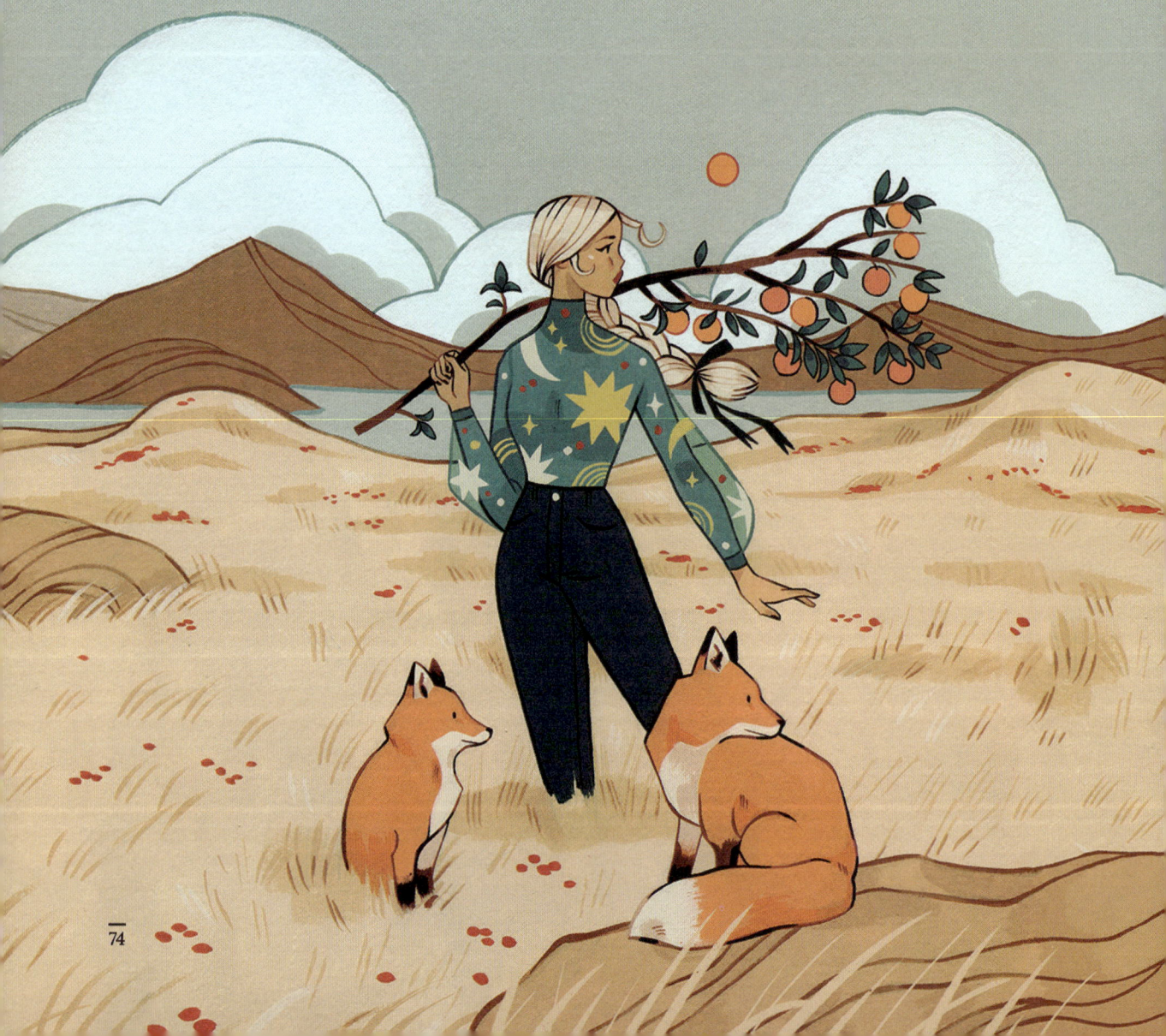

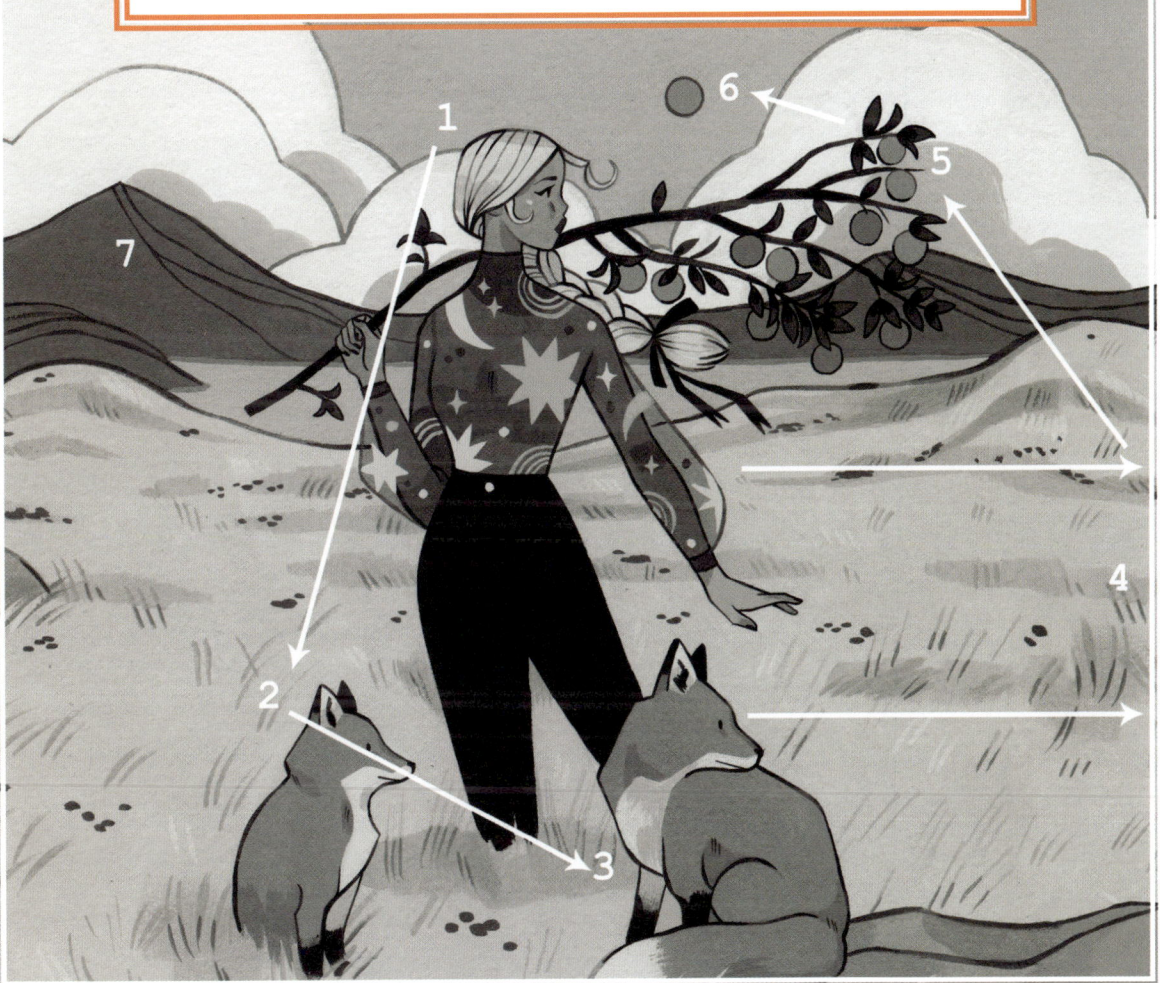

Reading direction breakdown

1 The first thing we look at in this piece is the main character because she stands in the center and takes up the most space. The bold pattern on her shirt also helps draw the eye in.

2&3 Next, the foxes at the bottom attract the eye because they are orange, and stand below the focal point: the main character.

4 We are naturally intrigued to find out what the characters are looking at, so follow their eyes to the right of the frame.

5 Next, we are pulled back to the center by the big branch, which fills a large space. With smaller details on the branch to decipher, naturally the eye lingers here.

6 After admiring the branch, taking in its complexities, we notice the sun because of its similarities to the orange fruits and proximity to the branch.

7 Lastly, we widen our view to look at the background and the painting as a whole.

STORYTELLING

WHAT I WANT TO TELL

Creating an image that tells a story without expressing a word can be challenging for some and easy for others. I'm a rather reserved person, so drawing has always been a very useful tool for me to express myself. What I want to convey through my work depends on what I'm experiencing at the time — both my mood and impactful events. Today I like to represent moments of well-being, escape, and peace with oneself, while adding a touch of adventure and fantasy. Themes such as waiting, thinking, and dreaming inspire me a lot, and I often use these ideas to tell stories in my drawings.

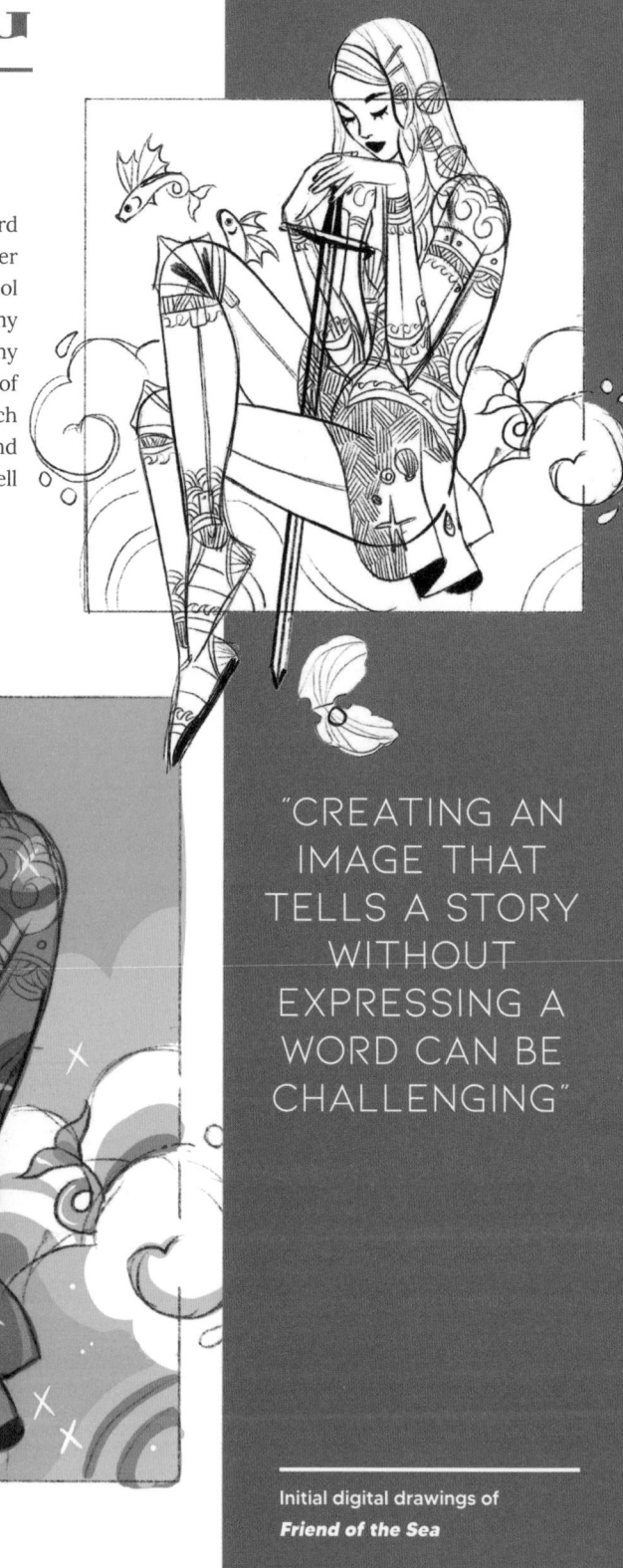

"CREATING AN IMAGE THAT TELLS A STORY WITHOUT EXPRESSING A WORD CAN BE CHALLENGING"

Initial digital drawings of
Friend of the Sea

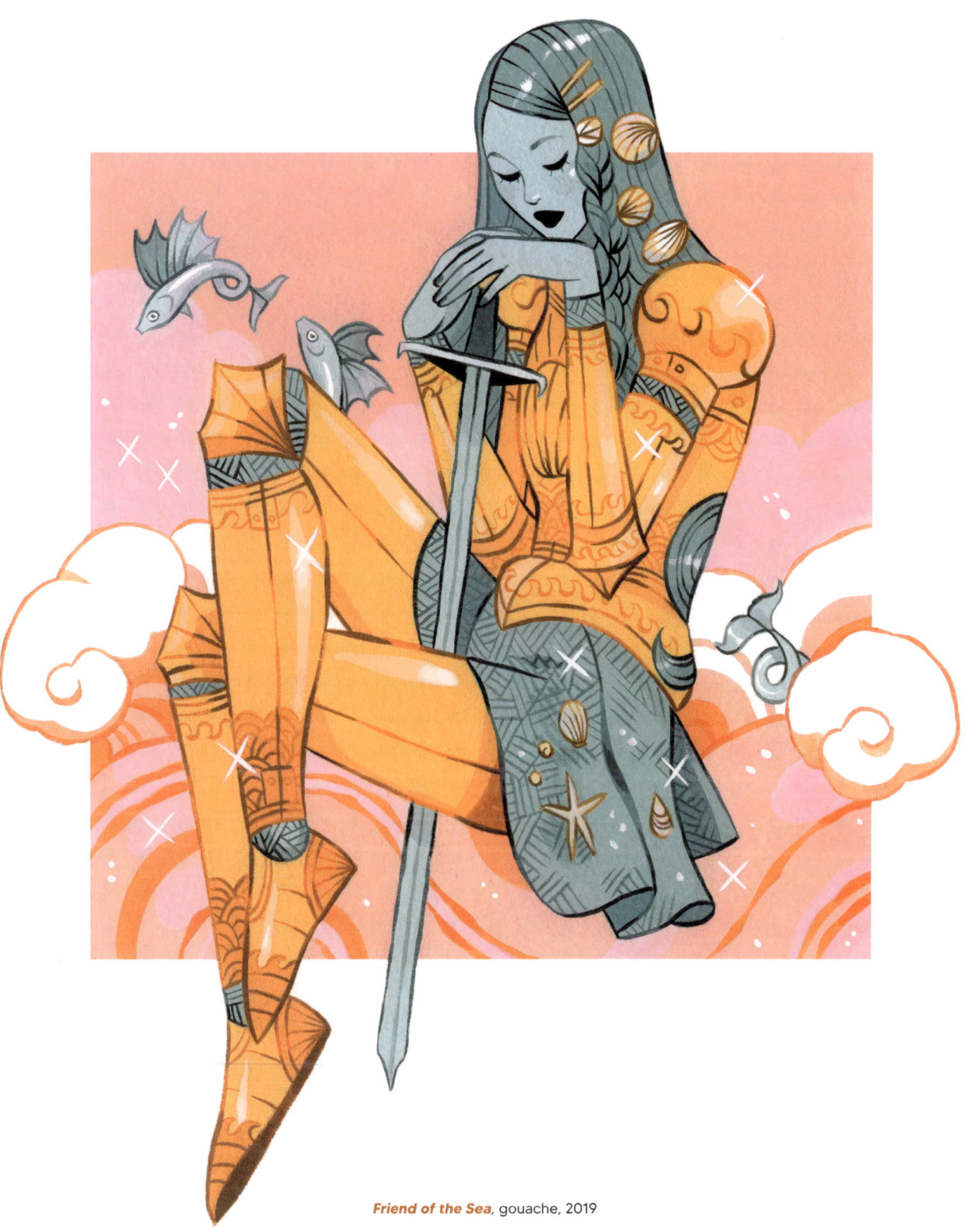

Friend of the Sea, gouache, 2019

CONVEYING A FEELING

CHARACTER

I believe it's easier to convey feelings through the use of a character — the facial expression or body language of a character can be used as a tool to display an emotion. Even subtle changes such as adjustments to posture, or the orientation of their face or direction of their gaze can impact the message they put across.

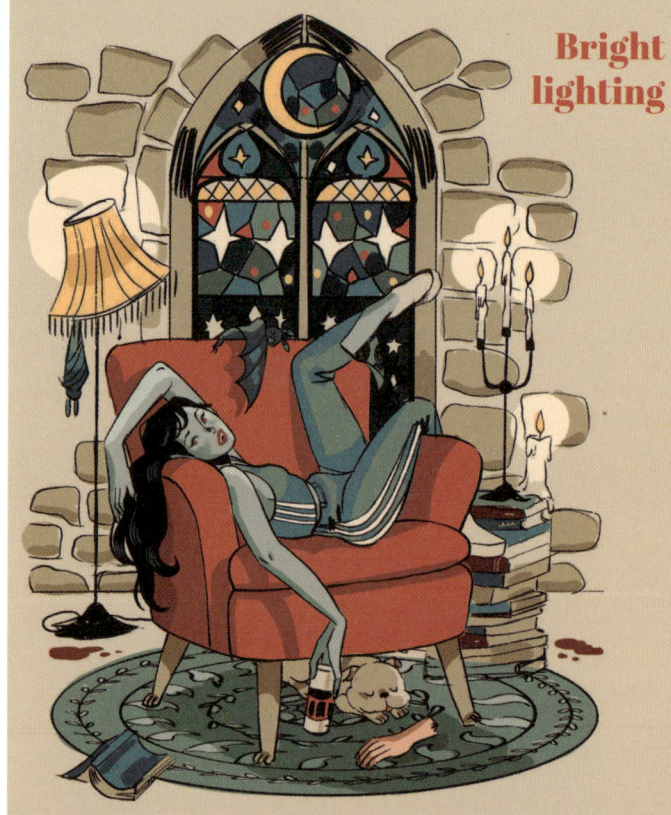

Bright lighting

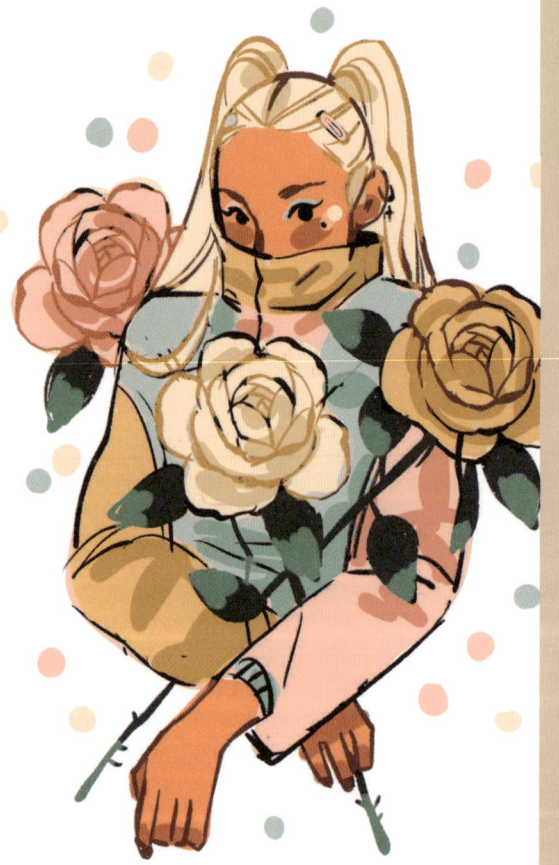

LIGHT

Lighting sets the tone of a design and creates an atmosphere. It can also be used to highlight a key element of the illustration. Dark lighting will portray a feeling of fear, sadness, anguish, or hopelessness. On the contrary, bright light will portray a sense of hope and joy.

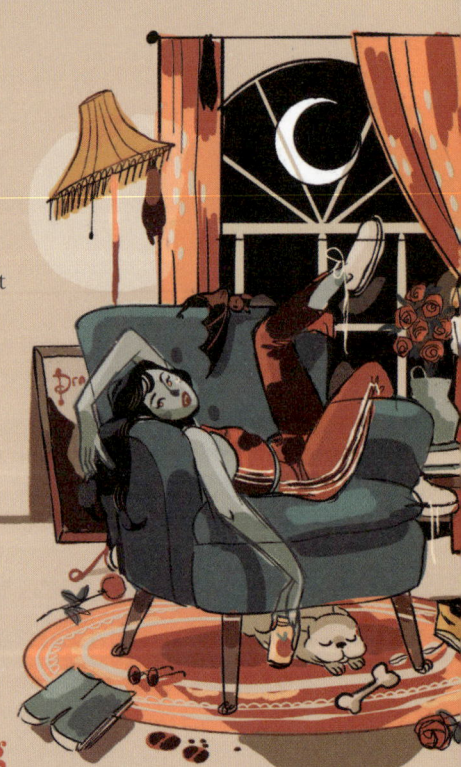

Dark lighting

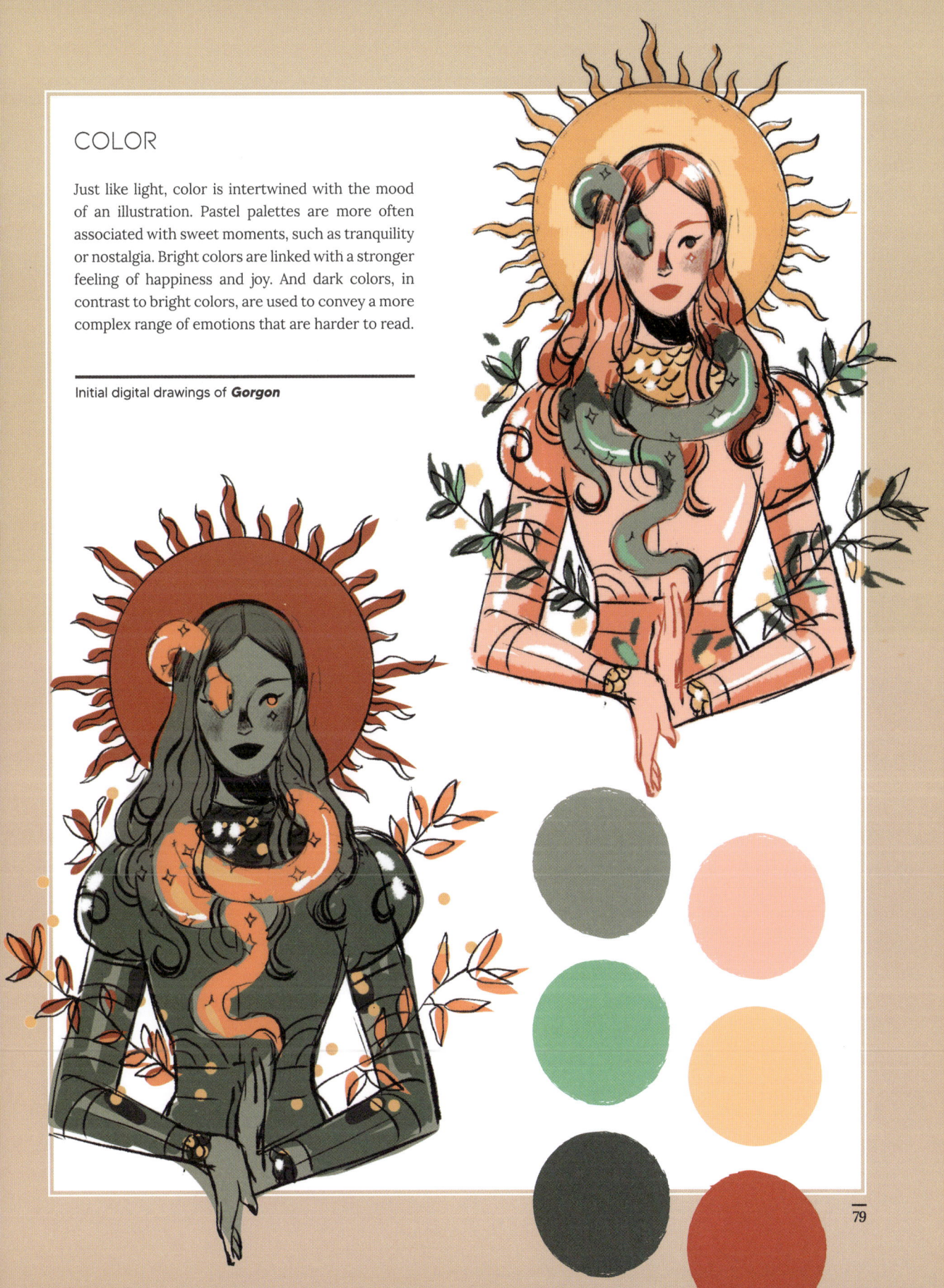

COLOR

Just like light, color is intertwined with the mood of an illustration. Pastel palettes are more often associated with sweet moments, such as tranquility or nostalgia. Bright colors are linked with a stronger feeling of happiness and joy. And dark colors, in contrast to bright colors, are used to convey a more complex range of emotions that are harder to read.

Initial digital drawings of **Gorgon**

LESS IS MORE

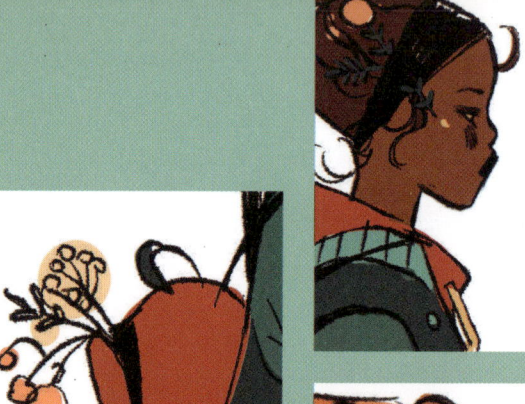

When I first developed my own artwork, I struggled with creating effective compositions, until one day I was told "less is more." I learned that including as few elements as possible makes a drawing easier to read and that limiting the color palette makes the drawing more efficient and cohesive. The same rule applies when aiming to convey a message through a single image. Telling a story while showing the minimum is difficult but not impossible. The personality of a character can be defined through their appearance and apparel, their attitude, as well as the elements that accompany them and act as a reflection and extension of them.

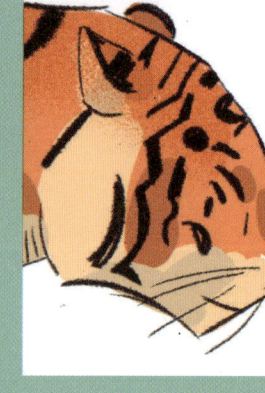

For example, here, I have drawn a girl walking with a tiger. The girl holds a map of the world in her hands. Around her neck and behind her head hangs a witch's hat, and she carries a backpack full of flowers with sparkles coming out of it. As indicated by different elements of the design, it could be interpreted that the girl is a young witch (the witch's hat and magical flowers) going on an adventure (map) with her friend or animal familiar (tiger walking calmly by her side).

Captured on a white background, this illustration depicts a clear moment in the life of this witch, who decides to go on a journey and discover the world with her friend. The viewer might contemplate what happened before or after this image. Is she delivering the flowers? Is she investigating the origin of the magical flowers? Has she collected ingredients to brew a potion? Where did the tiger come from, and why does it accompany the girl on her quest? What is certain is that her tiger friend will defend her if she encounters any unfriendly travellers.

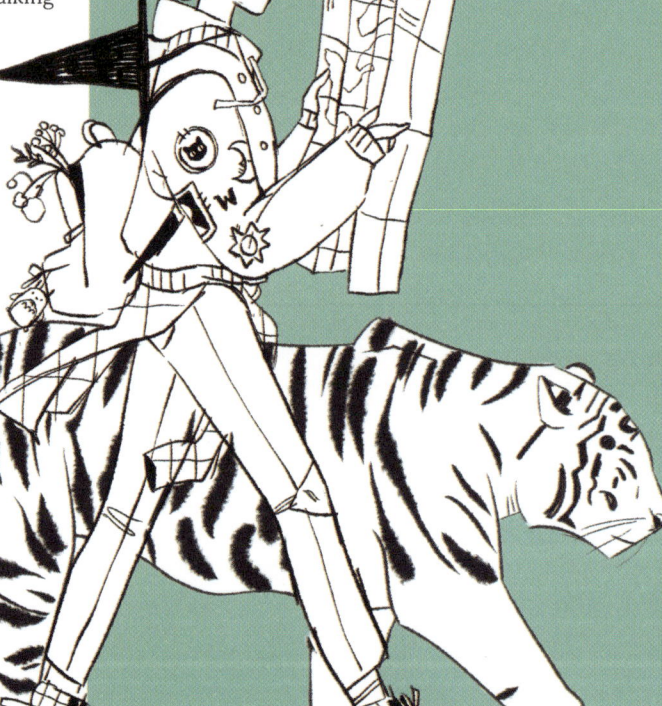

Initial digital drawings of
Witch and Friend

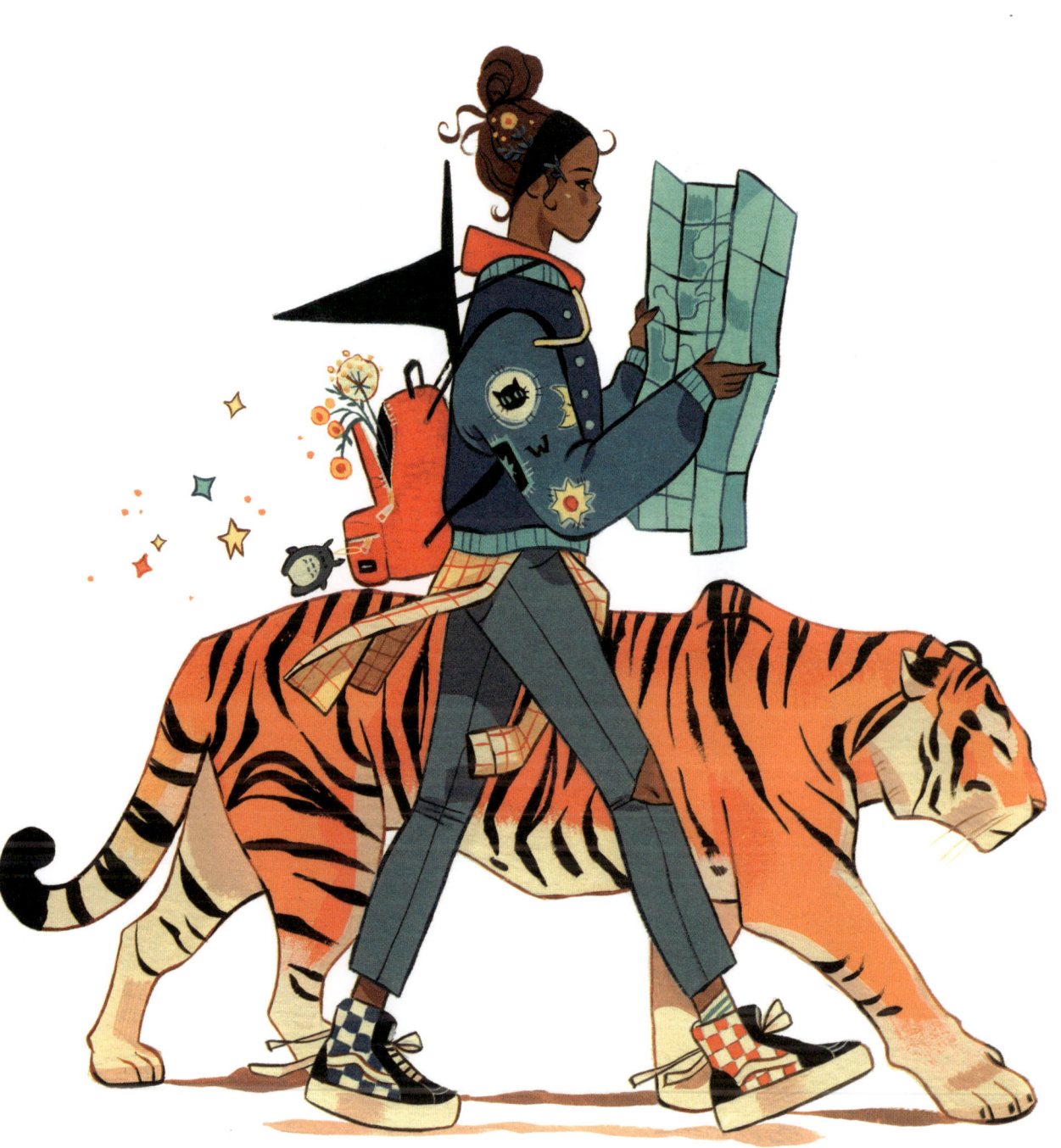

Witch and Friend, Acryla gouache, 2020

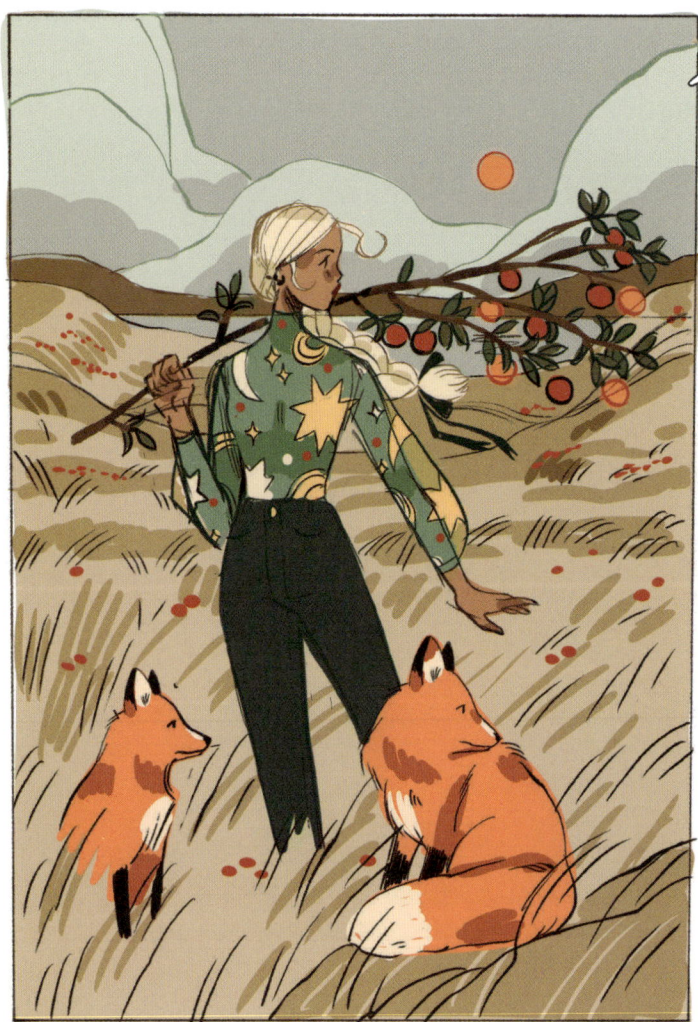

Foxes, digital sketch, 2020

In this illustration, a woman stands in a field. The scenery is rather vague, featuring a non-descript lake and mountain range in the distance. She holds a large branch covered in fruit. She and her fox friends are all looking in the same direction, to their left. They appear frozen, but not surprised. Did something happen to disrupt them in their mission? What is the branch for? Are the foxes leading the group's quest, or are they just accompanying the woman?

The woman's clothing suggests that she has some knowledge of magic, and the fruit-laden branch, which echoes the round orange sun in the background, could be of great importance in this story. This illustration, with a mysterious but rather calm atmosphere, could tell several stories.

Racoons, digital sketch (right) and gouache (opposite page), 2020

A girl, flanked by two curious-looking raccoons, seems to be spying on someone or something, hidden in the middle of a field. In her hands are a pair of binoculars. She looks just as mischievous as her friends. One raccoon seems focused while the other daydreams, gazing off into the middle distance. What are they looking at, or what are they hoping to see? This character seems to be looking for answers to her questions. She appears to have prepared for her outing: a bucket hat in case there is too much sun, and an umbrella in the bag in case they get caught in the rain.

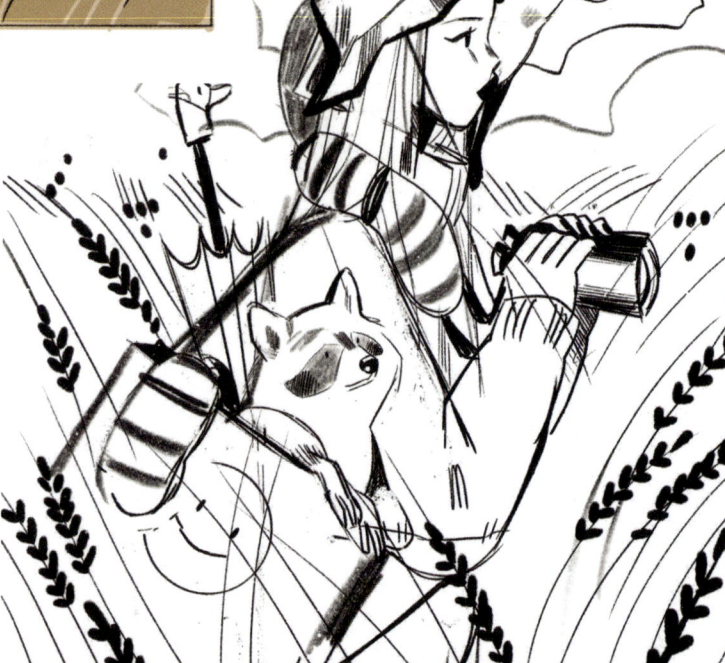

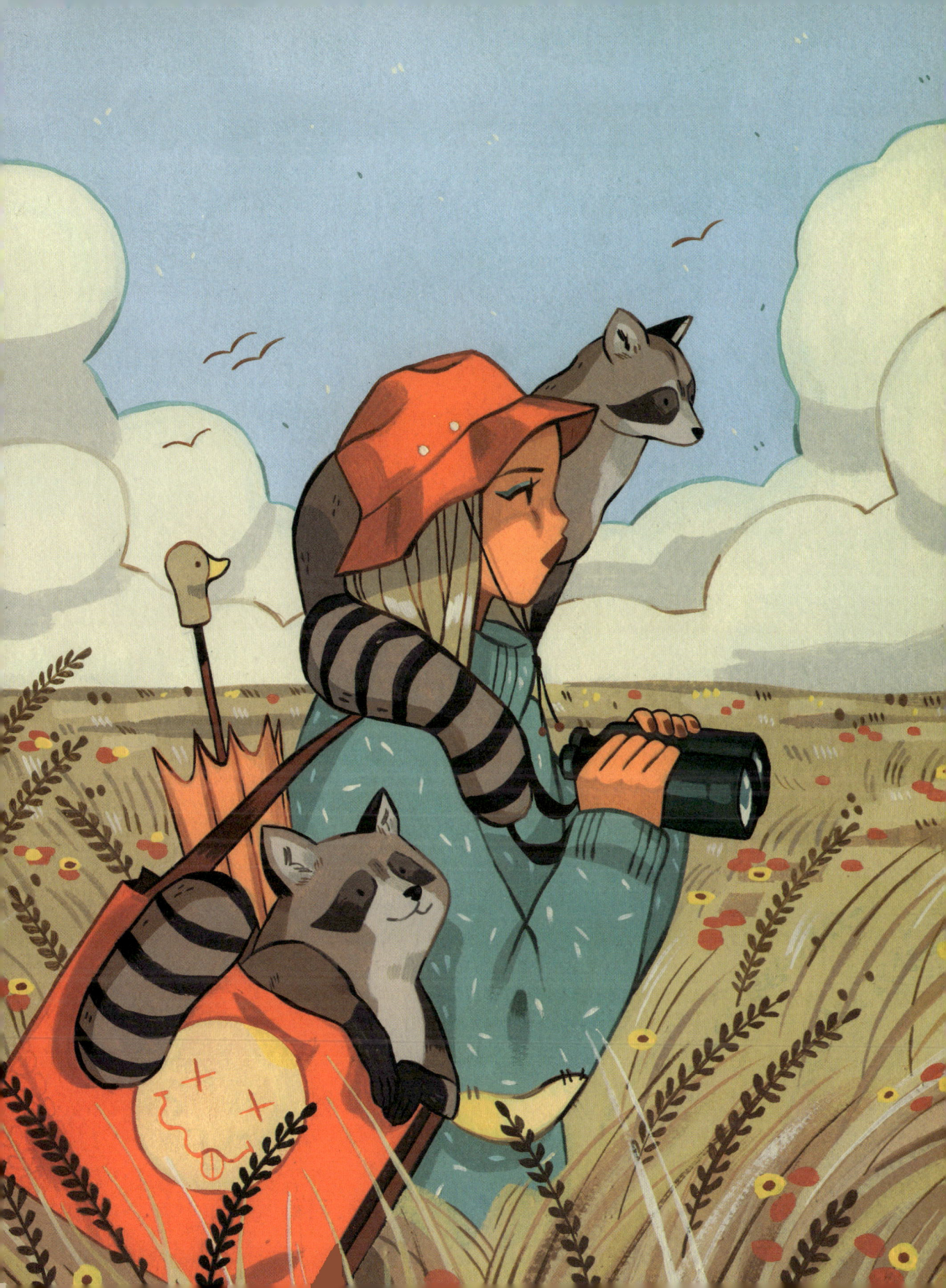

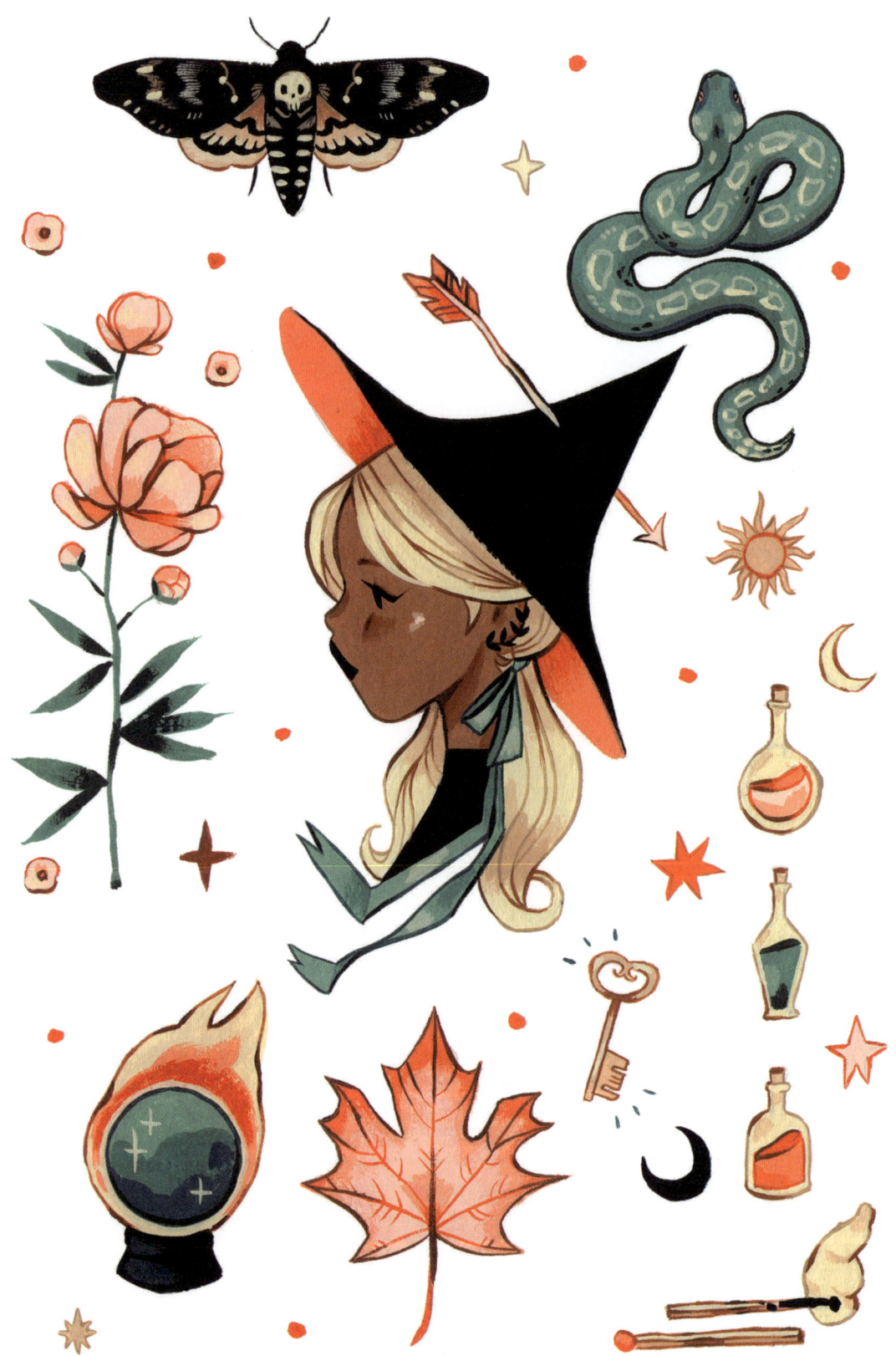

CHARACTER
DESIGN

Character design in my work is, above all, about giving the character a personality. Unlike character design for a movie, anime, or comic book where characters have to be drawn and viewed from all angles, with multiple expressions and feelings, I only draw my character once, under one particular angle. In the design process, the character is crystallized in a moment, like a memory.

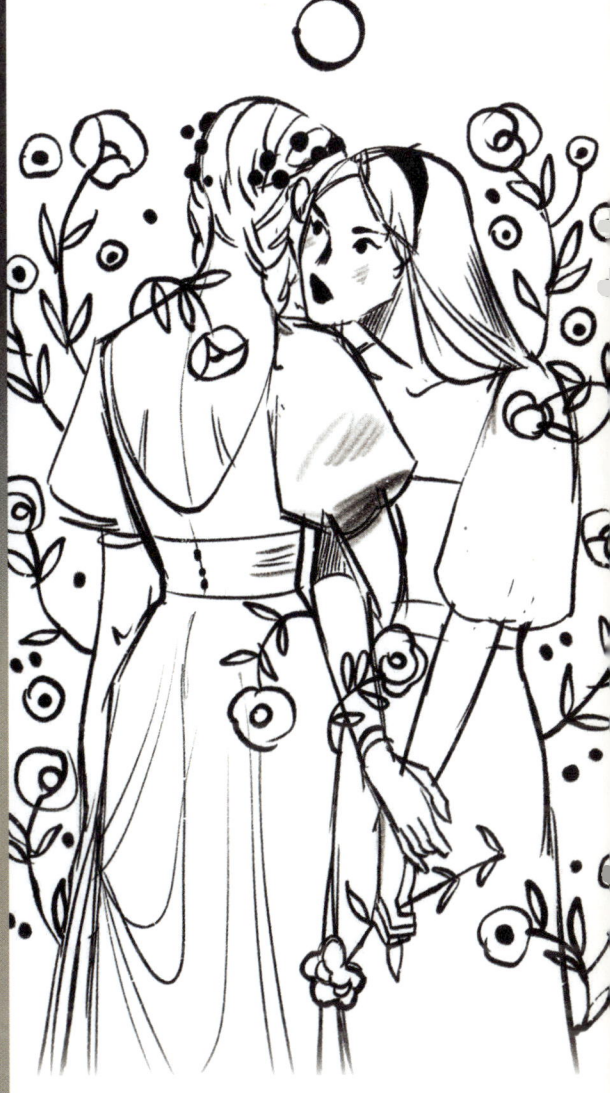

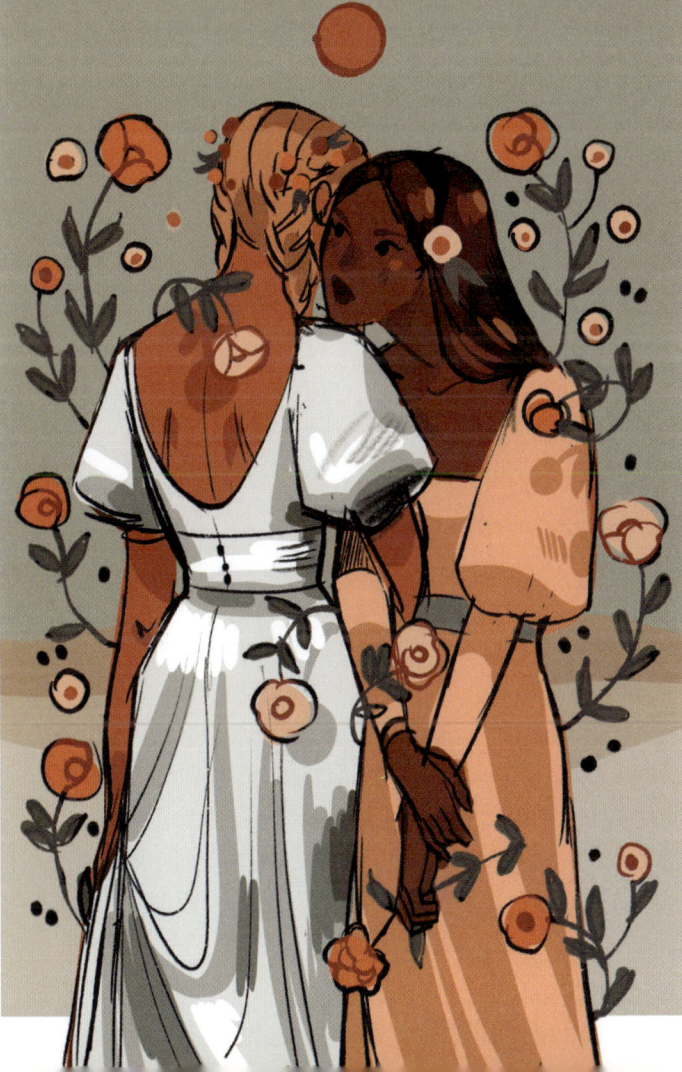

WOMEN

People often ask me why I almost exclusively draw women. In truth, I only share my drawings of women on social media because I feel they represent my personality the most. It's a personal choice and feeling, and I will always put women in the spotlight in my paintings because they constantly inspire me to tell stories.

I also draw men in my sketchbooks, and for comic book projects, and I really enjoy drawing my male friends, too.

ATTITUDE AND EXPRESSION

The body translates an emotion through its posture and attitude. Once I know what emotion I want to convey through the character, I consider how this can be read effectively through their design. Does their chest bulge with pride? Do they have their head up and ready to go on an adventure? Or is the body language closed, implying they might be shy? Perhaps they are bored or upset.

The face of the character can be a powerful tool in expressing an emotion. Even subtle changes in the face can convey their mood. Simply the orientation of their face or gaze can tell a tale — looking up toward the sky implies a sense of hope or dream of freedom, whereas looking down to the ground conveys feelings of quiet contemplation, serenity, or sadness. These complex emotions often feature in my illustrations.

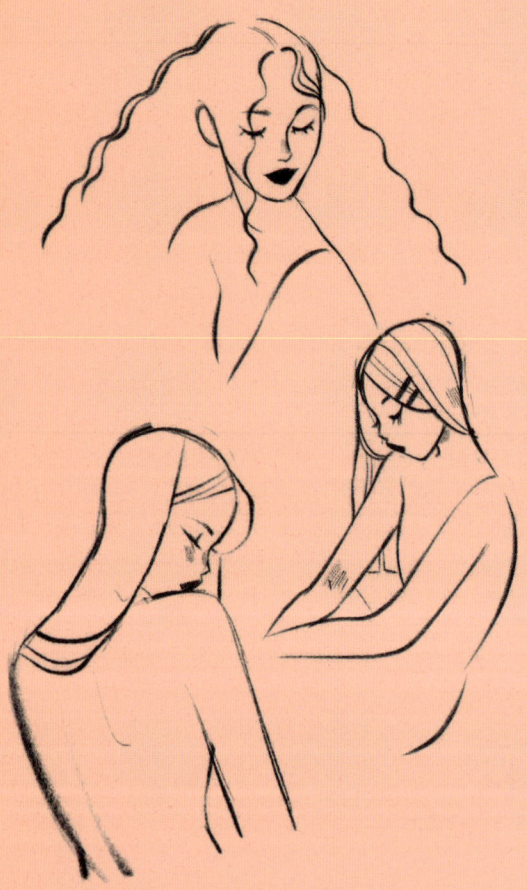

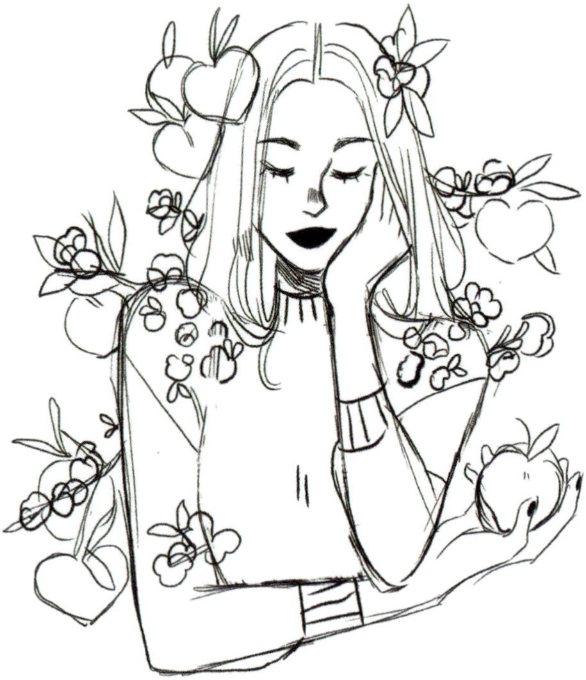

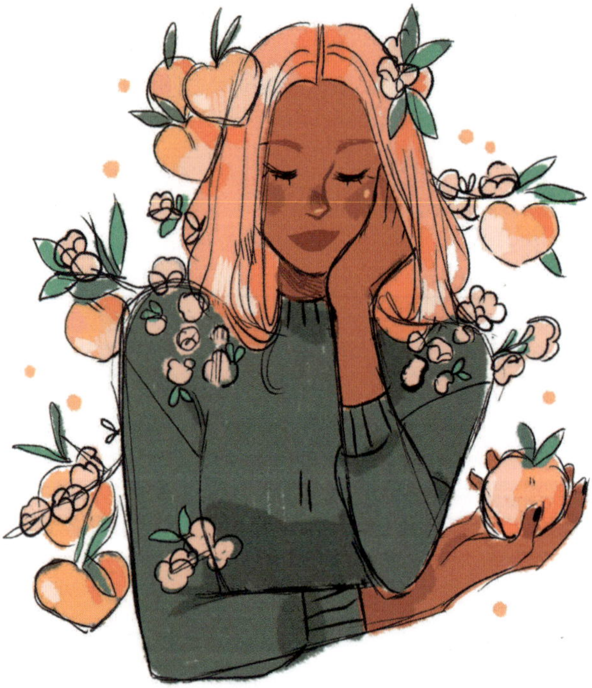

Peachy, digital sketch, 2019

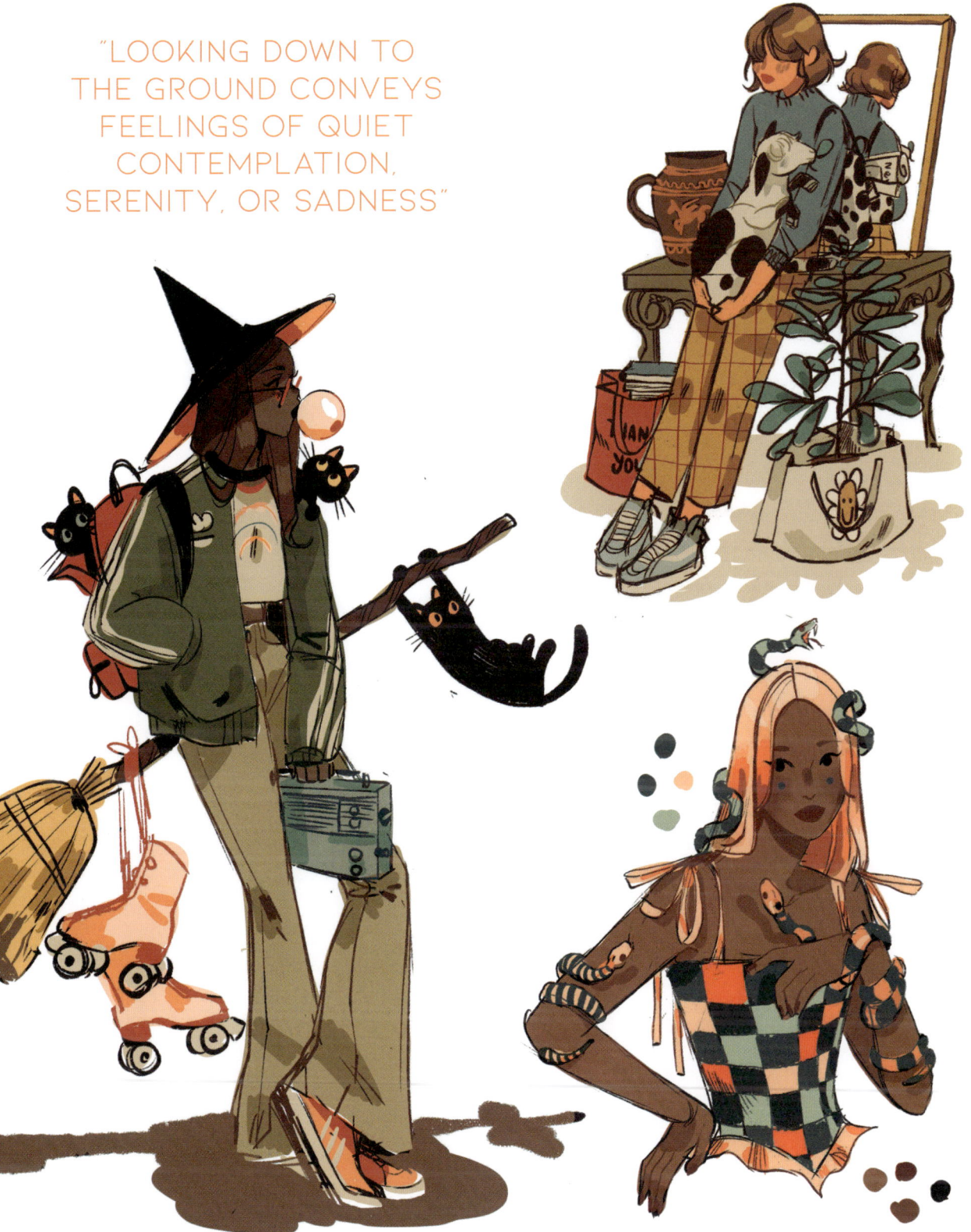

"LOOKING DOWN TO THE GROUND CONVEYS FEELINGS OF QUIET CONTEMPLATION, SERENITY, OR SADNESS"

CLOTHING

A character's clothes can also offer clues about their personality. Since I only have one picture to tell a story, I try to choose the style of each character wisely. Usually, their style is pretty close to my own style, and sometimes I create clothing for the characters that I would like to have myself!

Clothes can also reflect a specific style of the time and define the era of the design. If I draw a close-bodied gown, this garment will be used as a time indicator: the character is in France in the eighteenth century. If the character is dressed in a silver jumpsuit and wears fun neon makeup, they are probably from the future. Drawing an outfit from the 2020s is also a way to capture the era we are currently living in.

Clothing can also be used to interact with other key elements of the illustration and become an integral part of the design. For example, I like to use stripes, checks, or dots to create a contrast with the rest of my illustration, or to create a harmony and continuity. Sometimes my characters' outfits are linked to the design of their spirit animals.

Character inspired by Ms. Frizzle from the animated TV series, **The Magic School Bus.** The composition is inspired by John Singer Sargent's oil painting of Elizabeth Winthrop Chanler

Tic-Tac-Toe, digital sketch, 2021

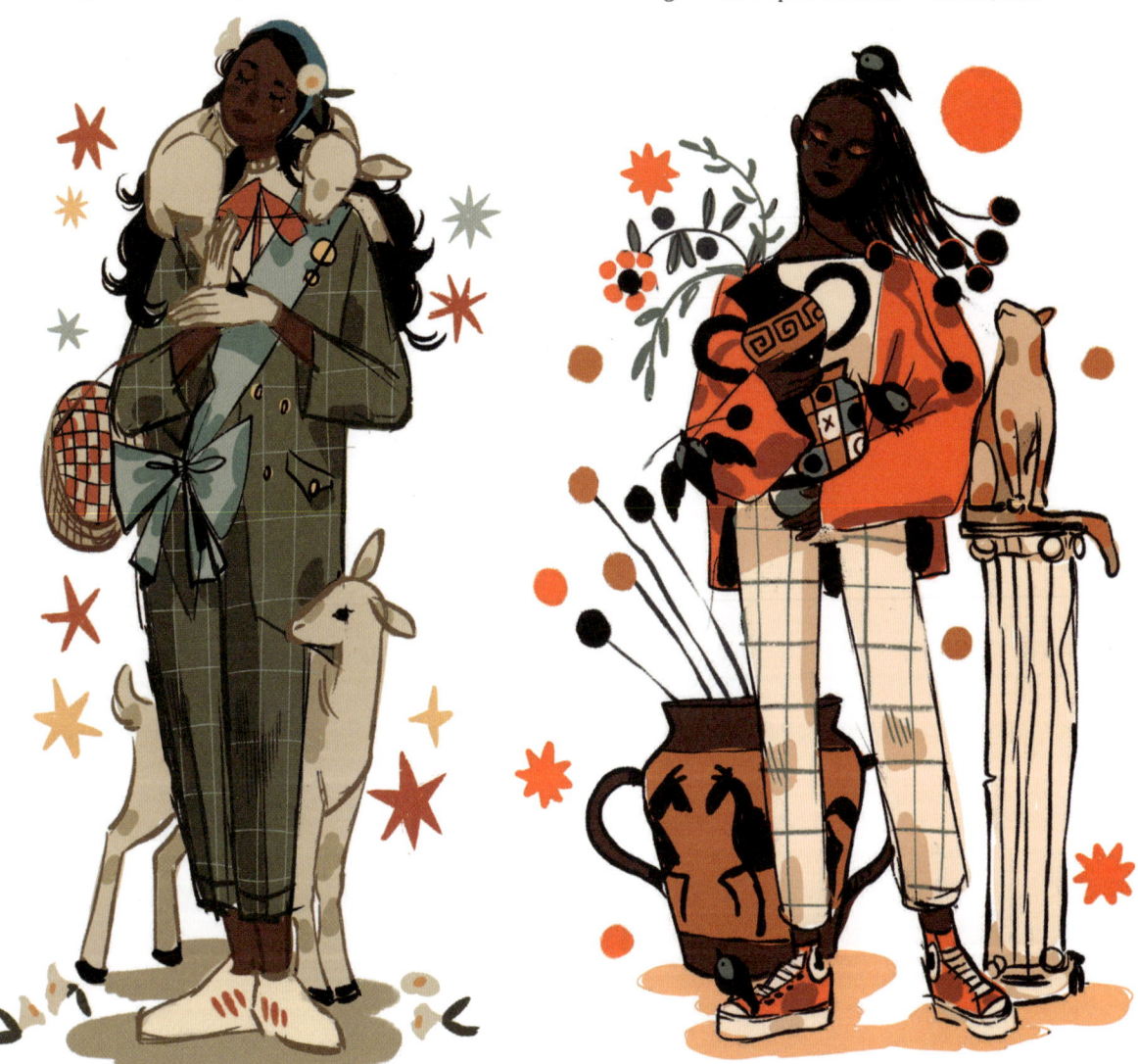

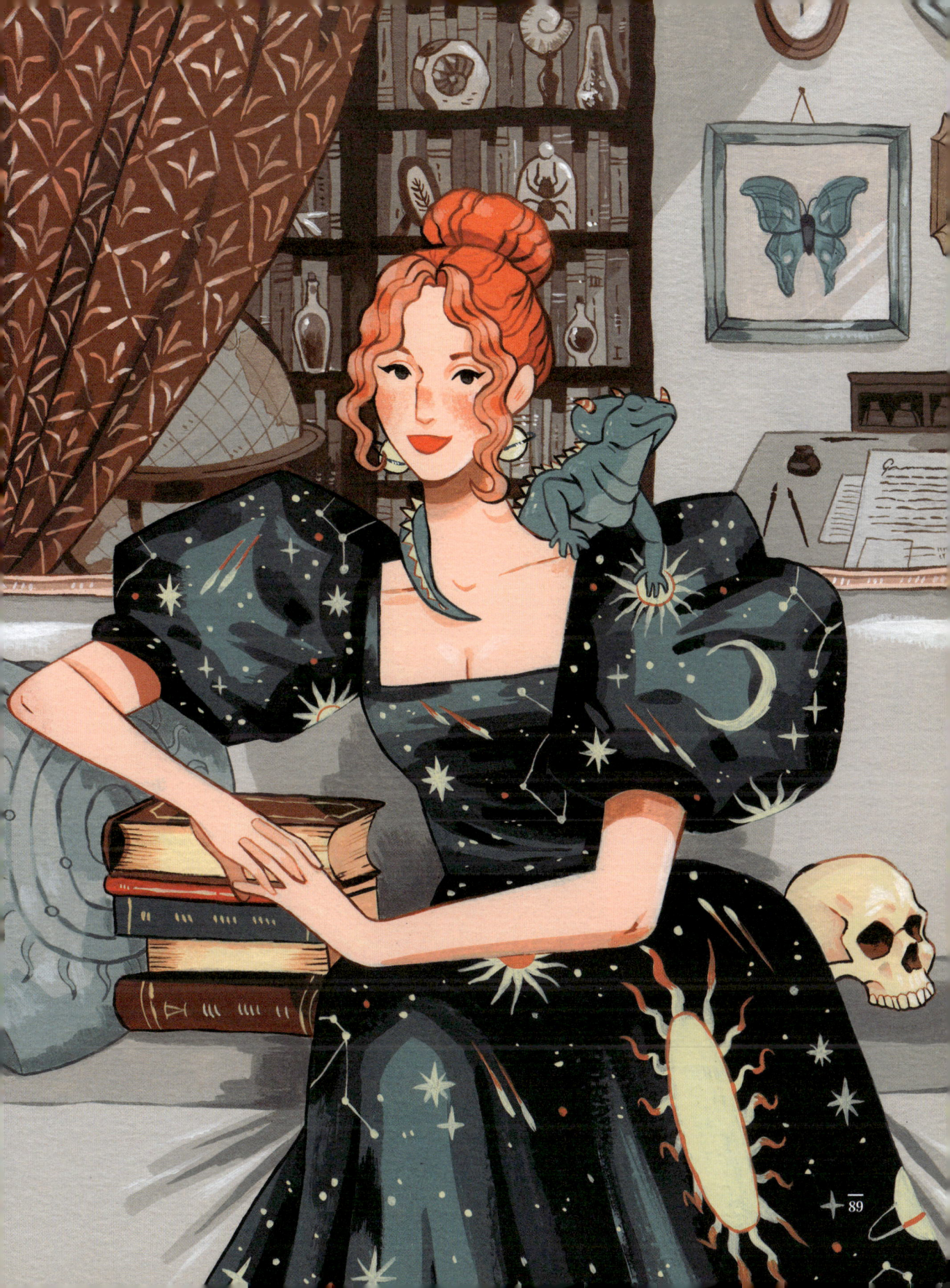

"ANIMALS ARE MAGICAL, MYSTERIOUS, AND IMPOSING, WHATEVER THEIR SIZE"

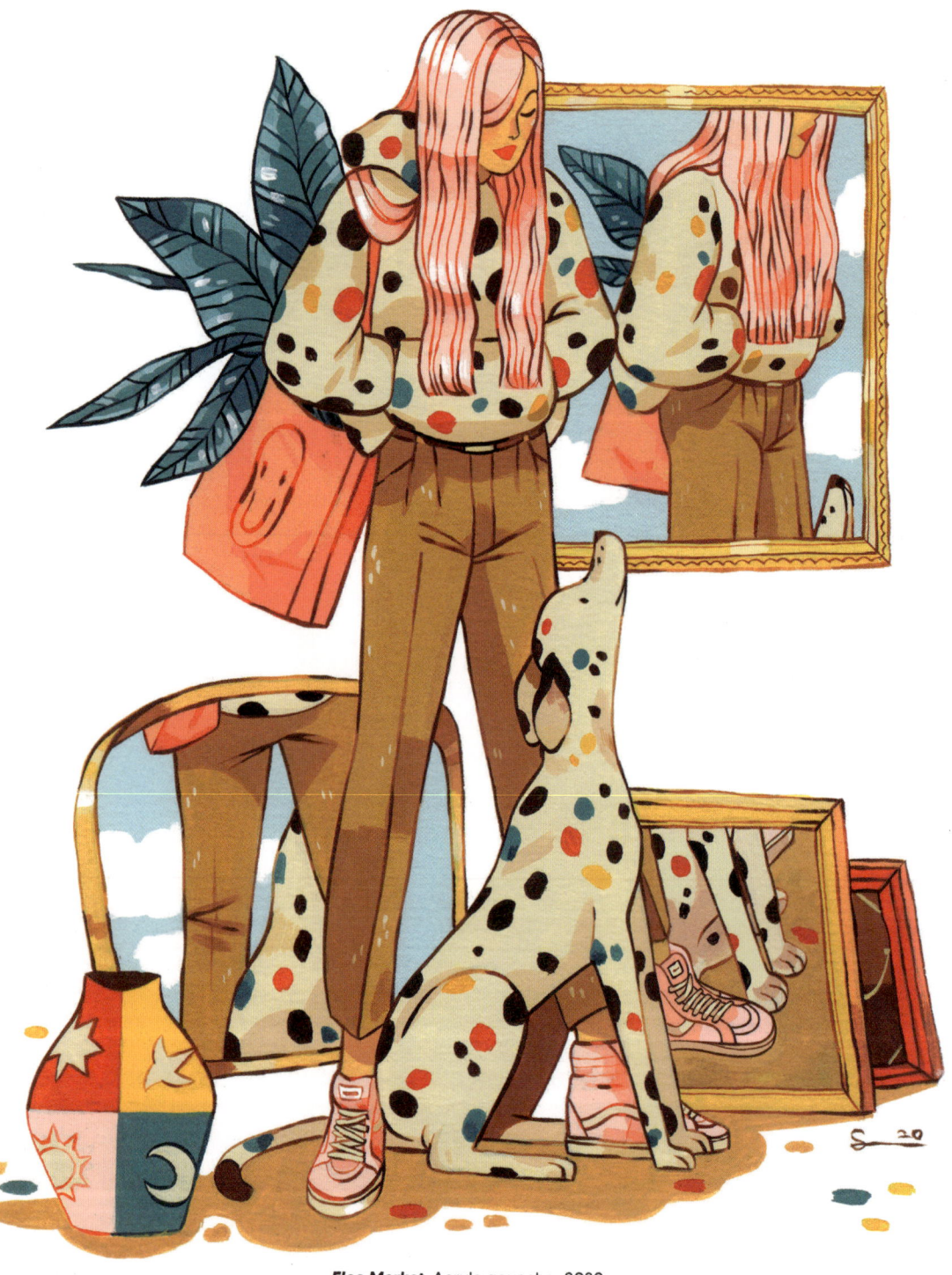

Flea Market, Acryla gouache, 2020

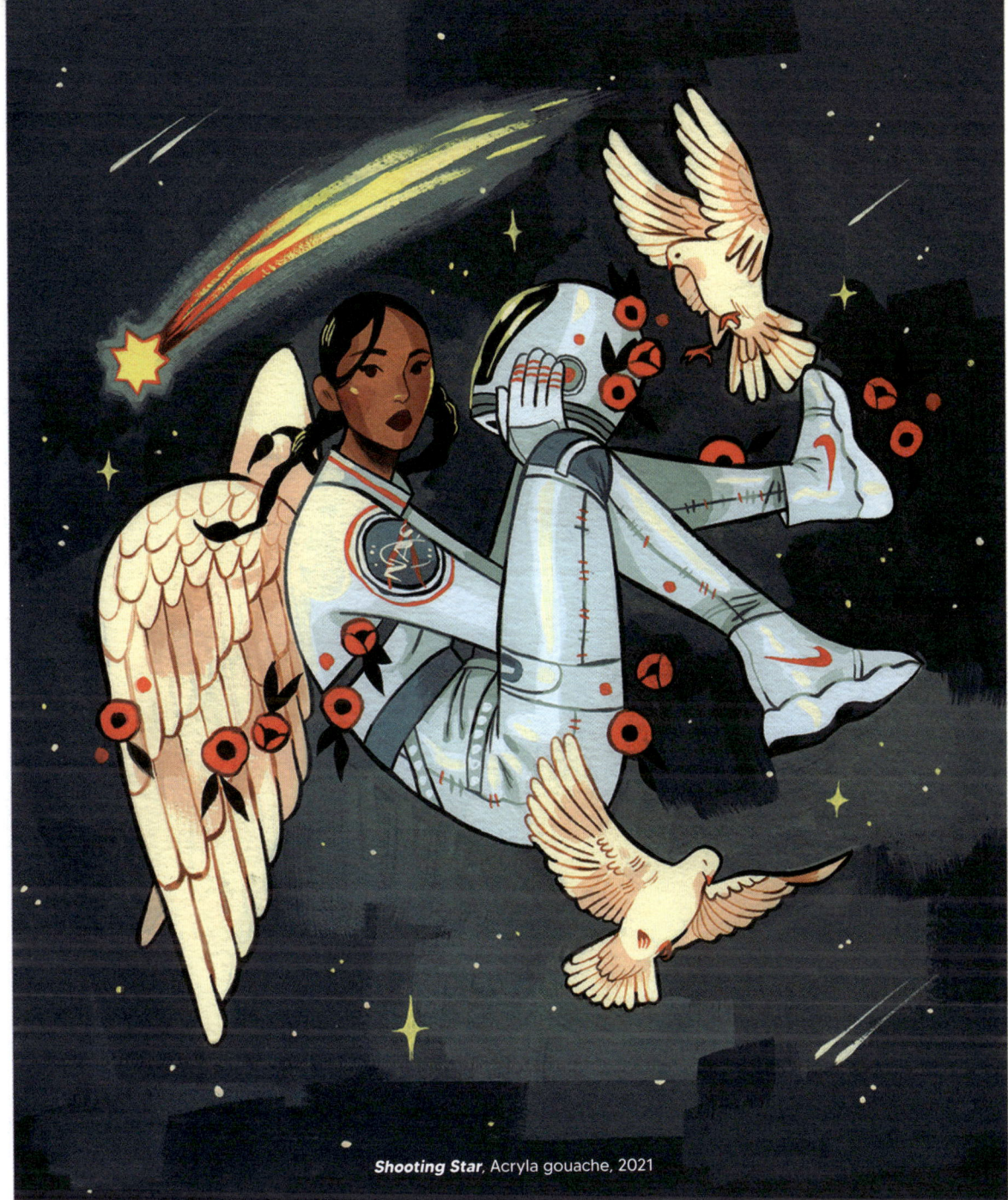

Shooting Star, Acryla gouache, 2021

ANIMALS

As previously mentioned, the animals in my illustrations are often used as an extension of the character, reflecting their unique personality and story in their design. They are often clearly visually linked by a pattern that crosses over onto the design of the character. This repeating pattern also provides continuity and harmony.

I like the idea of a spirit animals. I grew up surrounded by animals, and my pets have a big place in my life. Animals are magical, mysterious, and imposing, whatever their size. Every species has their own specificity, patterns, colors, and textures. Nature is beautiful and is an endless source of inspiration!

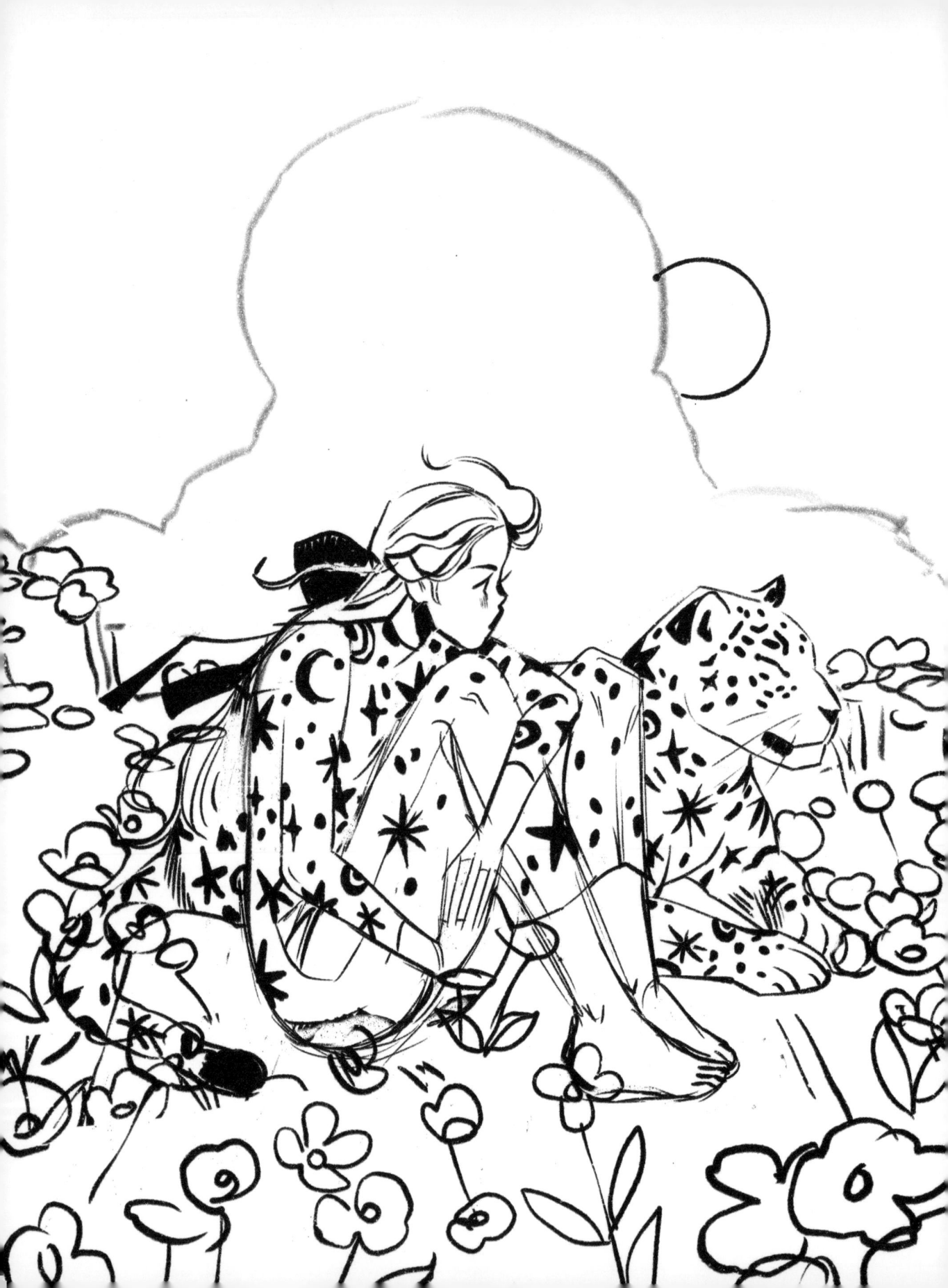

TECHNIQUES & TUTORIALS

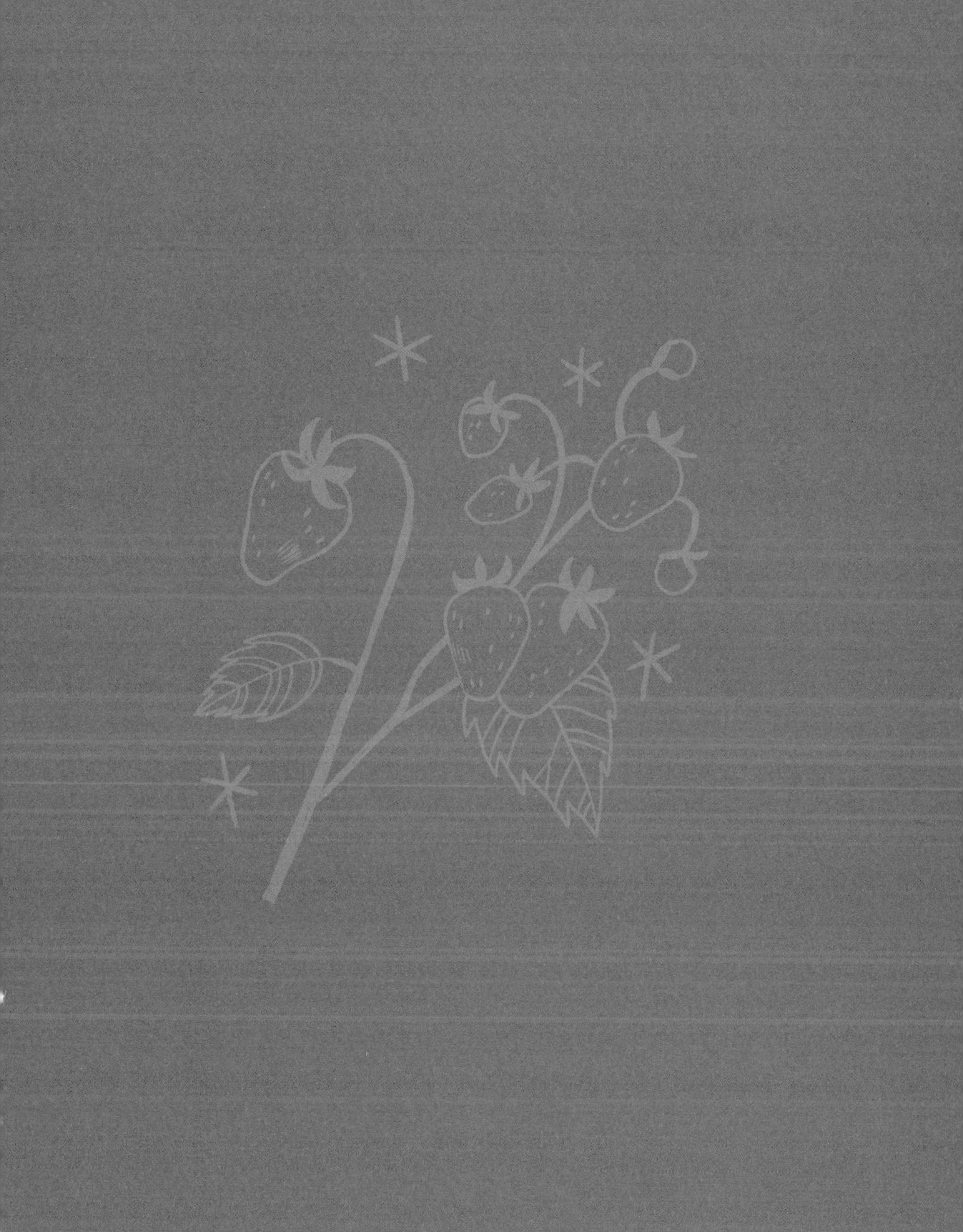

SKETCHING
& DOODLING

Sketching and doodling freehand allows me to find interesting shapes and compositions. I allow my mind to wander as I sketch on paper with a black pen. I know I won't be able to erase my doodles, so I keep the forms loose and simply have fun with shapes without thinking about what the final drawing might look like.

I always start my design process by sketching, as it is an exercise that offers me space to play and explore new leads for future illustrations without the need to create something technically perfect.

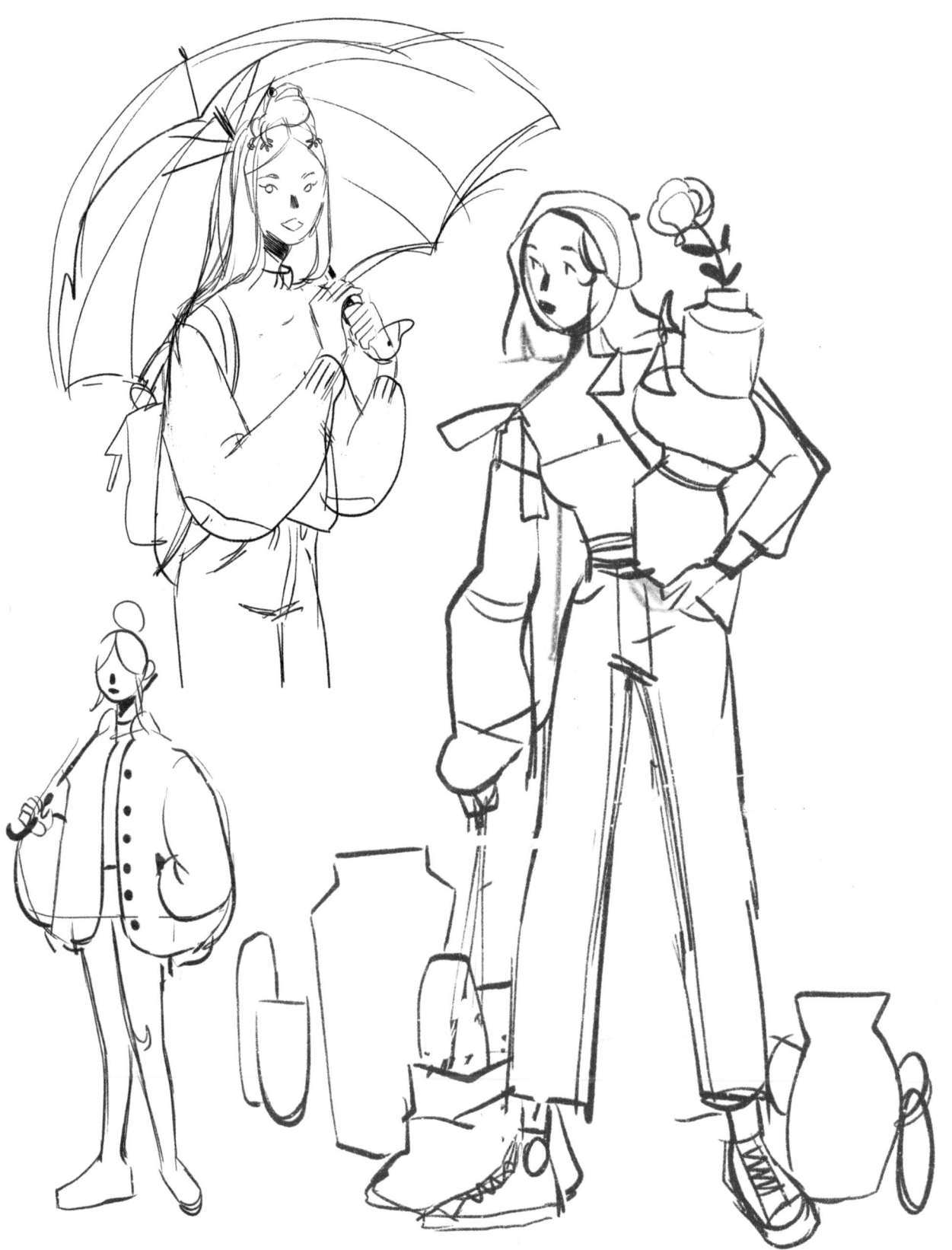

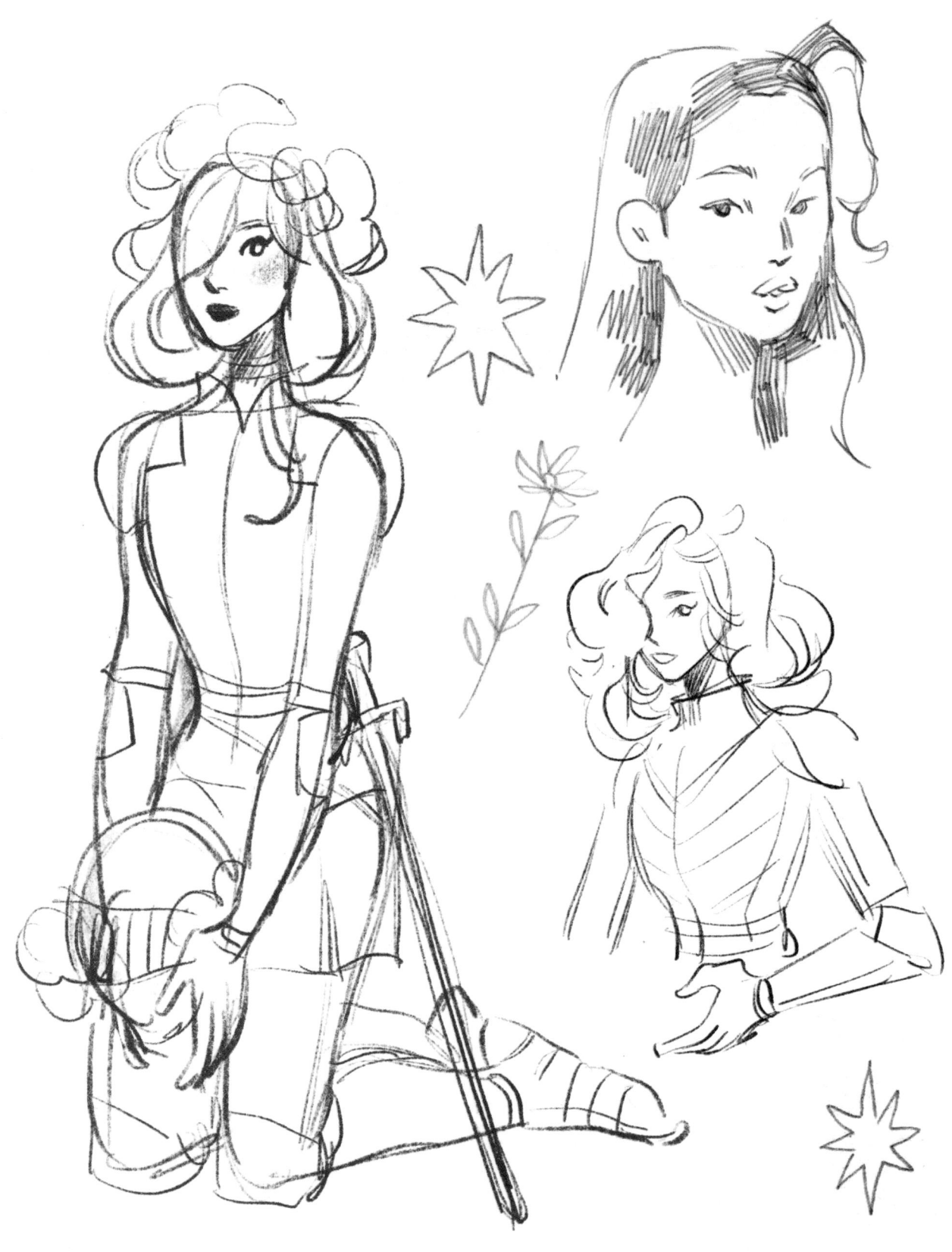

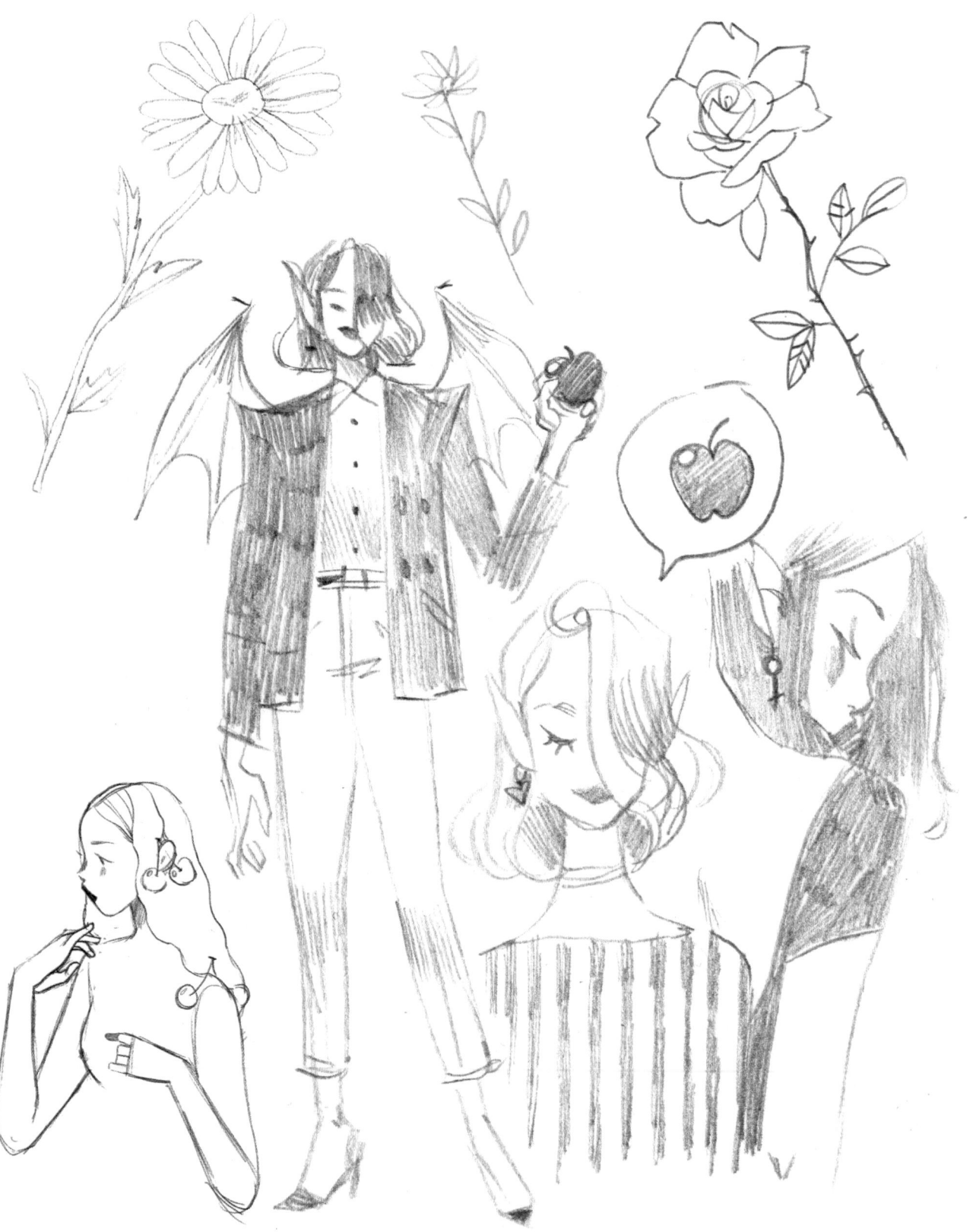

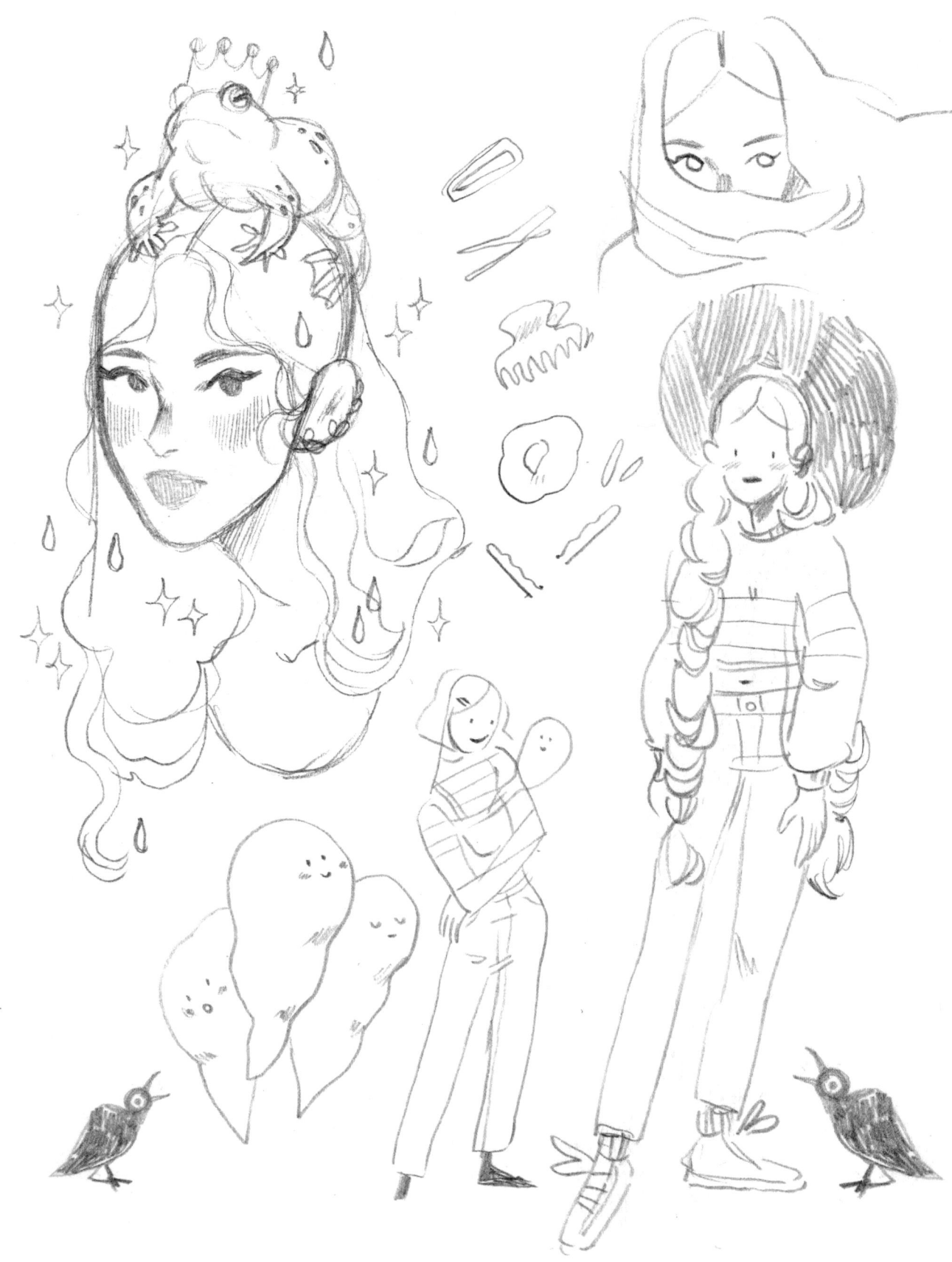

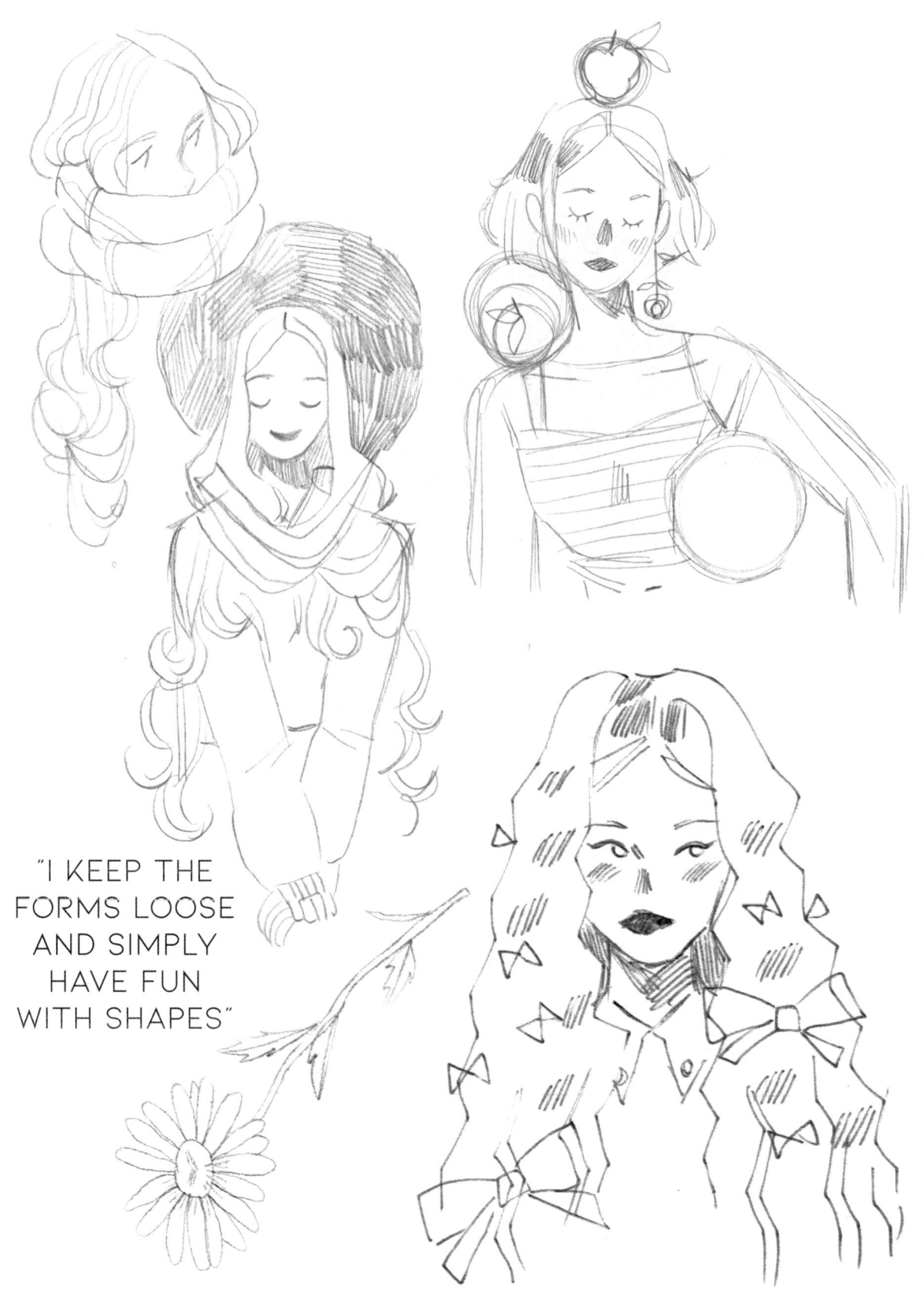

"I KEEP THE FORMS LOOSE AND SIMPLY HAVE FUN WITH SHAPES"

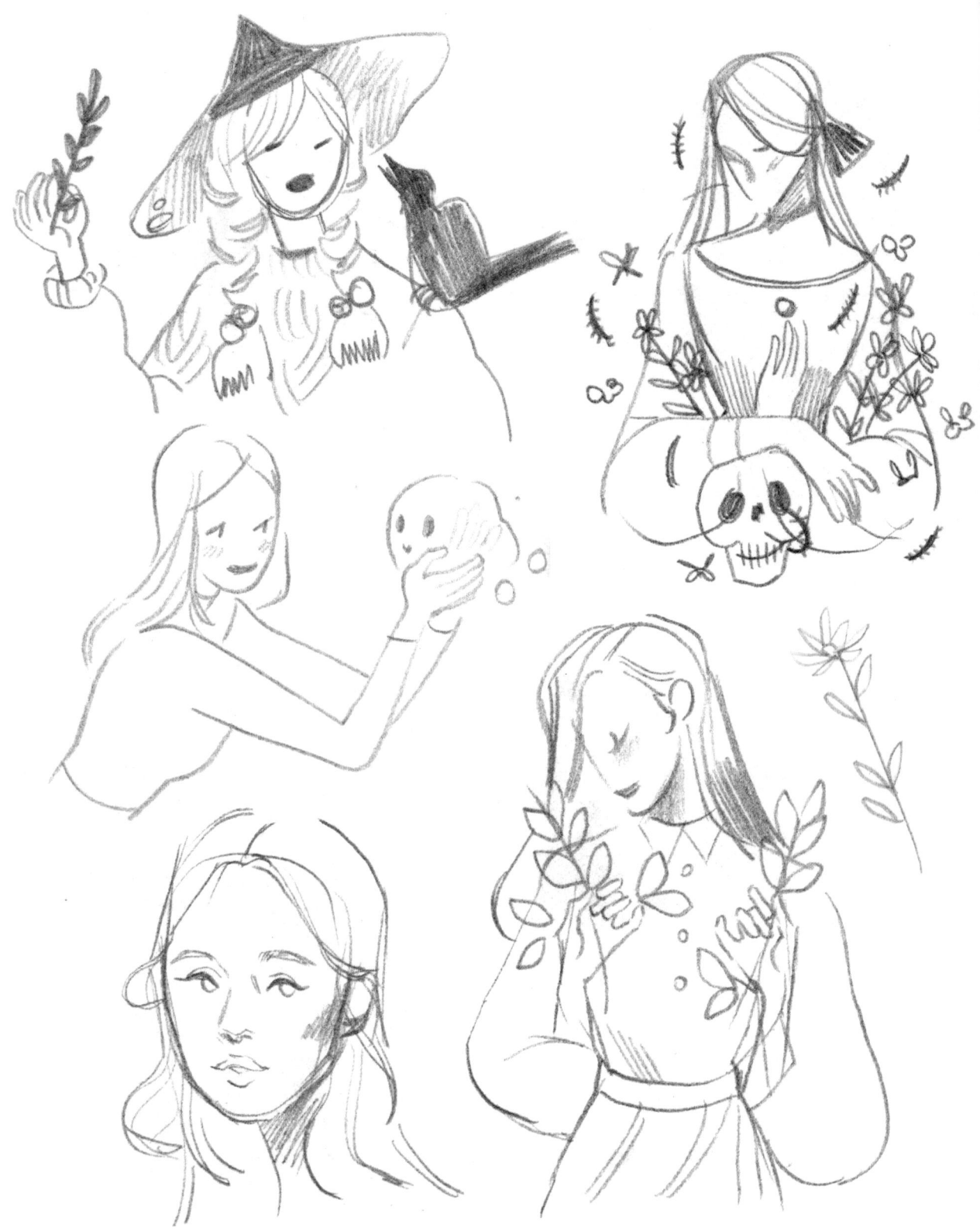

MOOD

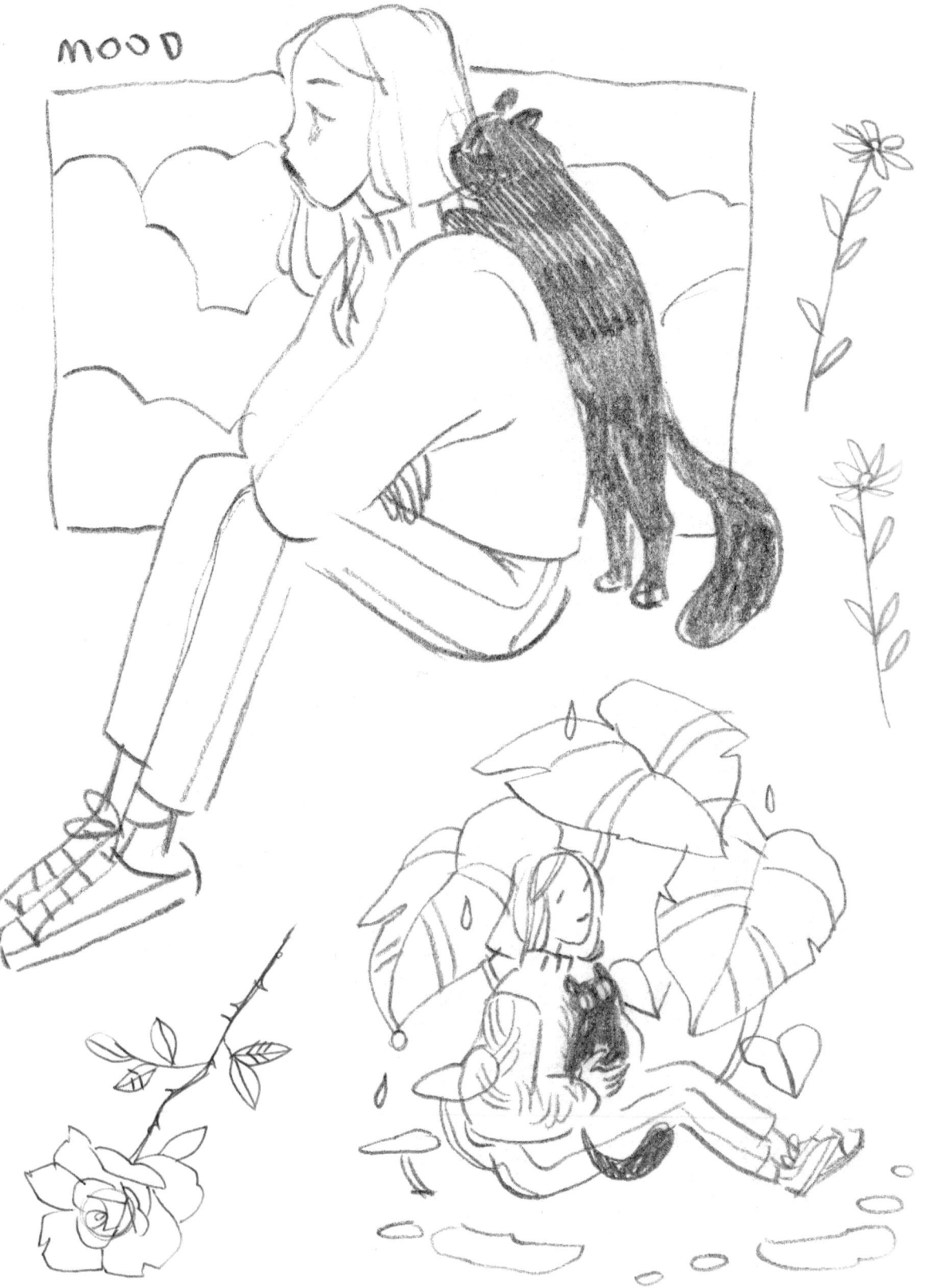

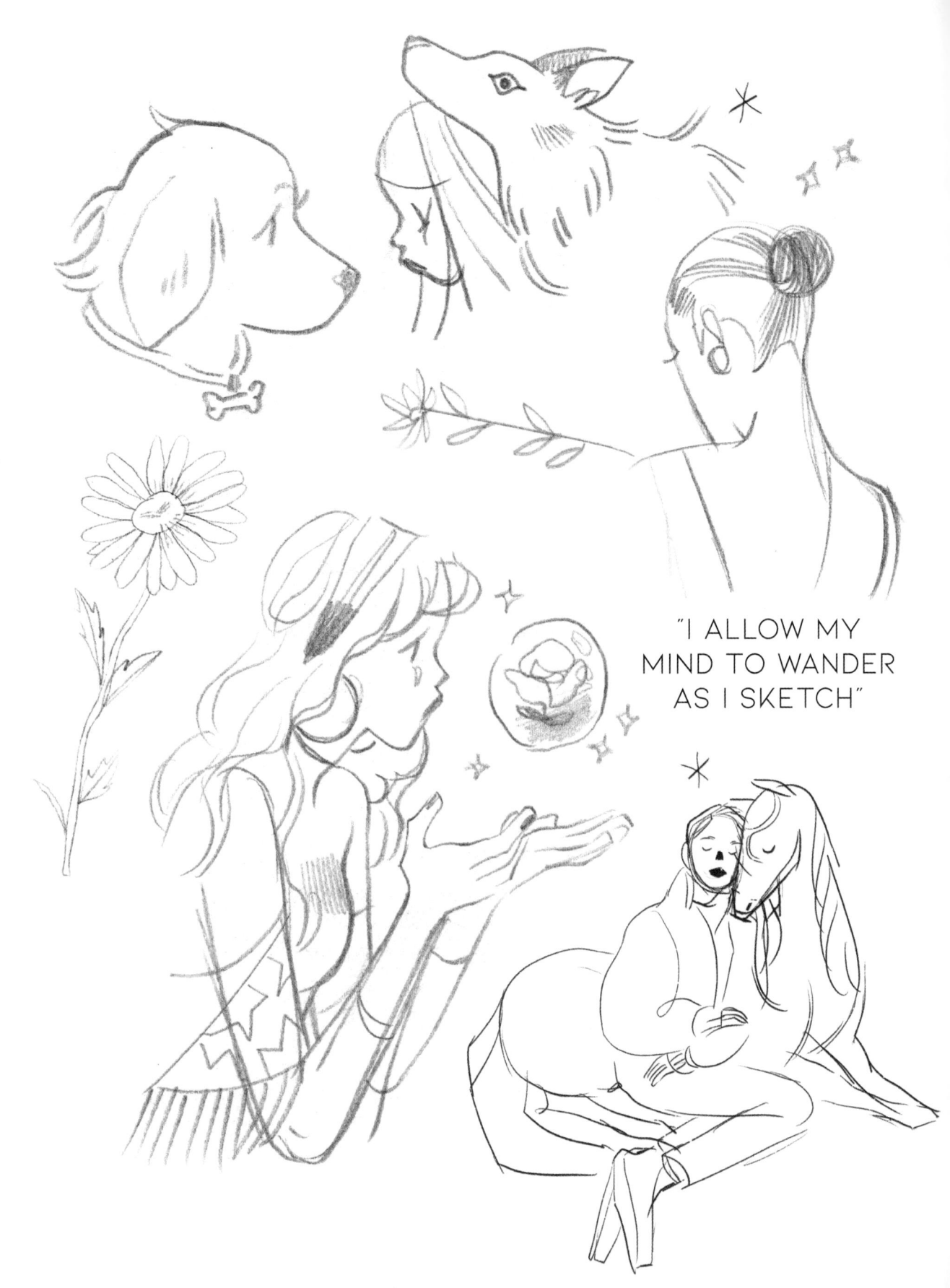

"I ALLOW MY
MIND TO WANDER
AS I SKETCH"

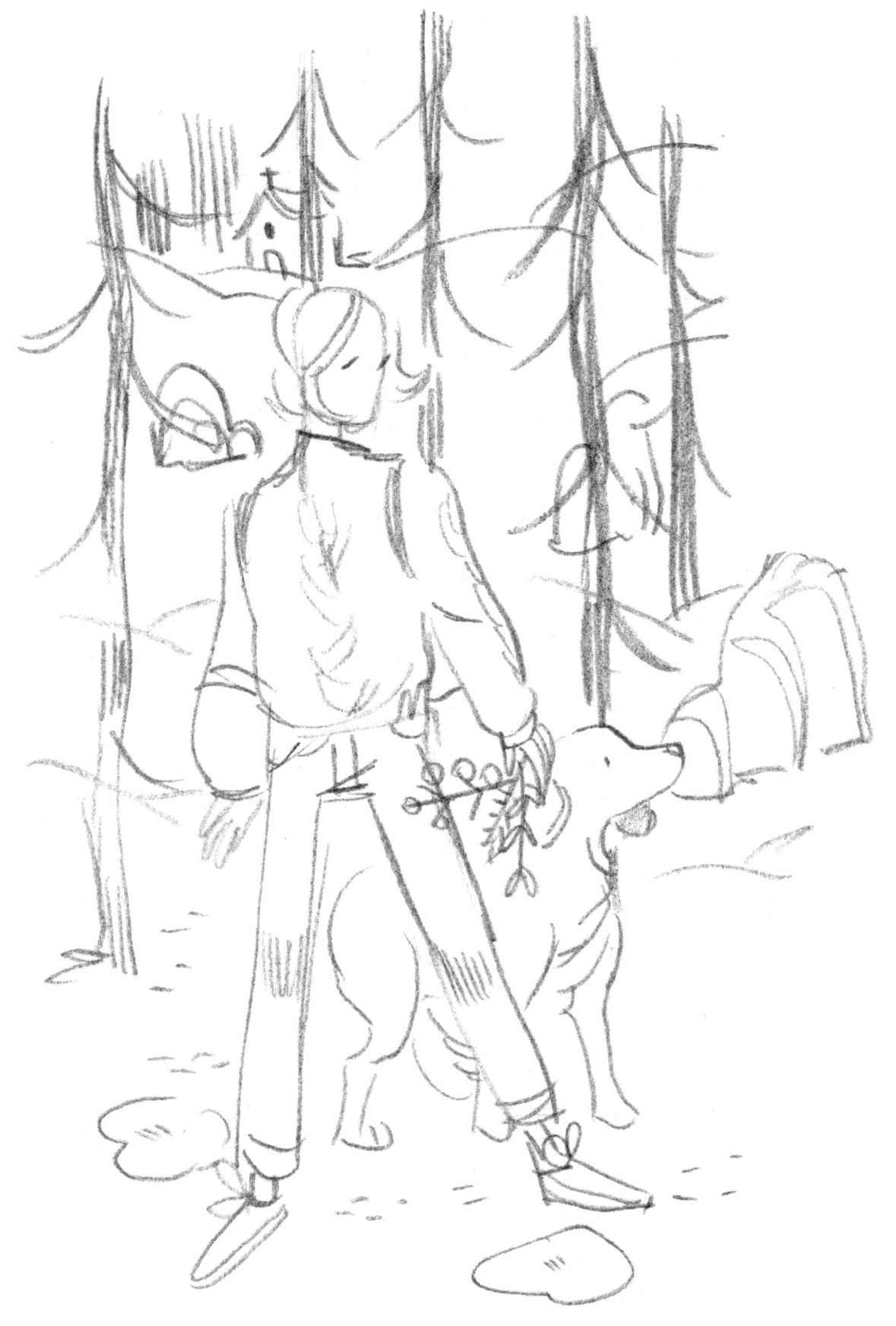

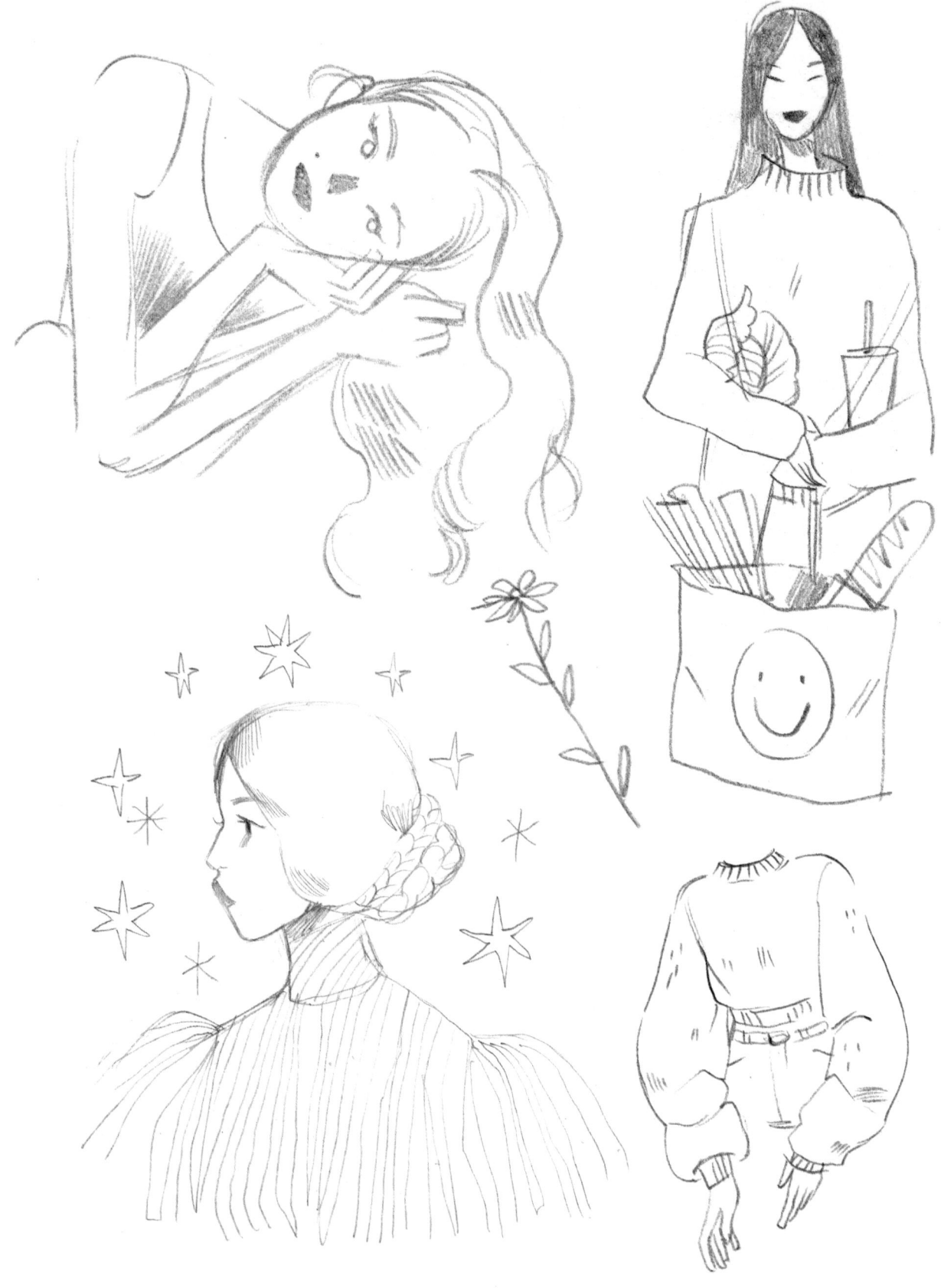

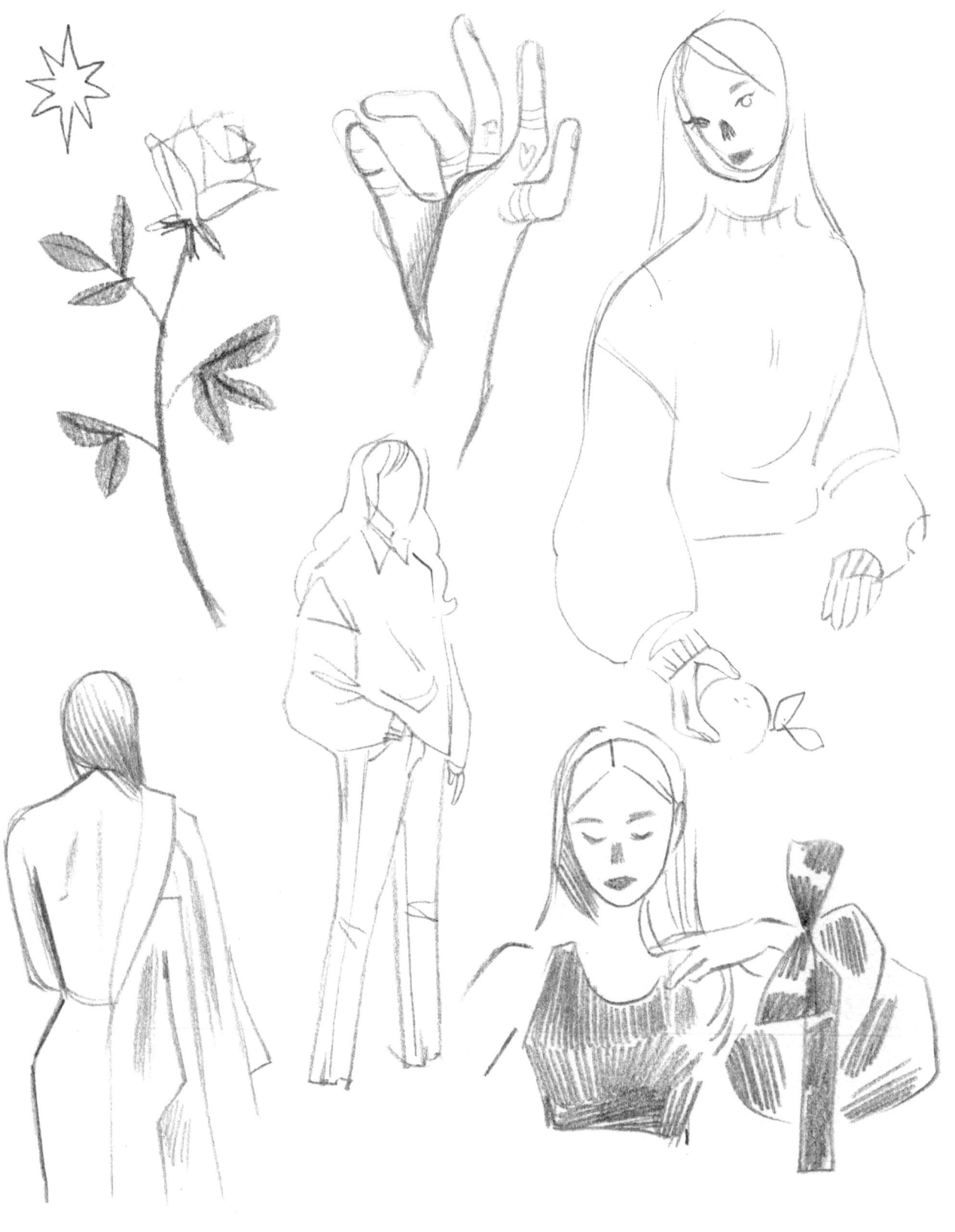

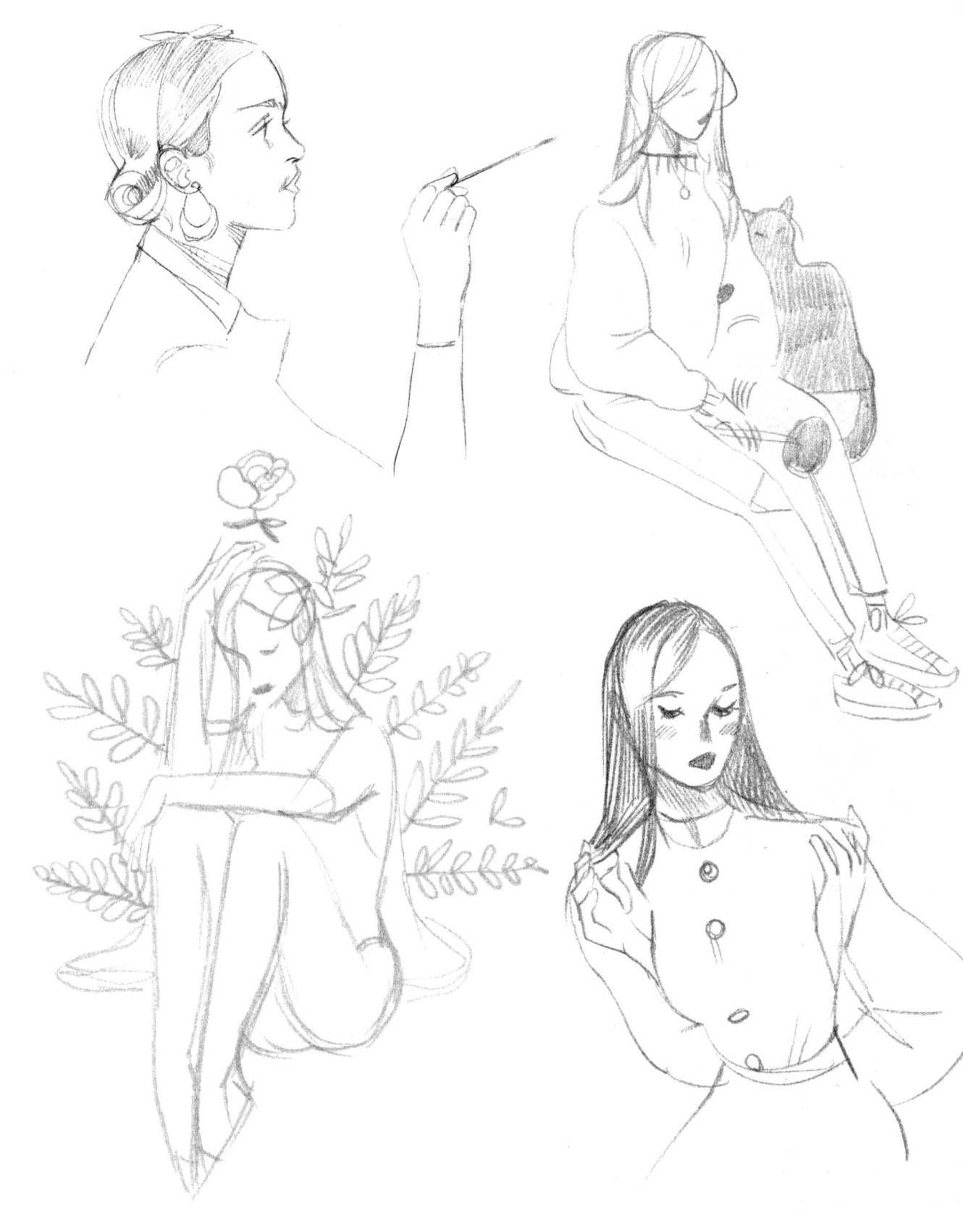

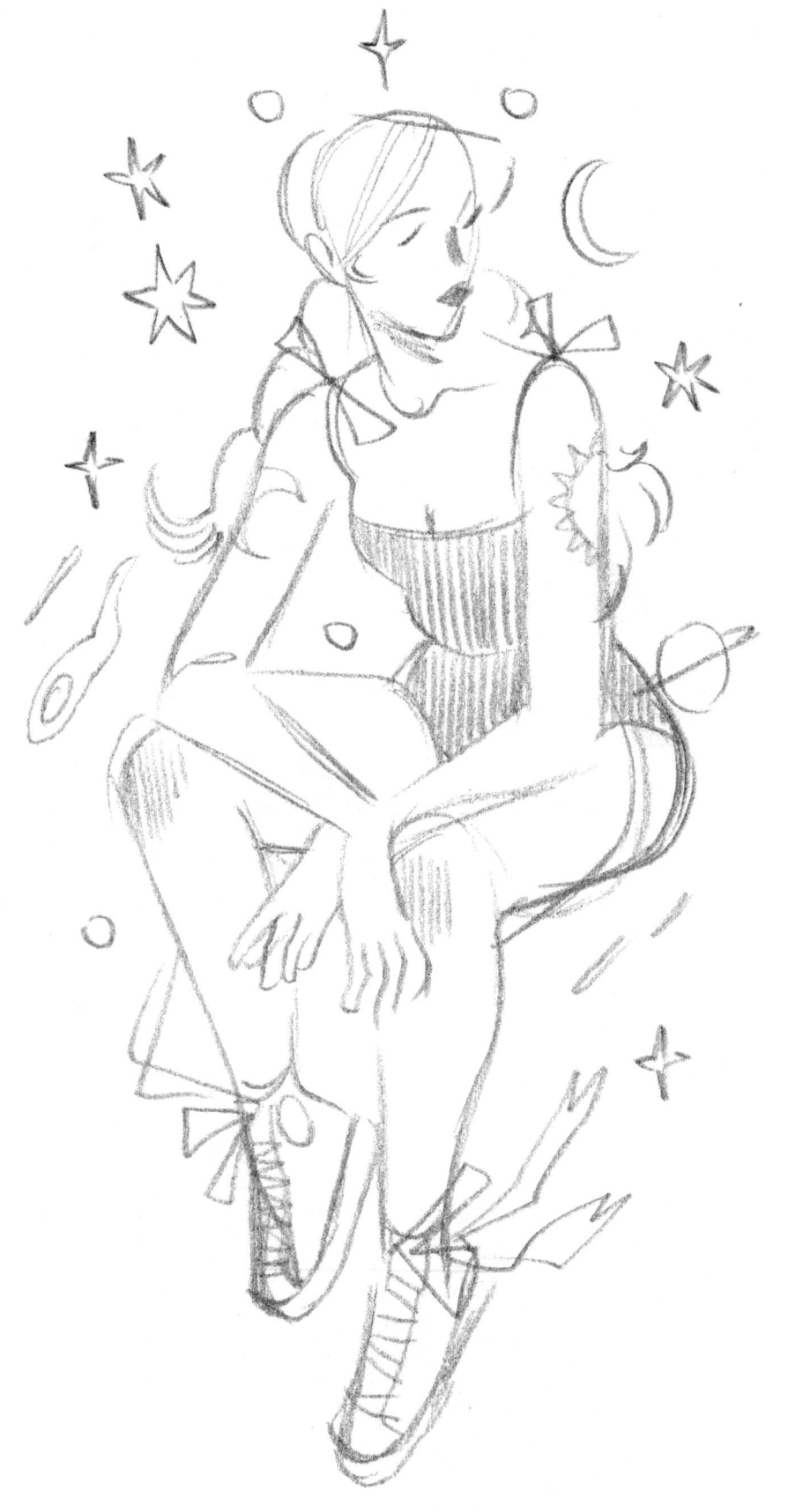

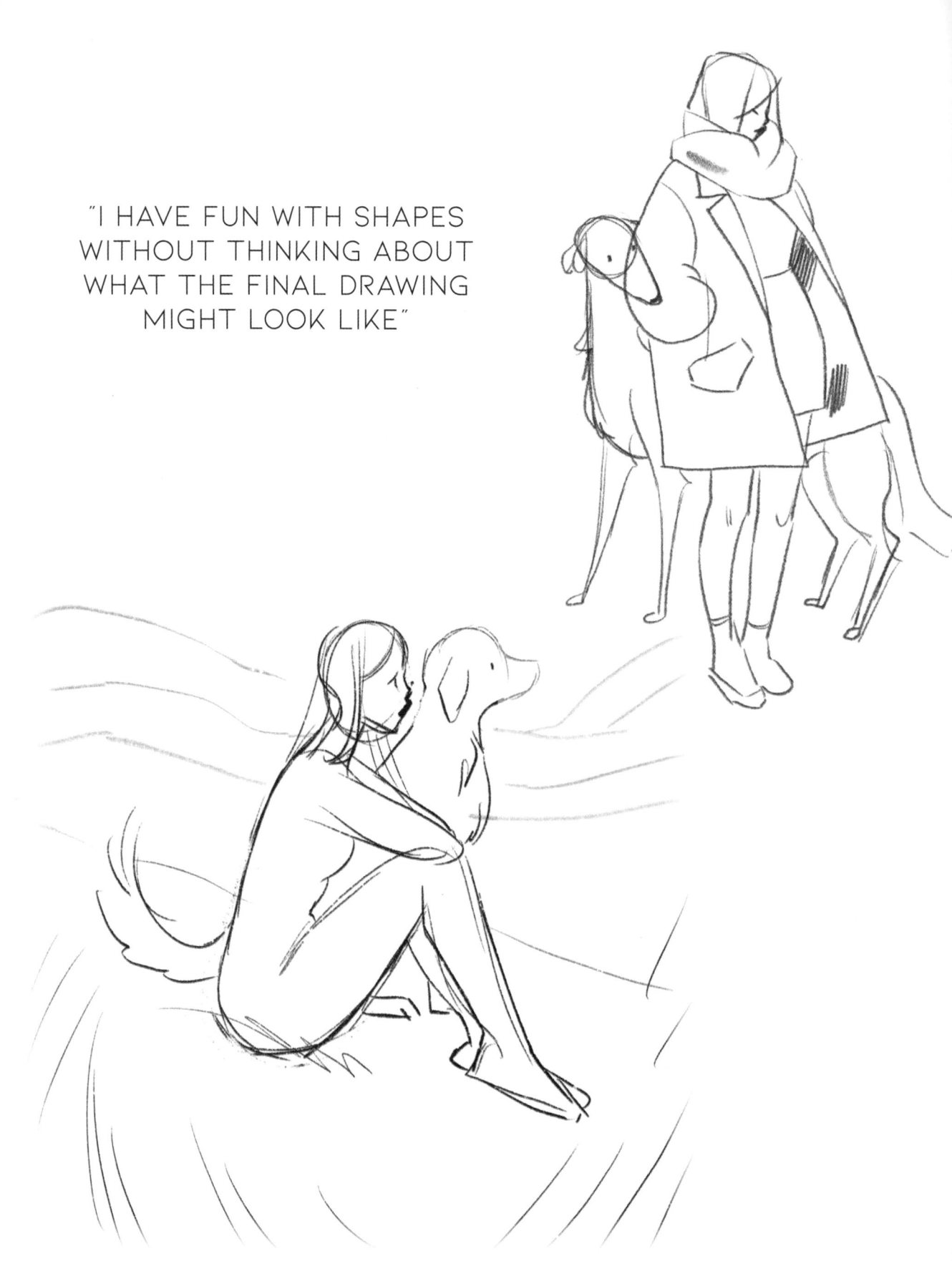

"I HAVE FUN WITH SHAPES WITHOUT THINKING ABOUT WHAT THE FINAL DRAWING MIGHT LOOK LIKE"

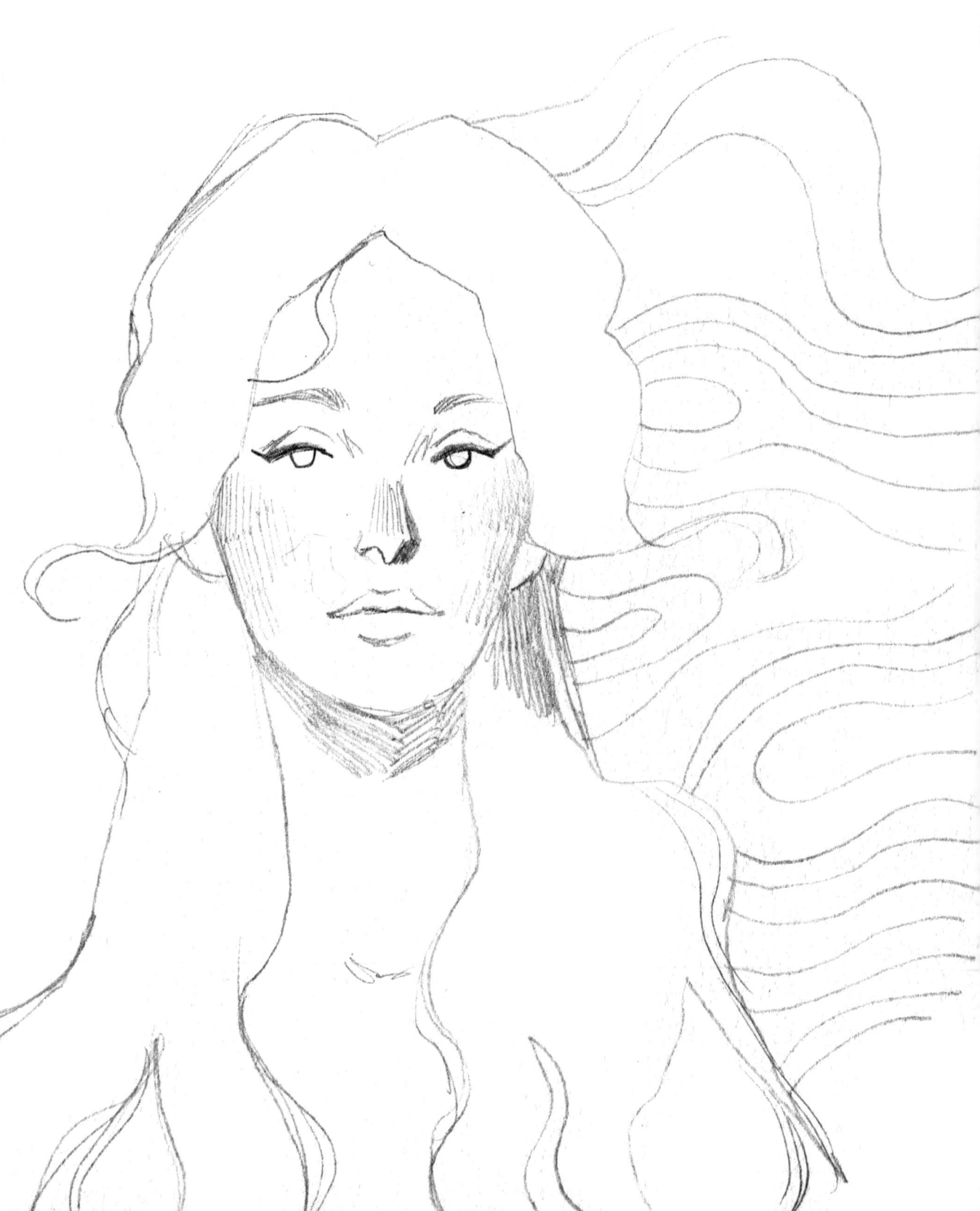

DIGITAL PAINTING

I use digital sketching and painting during the preparatory steps before painting a design traditionally on paper. Sketching on Procreate on my iPad offers so many possibilities, which makes it the best tool for perfecting a doodle I created on paper, and turning it into a rendered illustration.

Painting digitally allows me to experiment — color and compositional adjustments can be applied easily and often at the touch of a button! Once I'm happy with the final digital sketch, I transfer it to paper and embark on the traditional painting process using gouache.

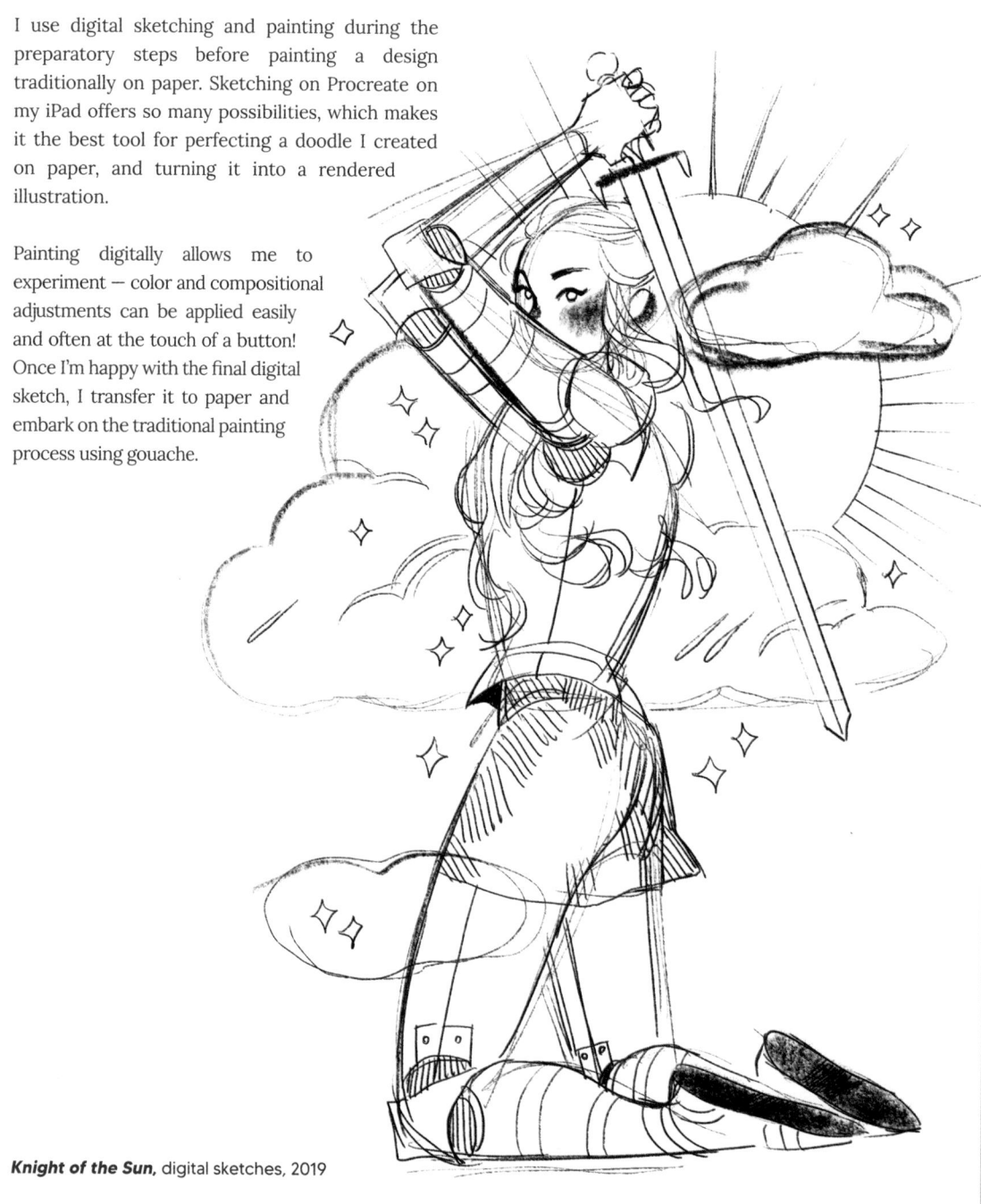

Knight of the Sun, digital sketches, 2019

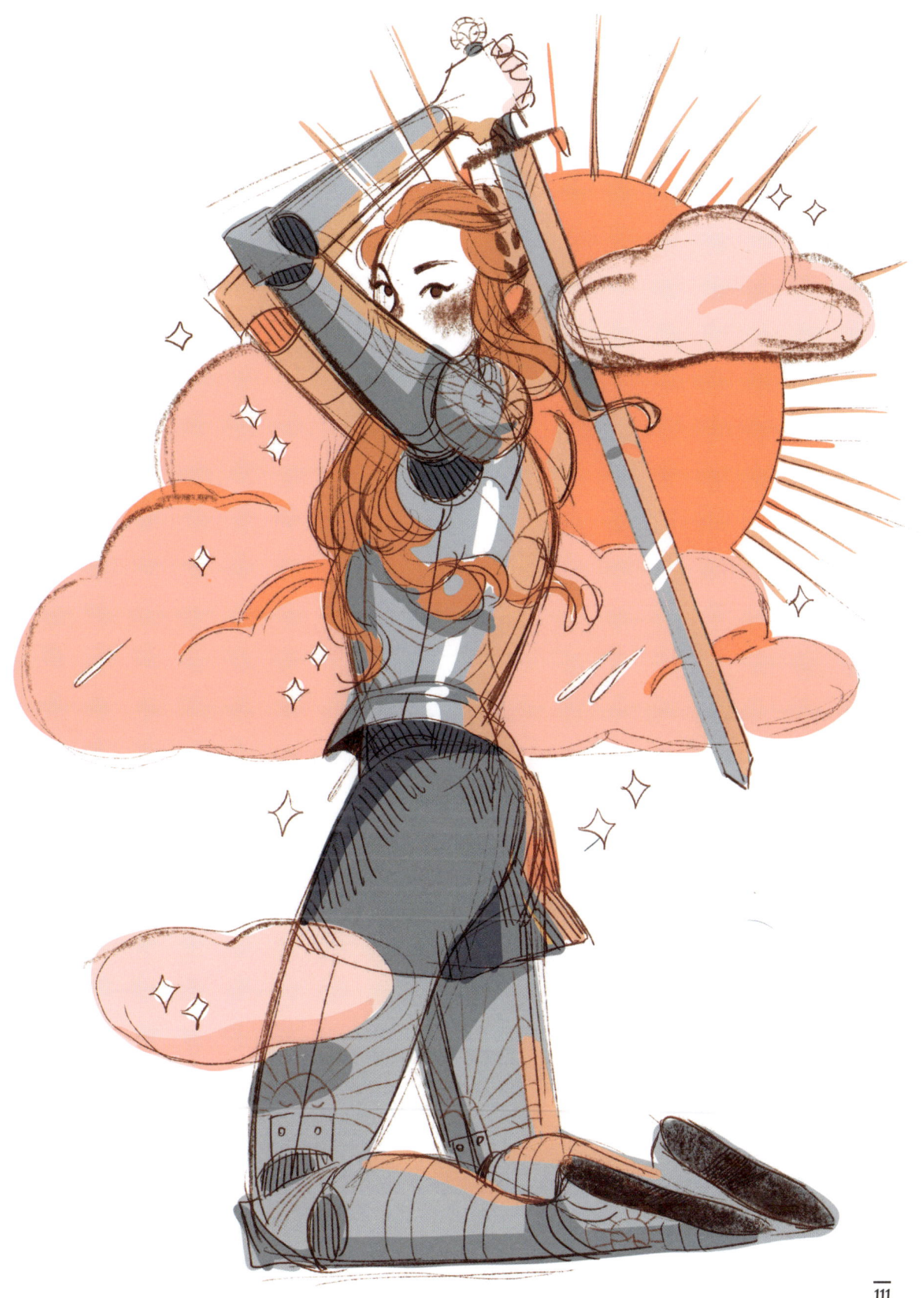

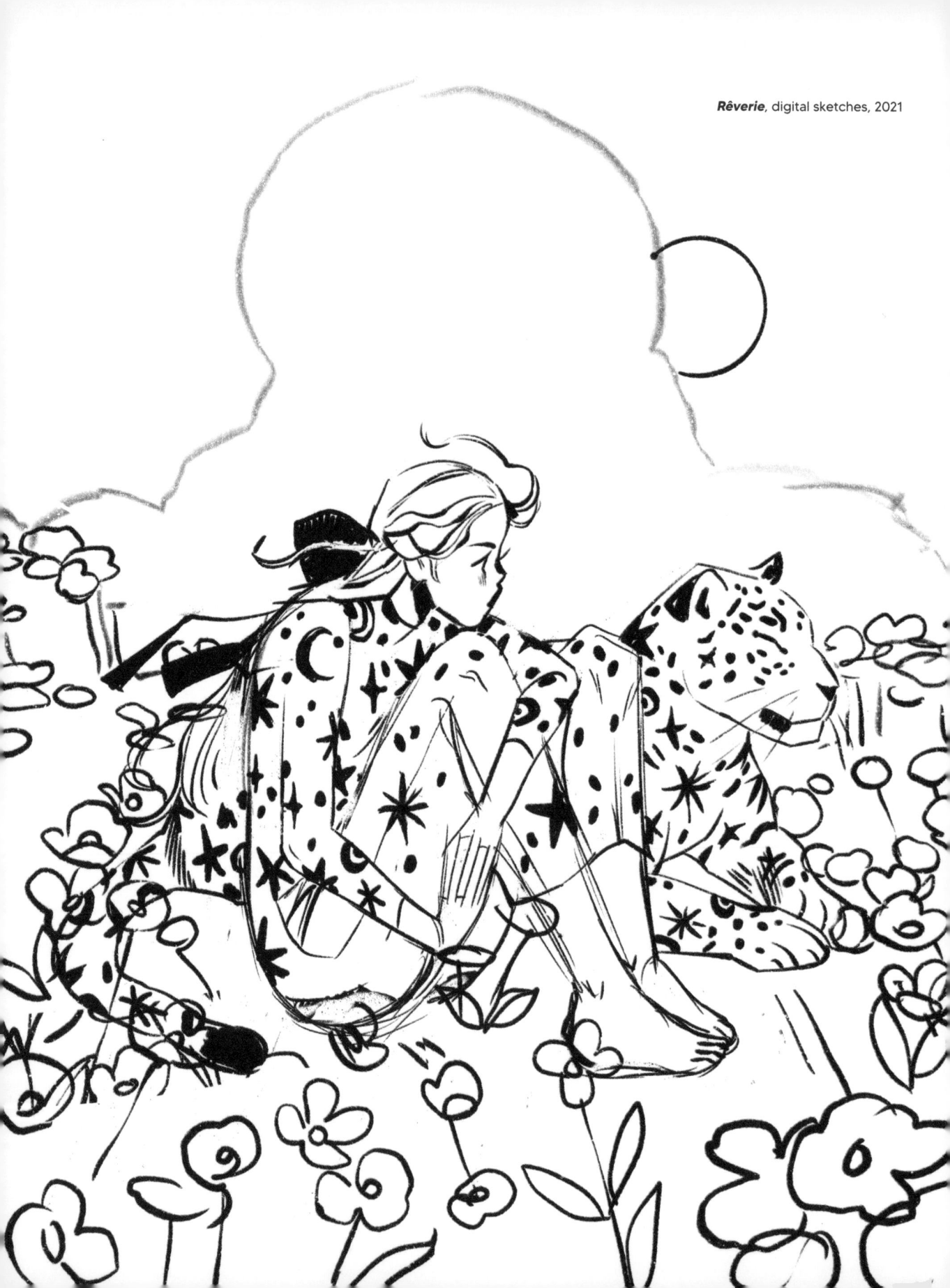

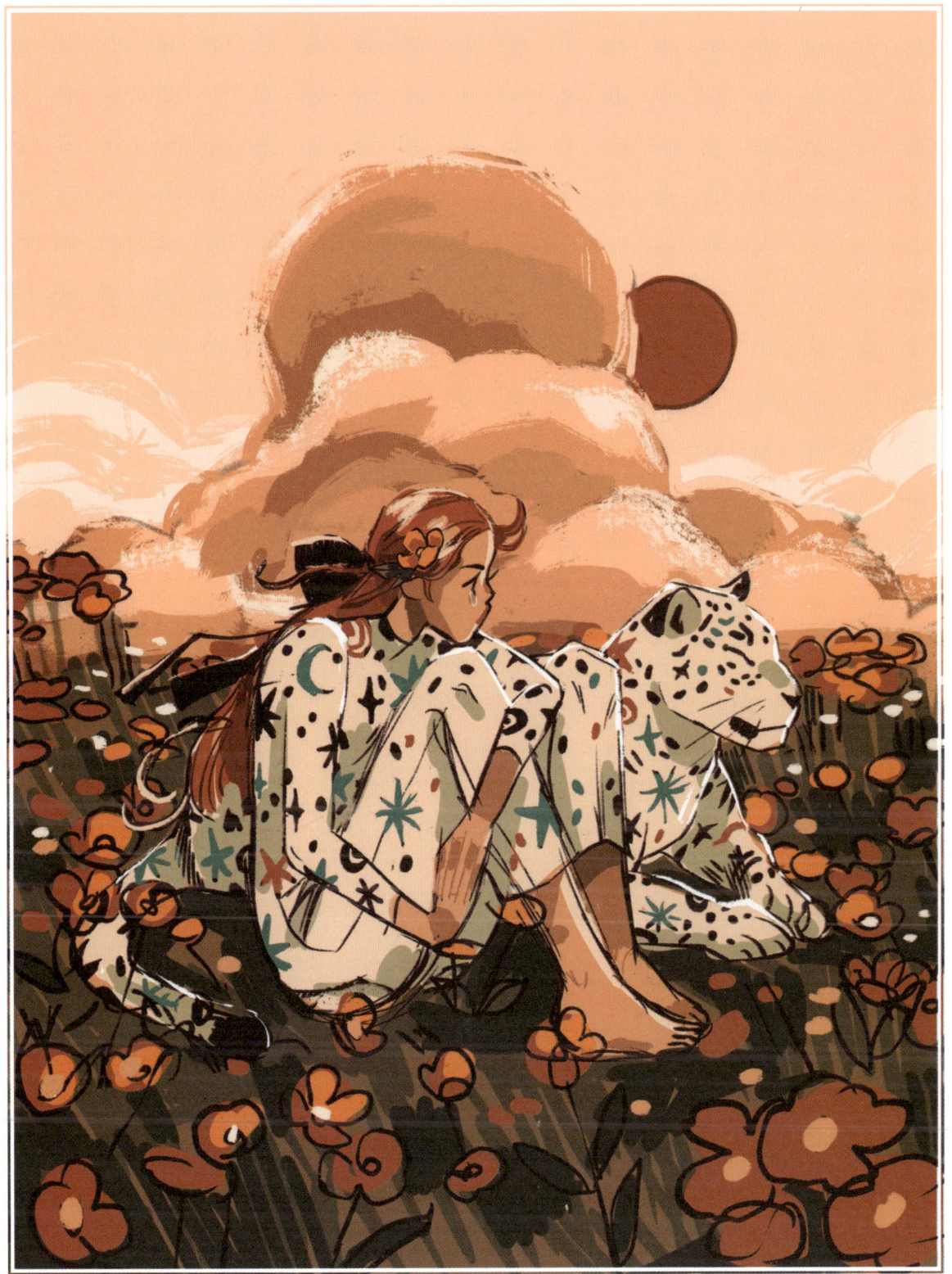

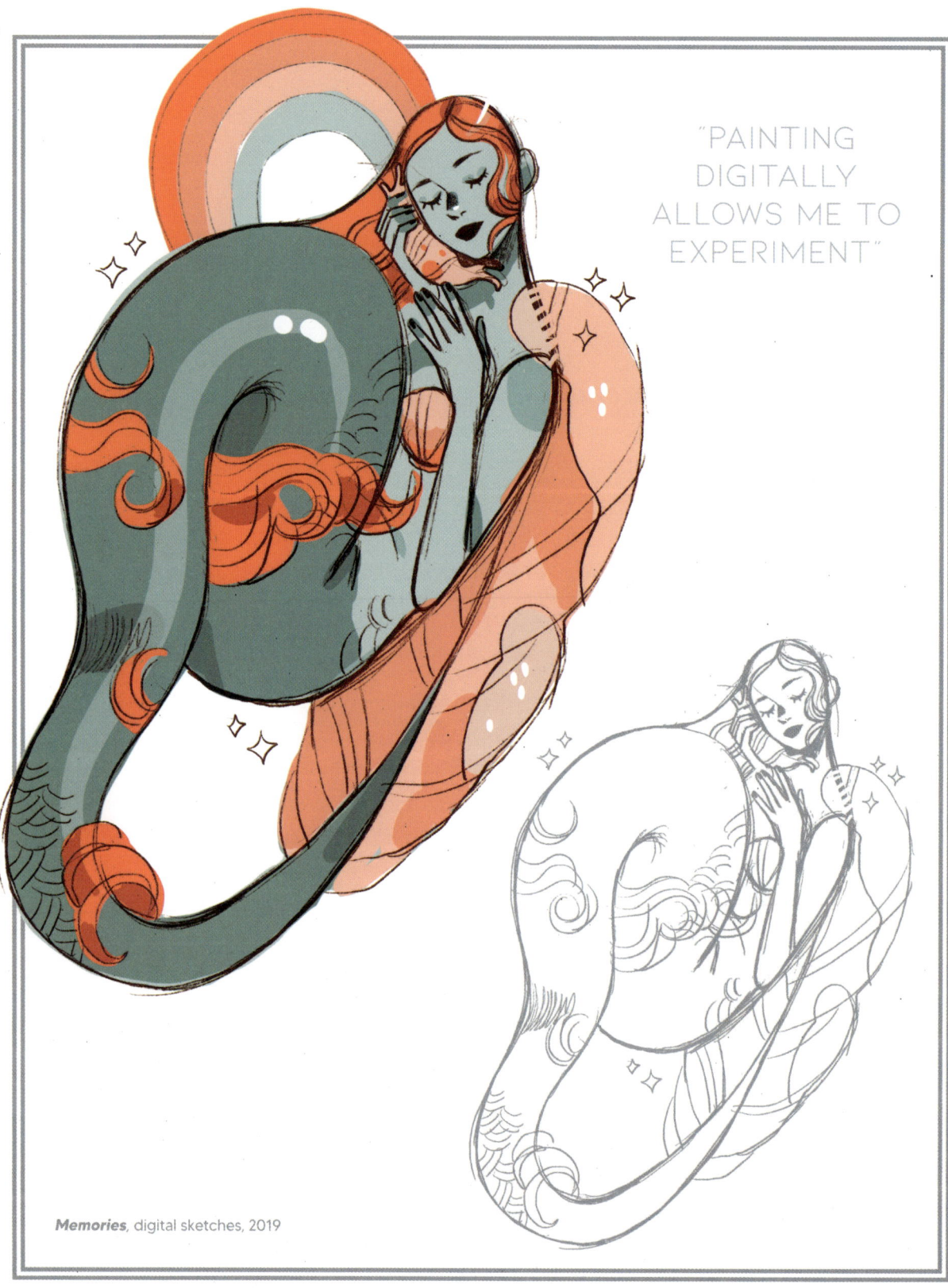

Memories, digital sketches, 2019

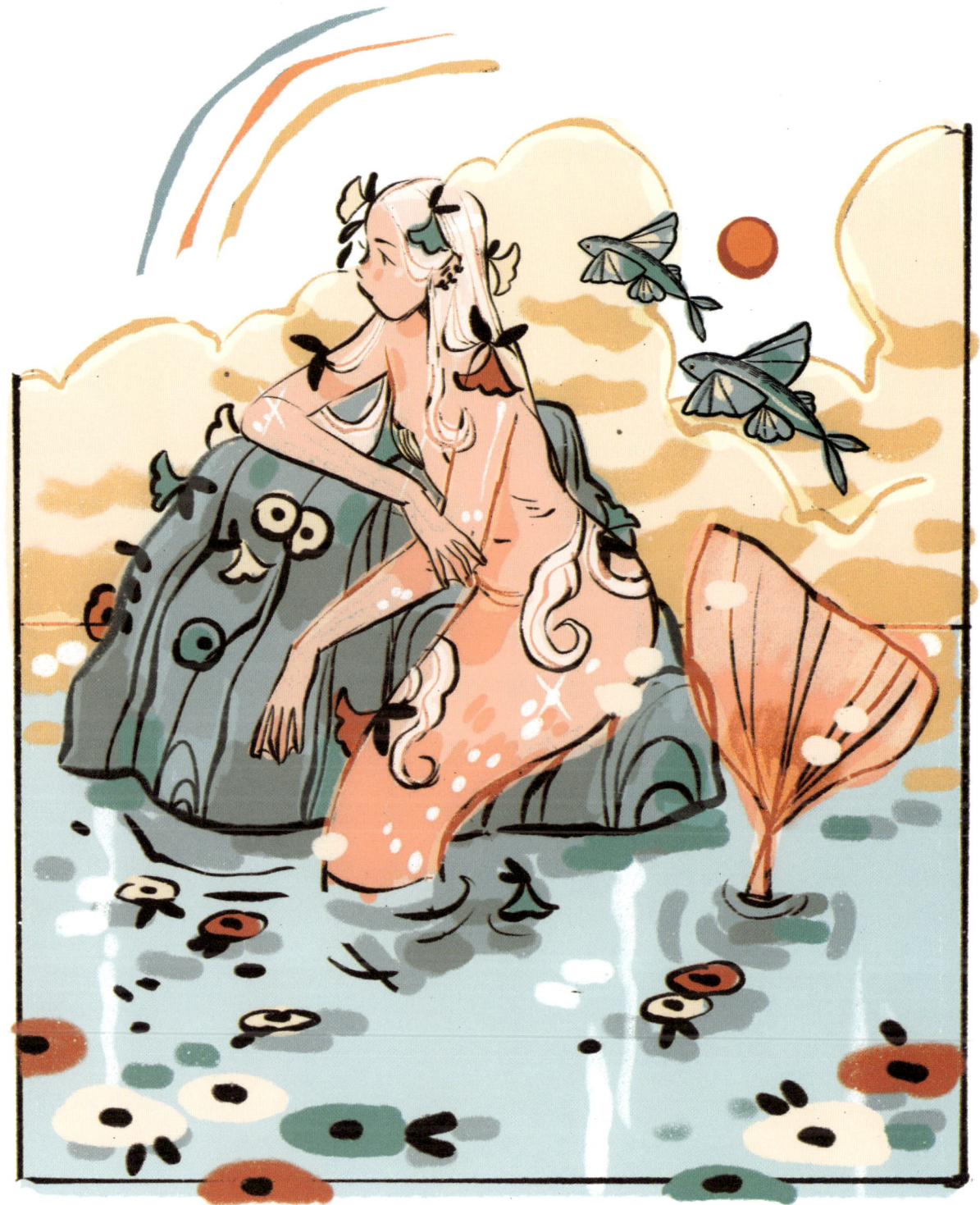

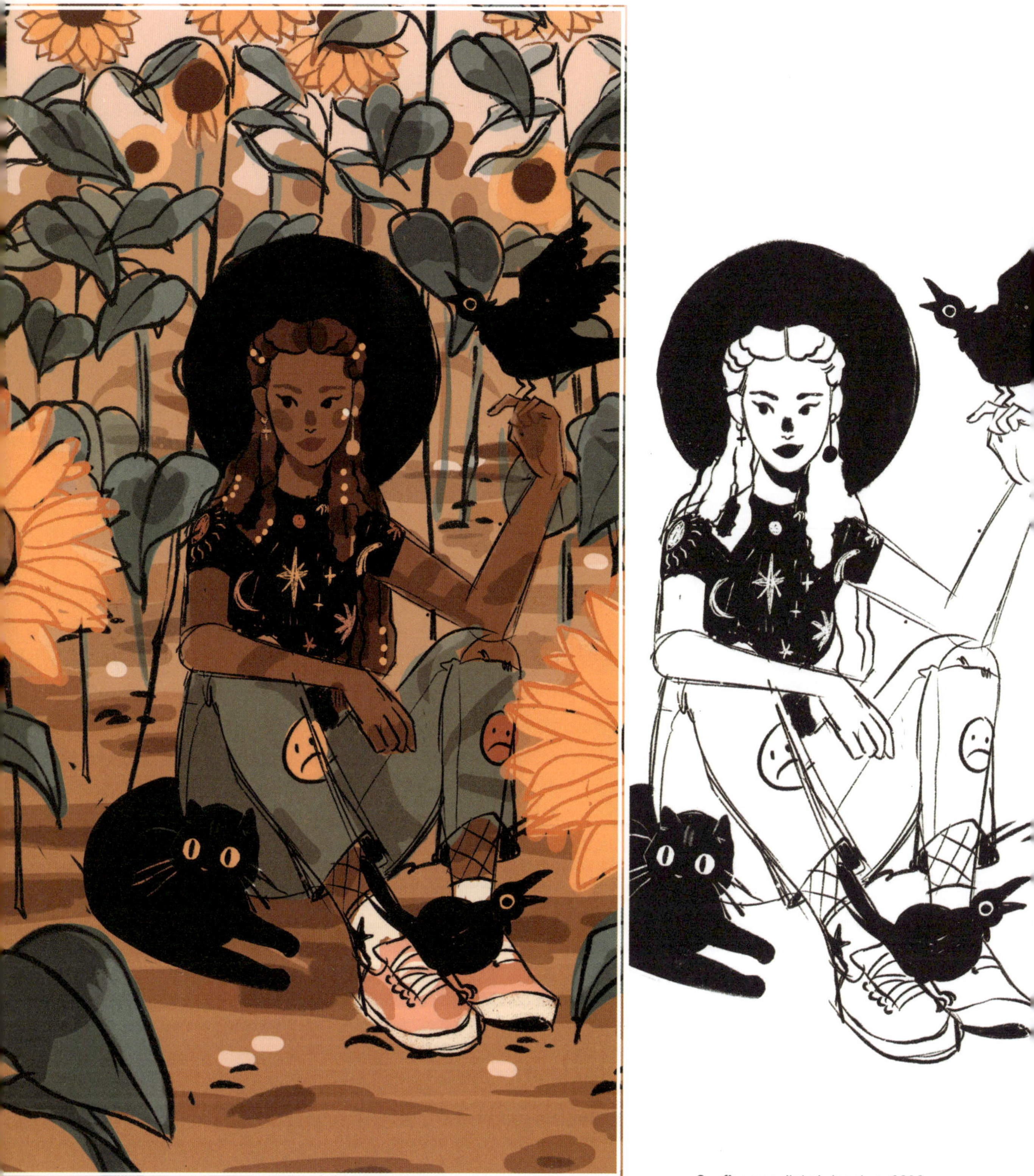

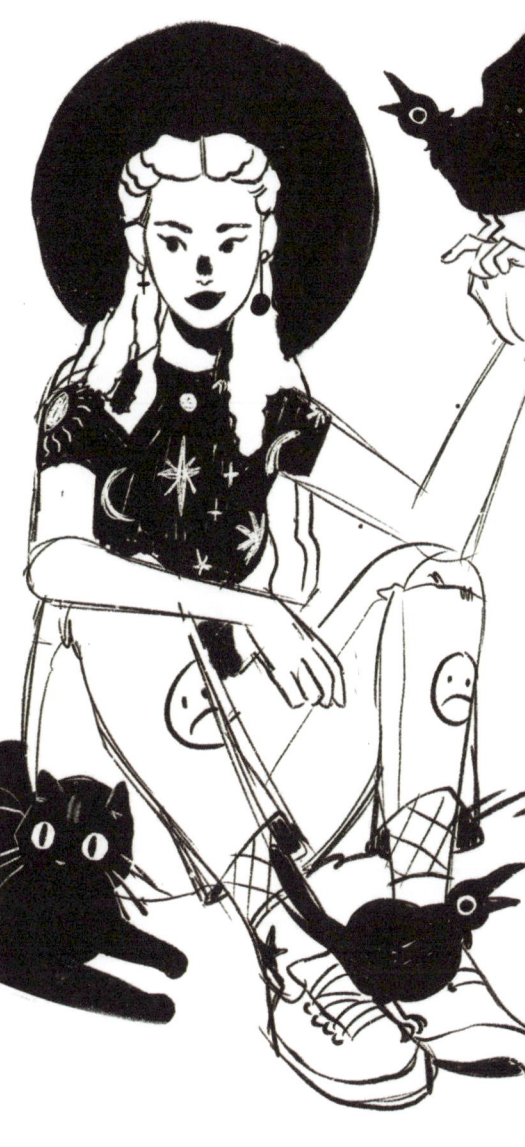

Sunflowers, digital sketches, 2020

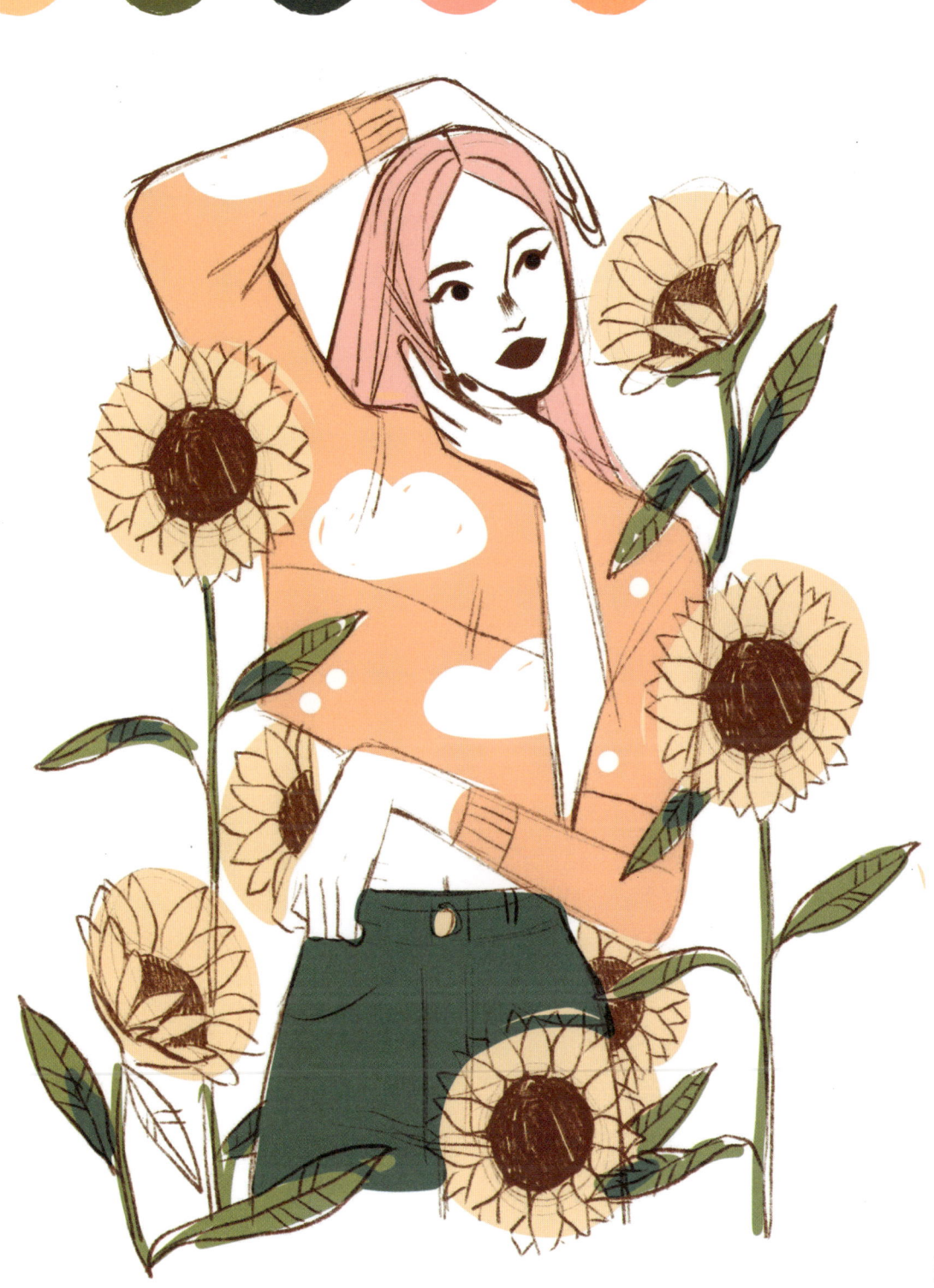

GOUACHE PAINTING

When painting on paper, I usually prepare the design beforehand so I can focus my attention purely on the painting process. As explained in the following tutorial on page 136, the digital sketch is printed, traced, and painted, using the original digital illustration as a guide for color and lighting.

My painting technique is simple, as I just add the colors one by one to fill the shapes. I apply two layers of slightly diluted gouache to create a smooth and opaque finish. The shadows and lights are not too complex in my paintings, which allows me to paint quite quickly.

When I paint a study, however, I am not usually as prepared because I want to explore the possibilities of techniques and color palettes as I go. I push myself to paint atmospheres that highlight shadows and lights because I almost never do this in my personal pieces. The challenge of working outside of my usual comfort zone offers a unique little adventure. These challenges teach me how to use gouache in new ways and expand my skillset.

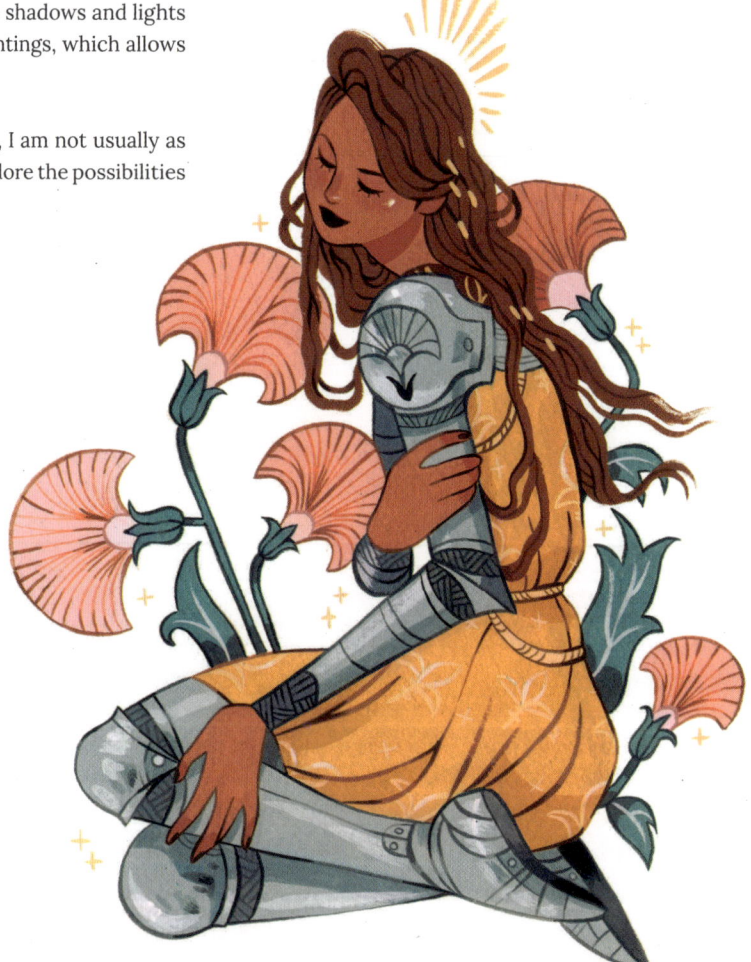

Lily, gouache, 2019

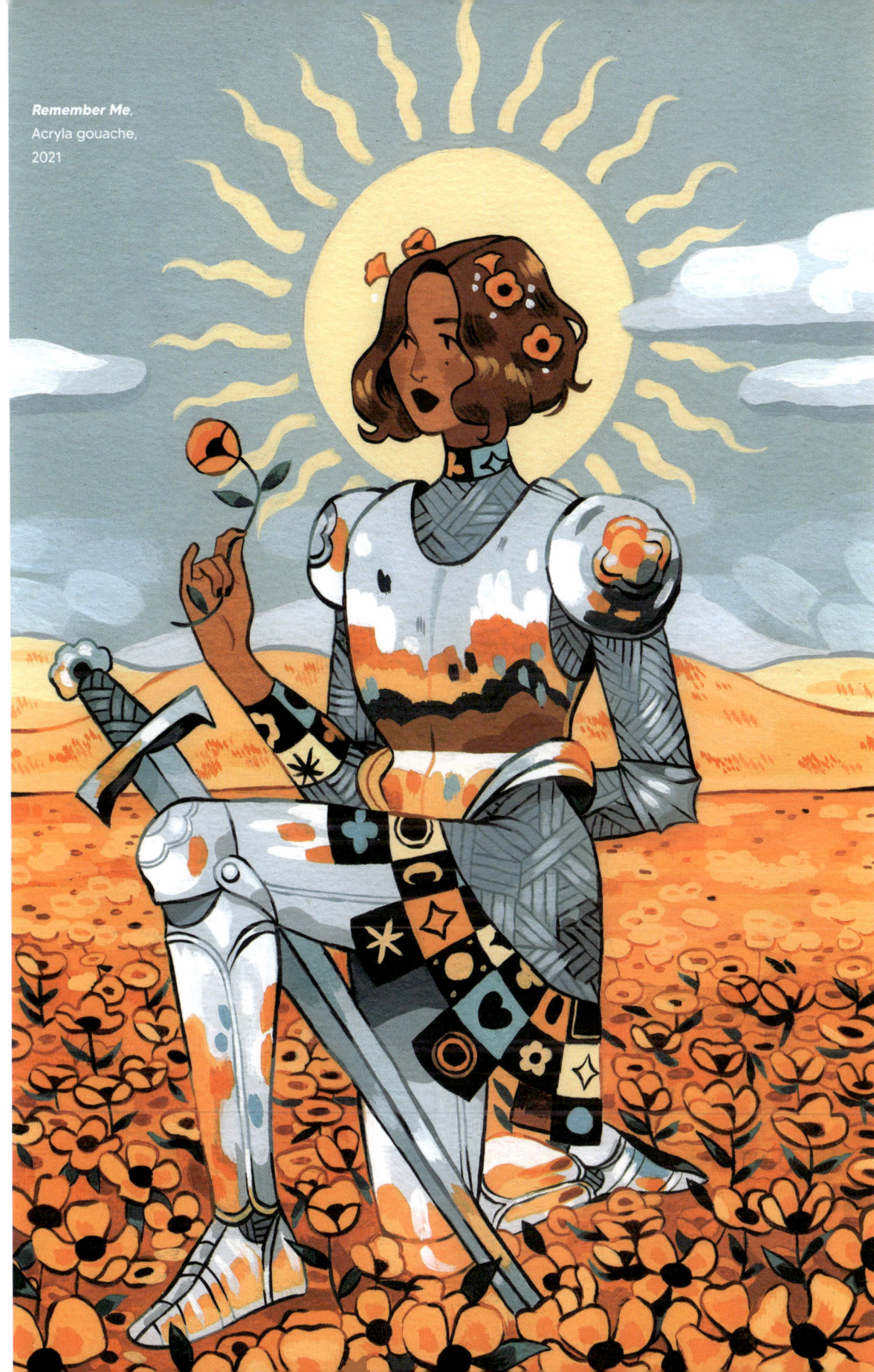

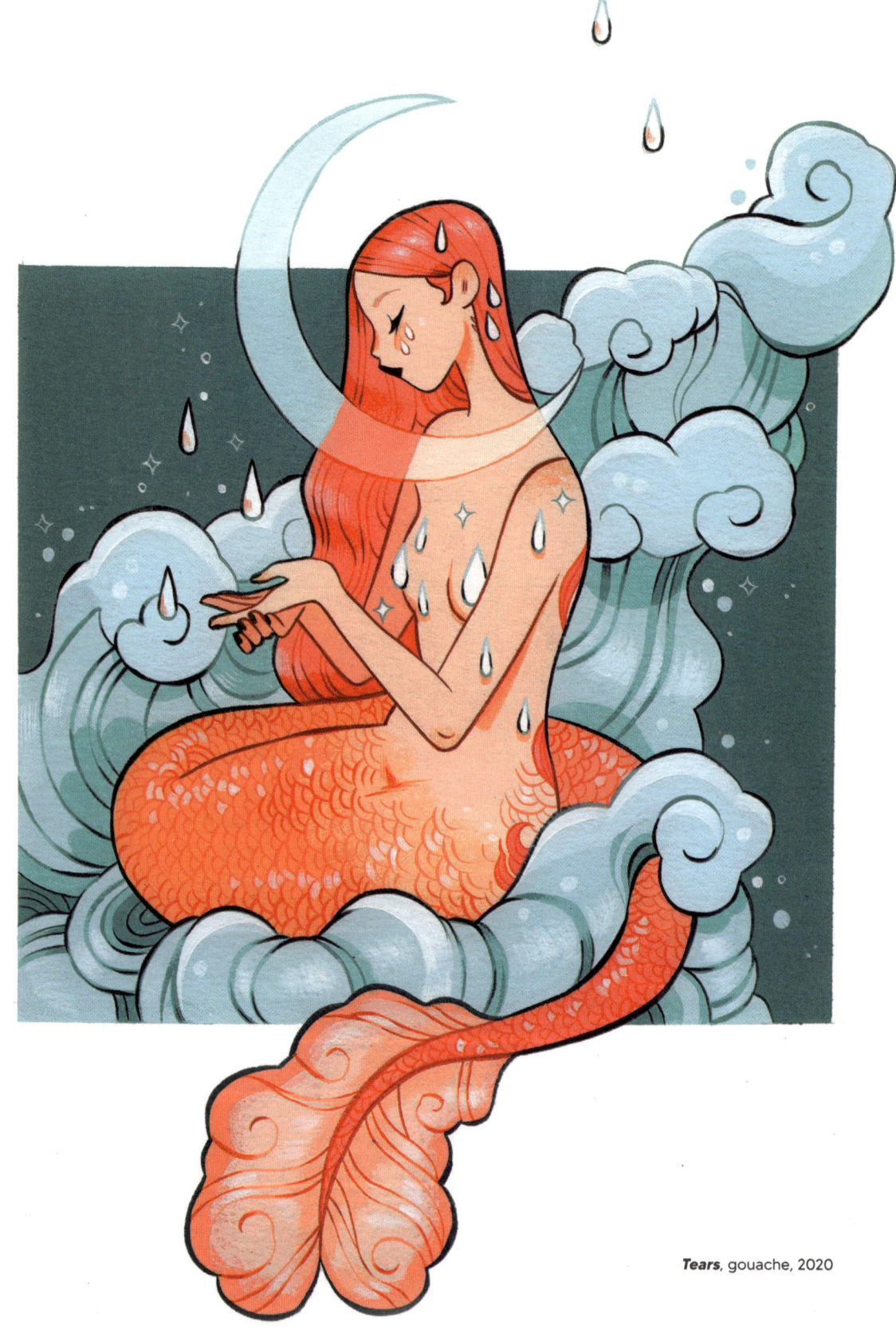

Tears, gouache, 2020

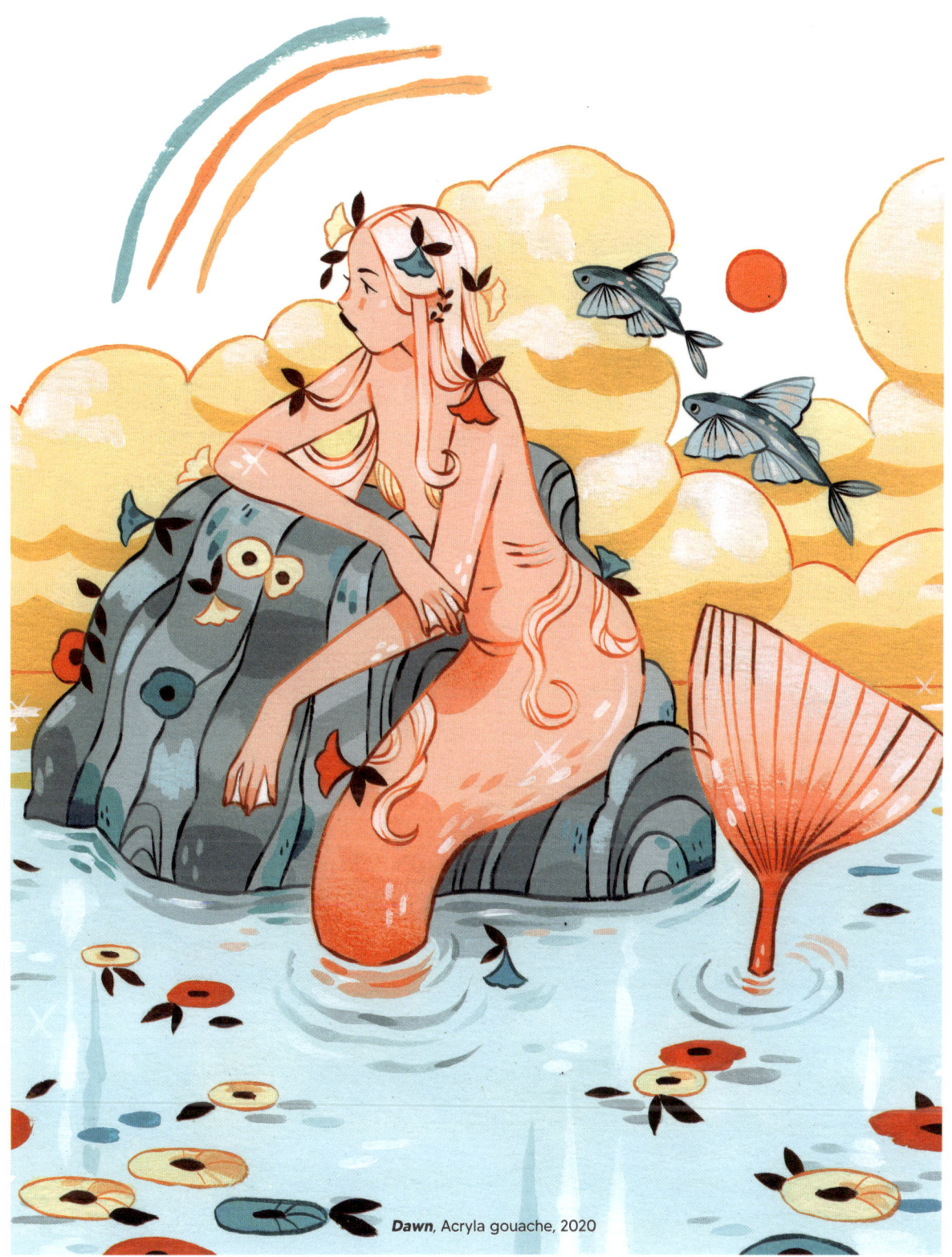

Dawn, Acryla gouache, 2020

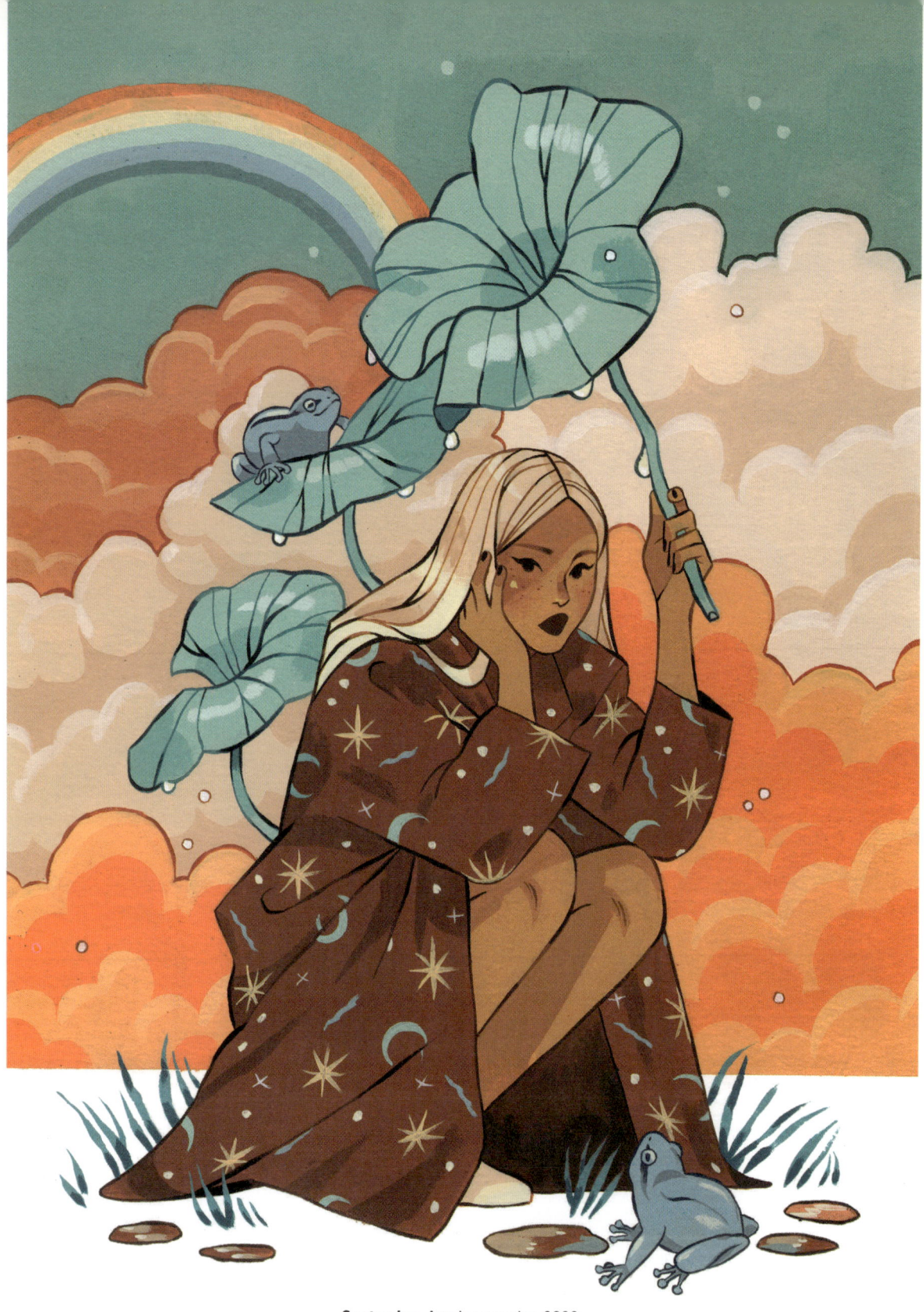

September, Acryla gouache, 2020

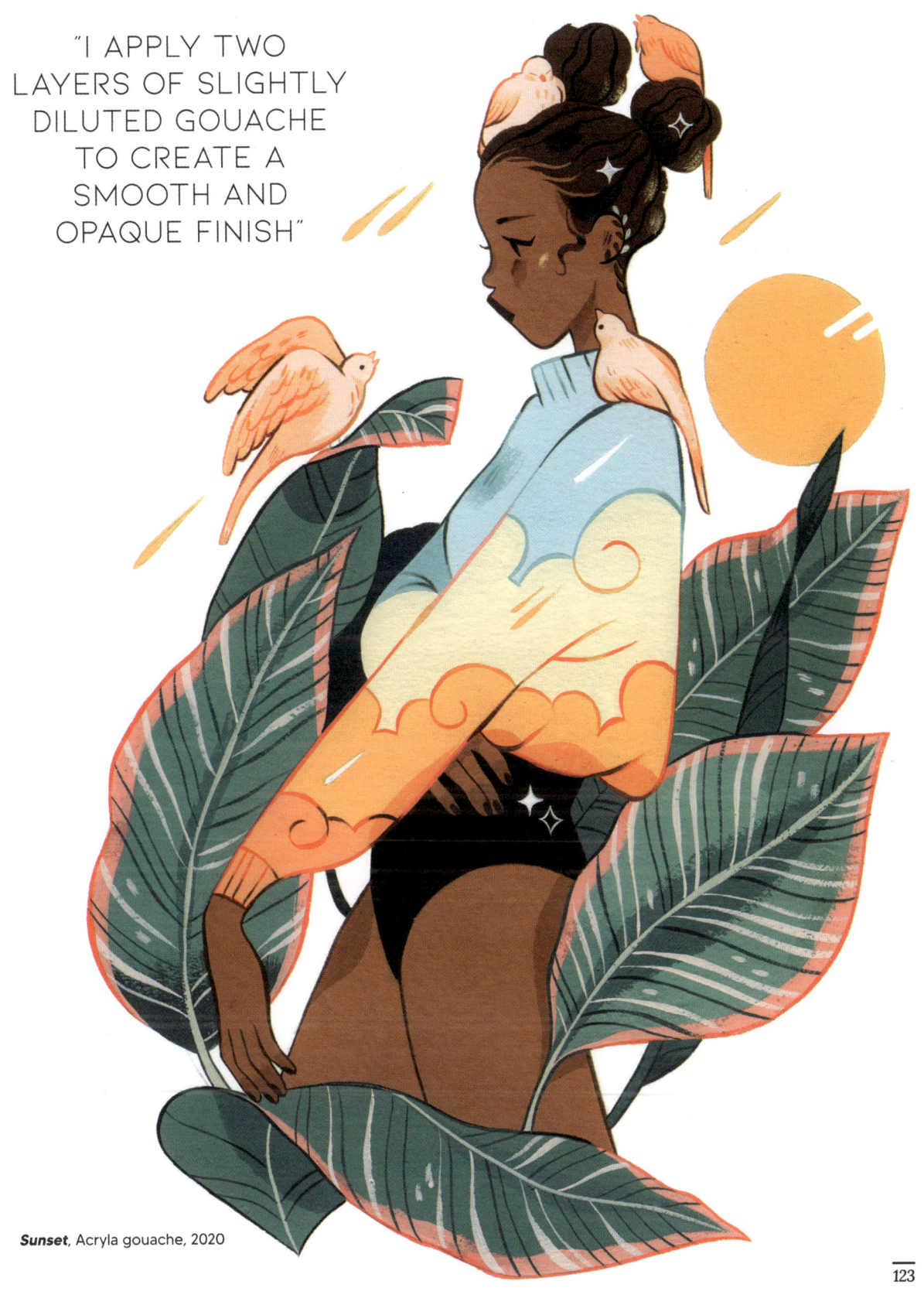

"I APPLY TWO LAYERS OF SLIGHTLY DILUTED GOUACHE TO CREATE A SMOOTH AND OPAQUE FINISH"

Sunset, Acryla gouache, 2020

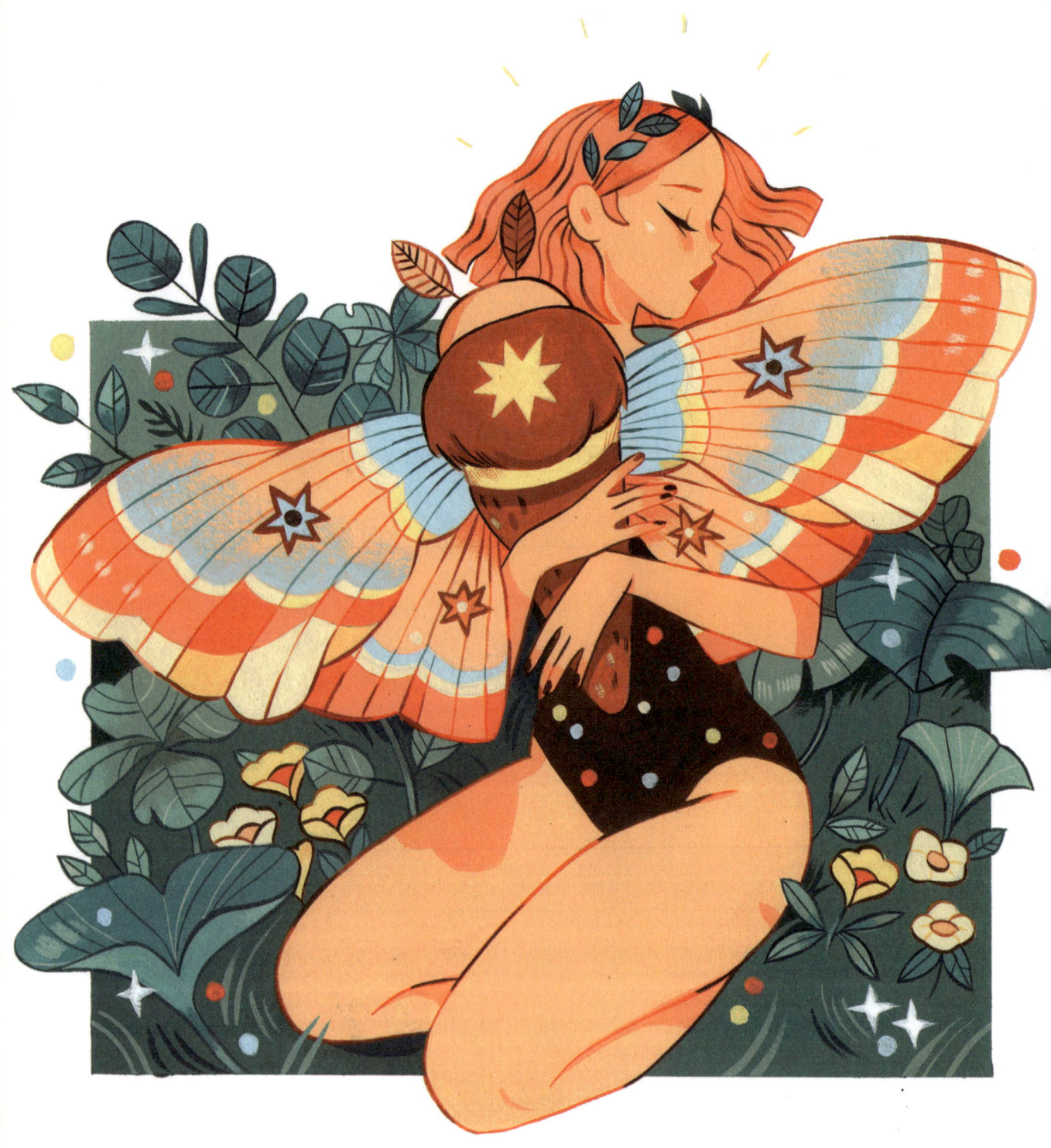

Moth, Acryla gouache, 2020

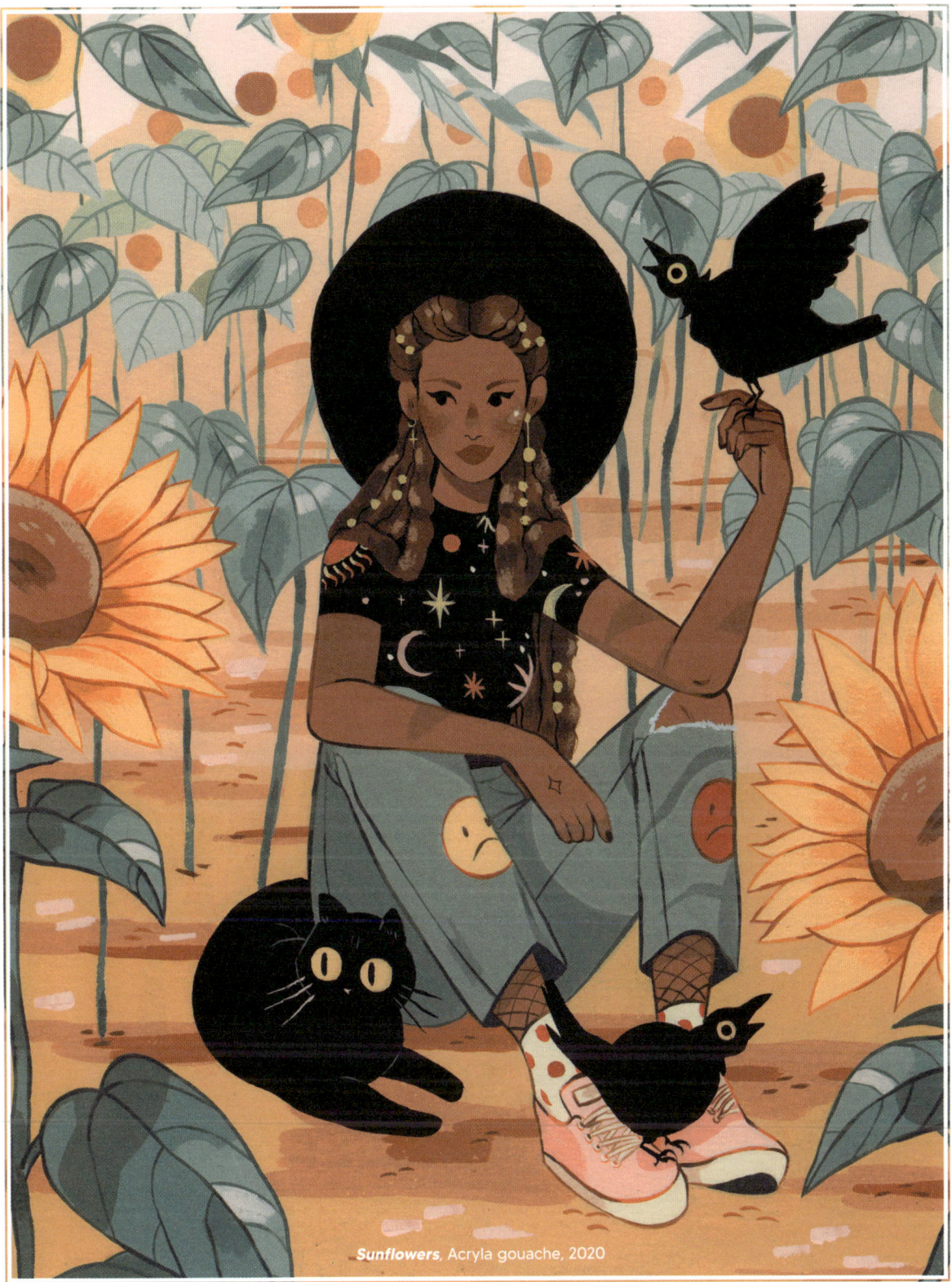

Sunflowers, Acryla gouache, 2020

tutorial
CREATING A DIGITAL ART PIECE

Through this tutorial I will explain how I create a digital art piece. I often call these designs "sketches" because I commonly use them to transfer the initial design to paper. Once a digital design is complete, I simply print the design out and trace the sketch onto paper. I then use the sketch as a guide while I paint the image again traditionally on paper. This has been a method I have used consistently recently, and every one of my latest pieces was created digitally first.

To draw digitally, I use Procreate on my iPad, and sketch with an Apple pencil. My favorite brush in Procreate to sketch with is the Dry Ink brush in the Ink category of brushes.

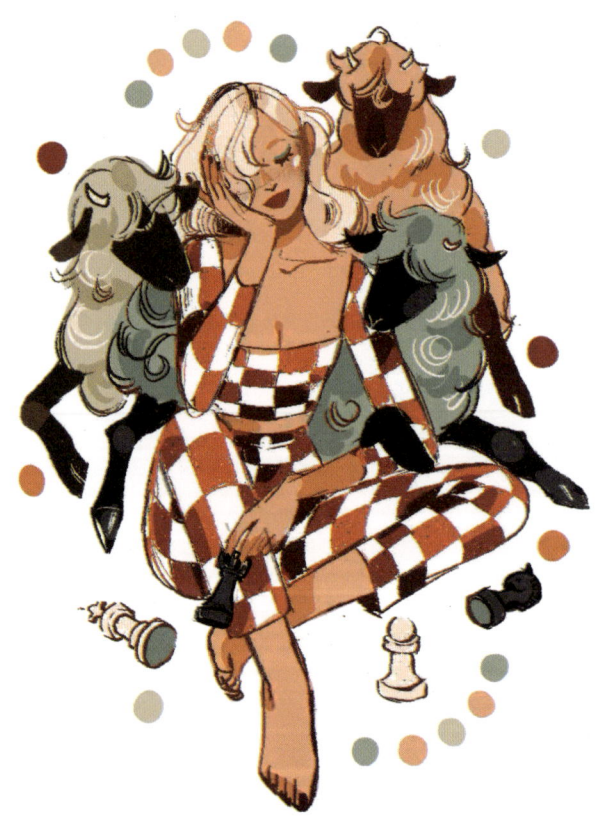

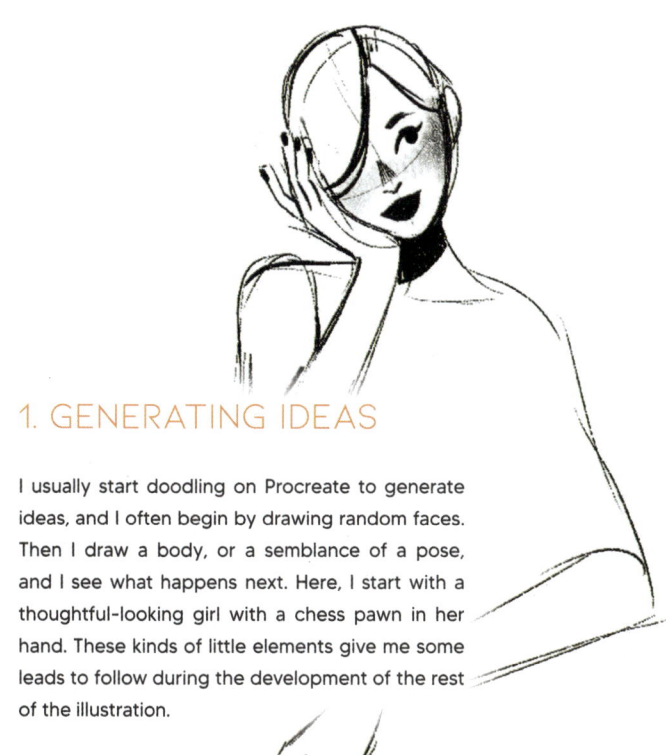

1. GENERATING IDEAS

I usually start doodling on Procreate to generate ideas, and I often begin by drawing random faces. Then I draw a body, or a semblance of a pose, and I see what happens next. Here, I start with a thoughtful-looking girl with a chess pawn in her hand. These kinds of little elements give me some leads to follow during the development of the rest of the illustration.

2. EXPLORATION

Searching for an appealing pose, I keep drawing the body. I play around with different items of clothing and hairstyles. Sometimes I use reference images as inspiration, and to help guide the drawing of the body if I'm in doubt. Here, I simply draw from my imagination.

3. DESIGN DEVELOPMENT

To introduce a visual connection to the chess pawn, I add a checkered print to the girl's clothing. I ask my patrons on Patreon what species of animal they would like to see in my next illustration, and several of them ask for sheep. So, I draw one, then two, then three, to balance the composition and bring life and energy to the drawing. I give them a curious appearance — they probably wonder what she's doing with her chess pawn (me too!).

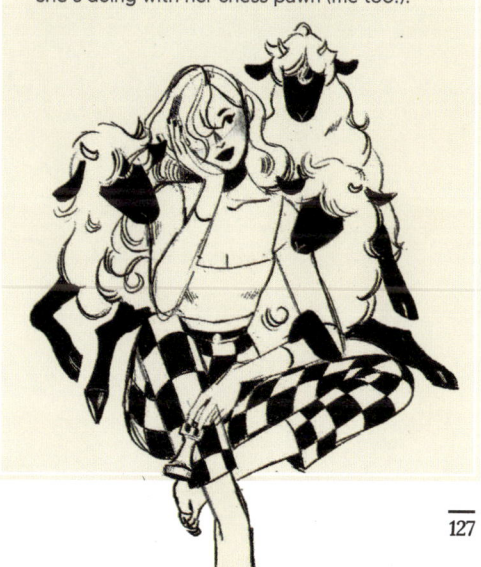

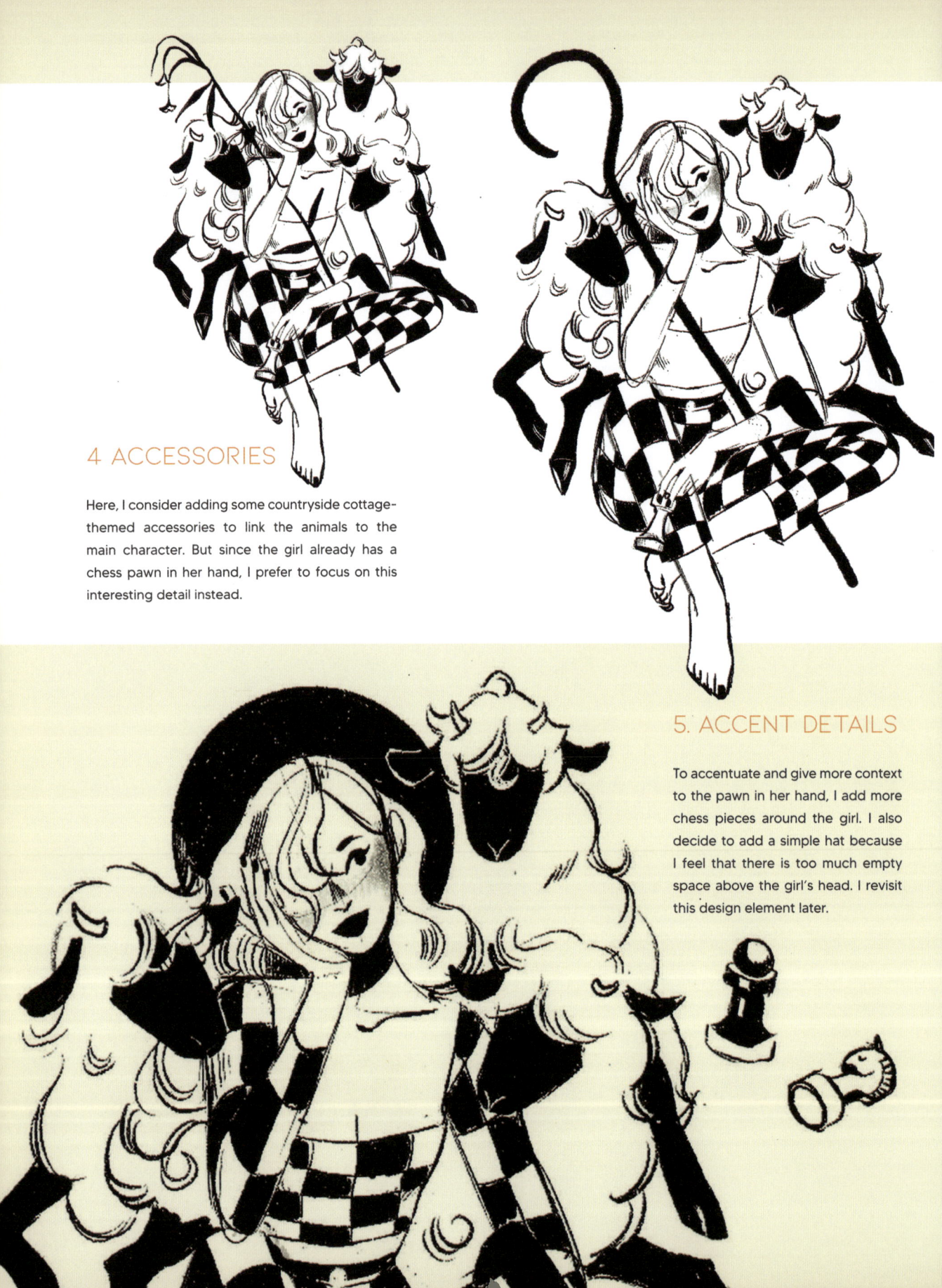

4 ACCESSORIES

Here, I consider adding some countryside cottage-themed accessories to link the animals to the main character. But since the girl already has a chess pawn in her hand, I prefer to focus on this interesting detail instead.

5. ACCENT DETAILS

To accentuate and give more context to the pawn in her hand, I add more chess pieces around the girl. I also decide to add a simple hat because I feel that there is too much empty space above the girl's head. I revisit this design element later.

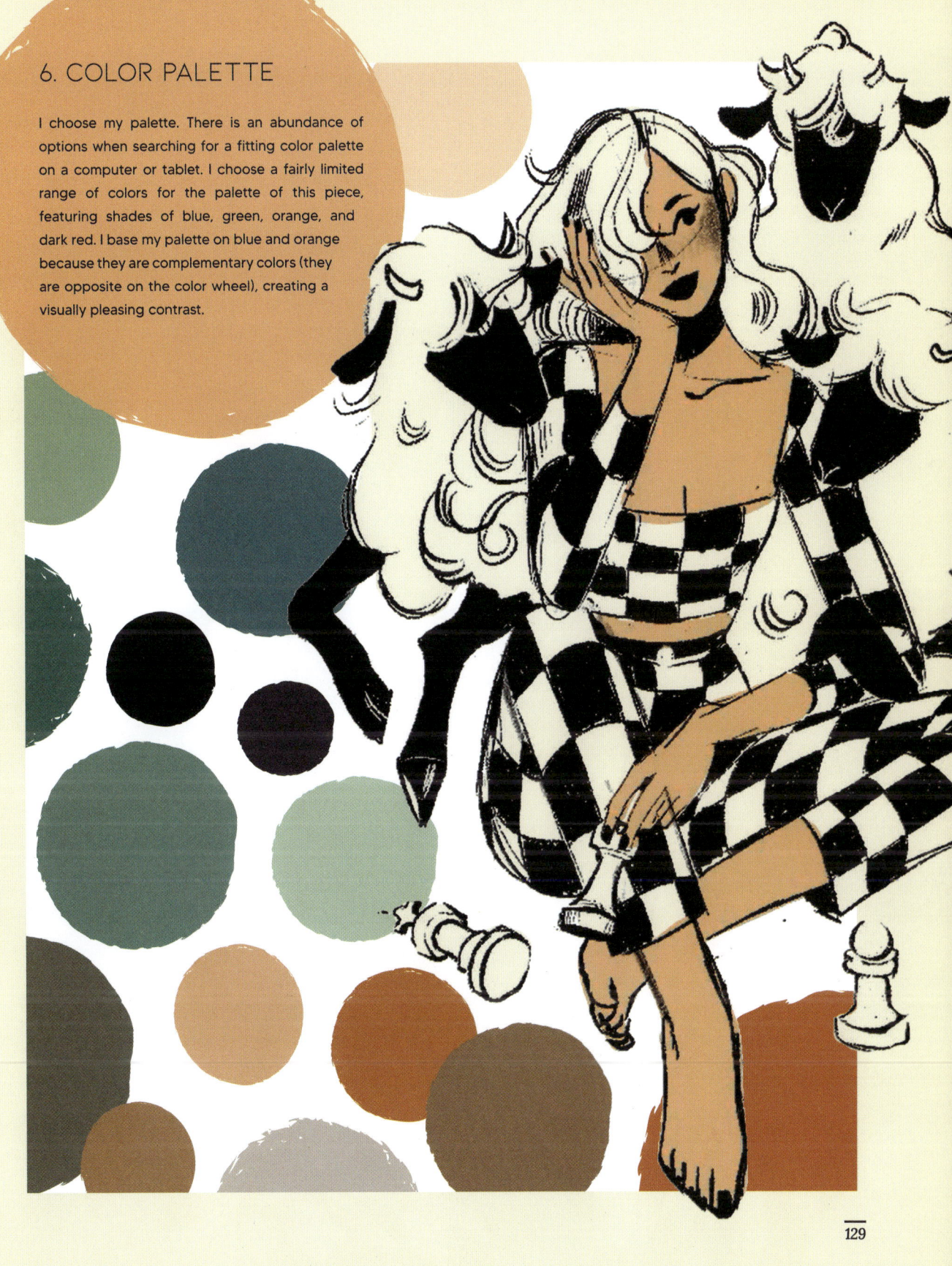

6. COLOR PALETTE

I choose my palette. There is an abundance of options when searching for a fitting color palette on a computer or tablet. I choose a fairly limited range of colors for the palette of this piece, featuring shades of blue, green, orange, and dark red. I base my palette on blue and orange because they are complementary colors (they are opposite on the color wheel), creating a visually pleasing contrast.

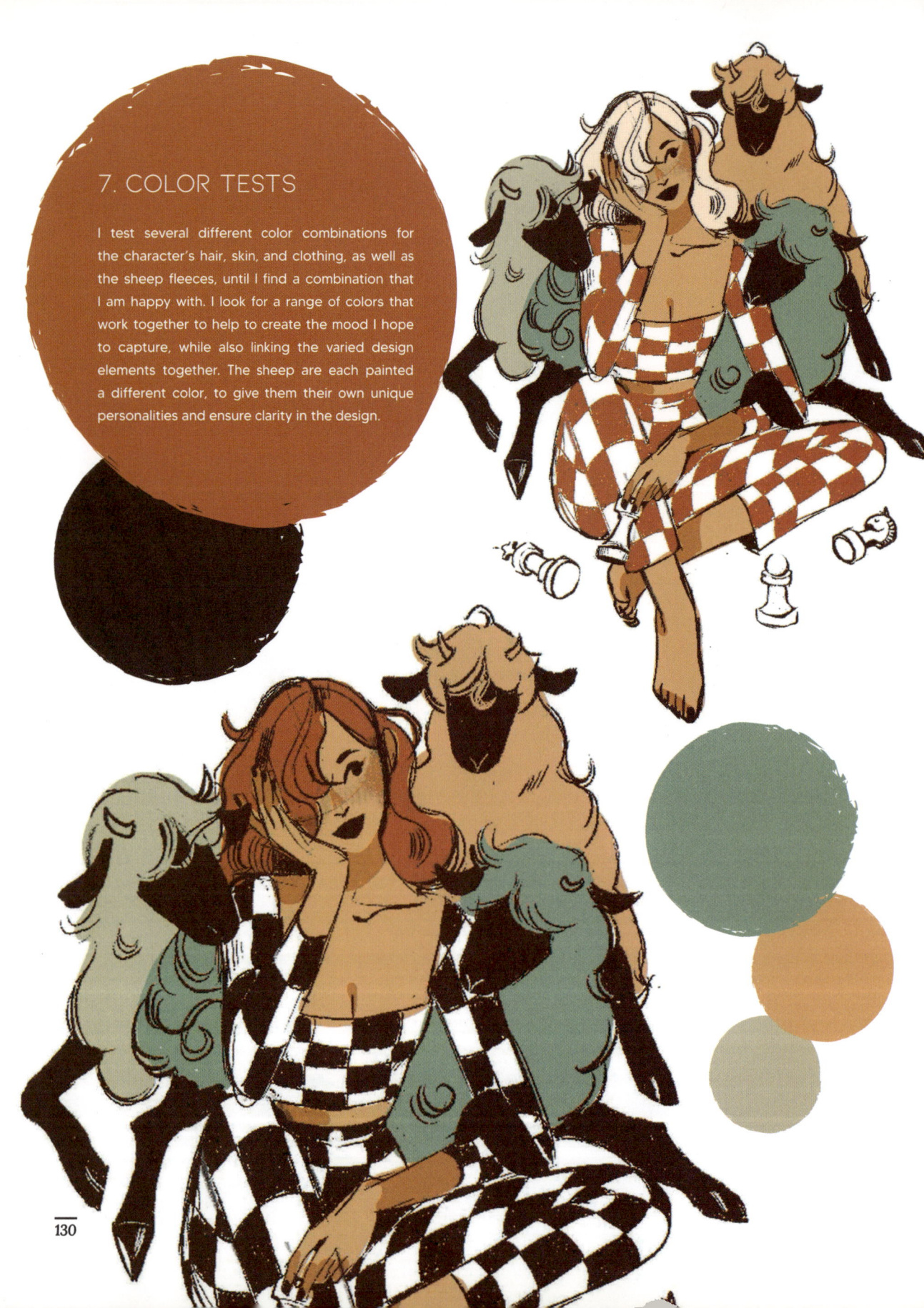

7. COLOR TESTS

I test several different color combinations for the character's hair, skin, and clothing, as well as the sheep fleeces, until I find a combination that I am happy with. I look for a range of colors that work together to help to create the mood I hope to capture, while also linking the varied design elements together. The sheep are each painted a different color, to give them their own unique personalities and ensure clarity in the design.

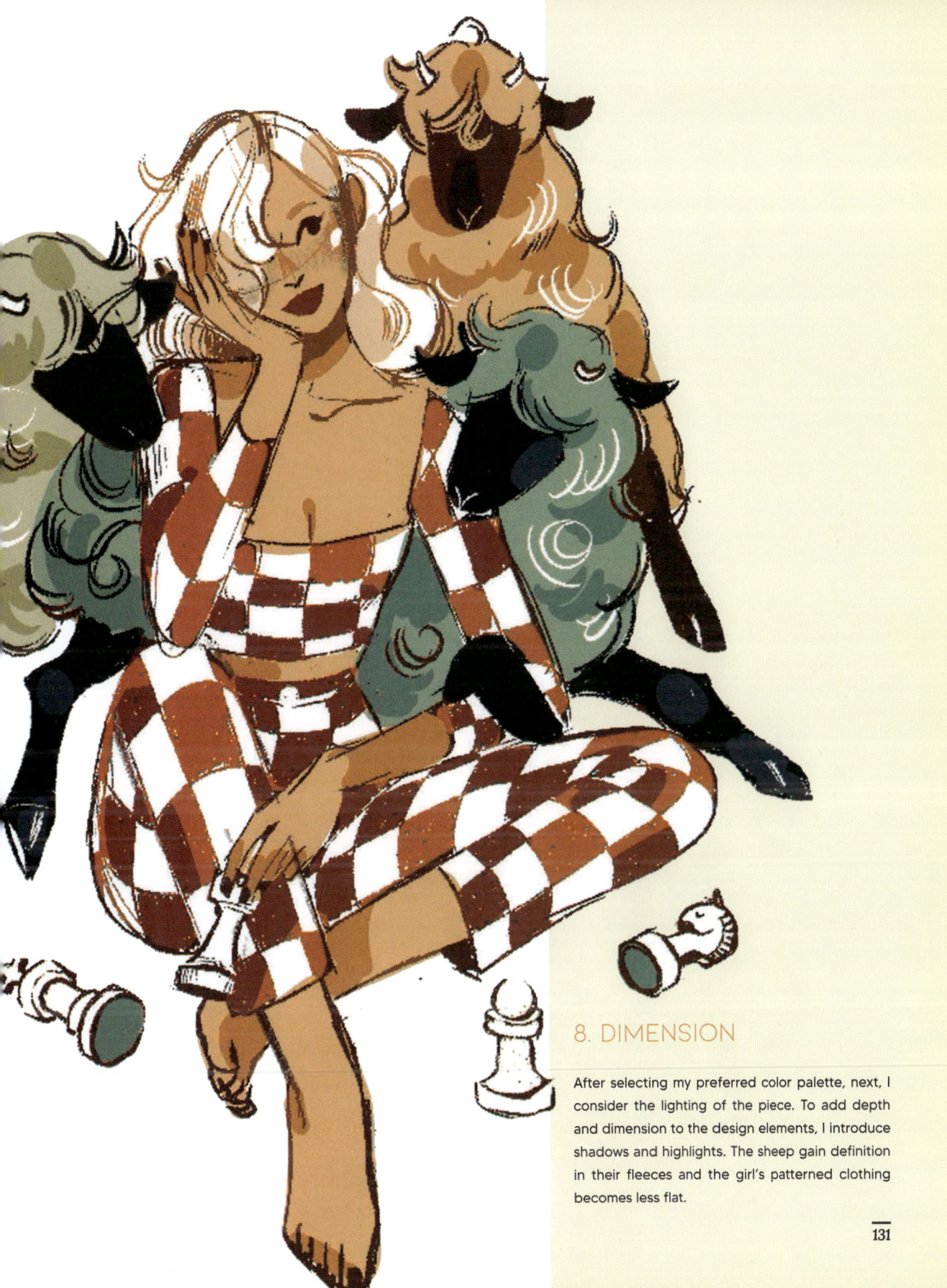

8. DIMENSION

After selecting my preferred color palette, next, I consider the lighting of the piece. To add depth and dimension to the design elements, I introduce shadows and highlights. The sheep gain definition in their fleeces and the girl's patterned clothing becomes less flat.

9. FINISHING TOUCHES

I decide to close the girl's eyes so that she appears more peaceful and thoughtful. I then add colored dots to decorate and frame my illustration. The dots recall the roundness of the sheep's curls, and create a contrast with the angular forms on the girl's bold clothing.

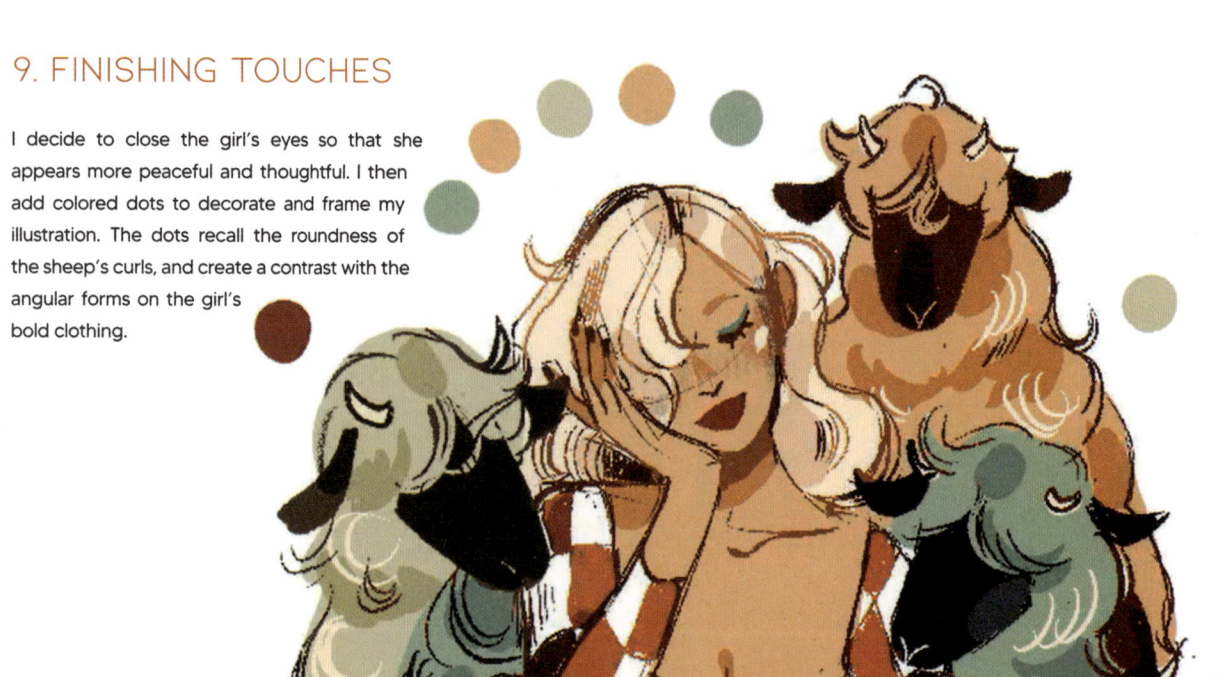

10. ADJUSTMENTS

As the colors appear a little too yellow for my liking, I add a Tint layer that I fill in with red to eliminate the excess yellow across the illustration. The image now appears to contain more reds, has greater interest, and the colors are more consistent with each other.

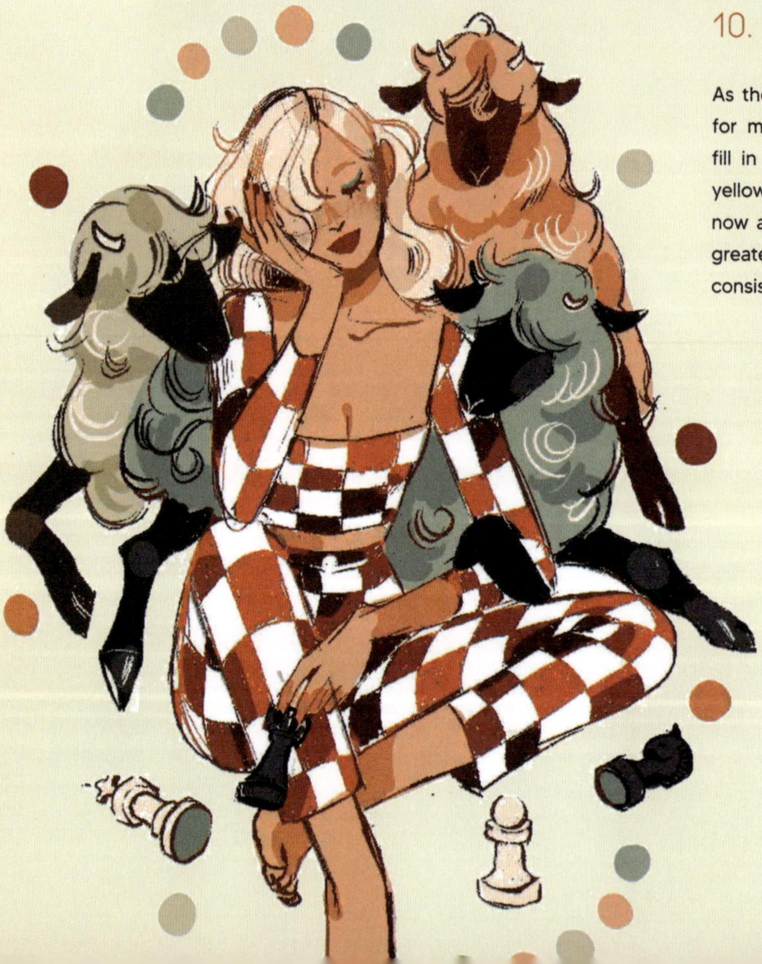

DIGITAL TO TRADITIONAL

After completing and refining the digital sketch, I use it to transfer the design to gouache paint on paper. Selecting and perfecting a color palette digitally before starting a traditional gouache painting is a time-saving technique that I can't live without! I use this digital design workflow for every piece I want to paint traditionally. What I enjoy about drawing digitally is the endless possibilities — layers can be duplicated, the canvas can be resized, and elements can be easily moved around. When combining with traditional painting, however, some of the functions of digital painting software can be a hinderance, and attempting to recreate a digital effect with traditional materials can require additional time, patience, and energy.

Painting traditionally will always be my favorite way to create art, even though it has its obstacles sometimes. I enjoy the feeling of working on paper, using physical tools, and find the whole process relaxing. I also find being able to hold a finished piece in my hands incomparable to digital art.

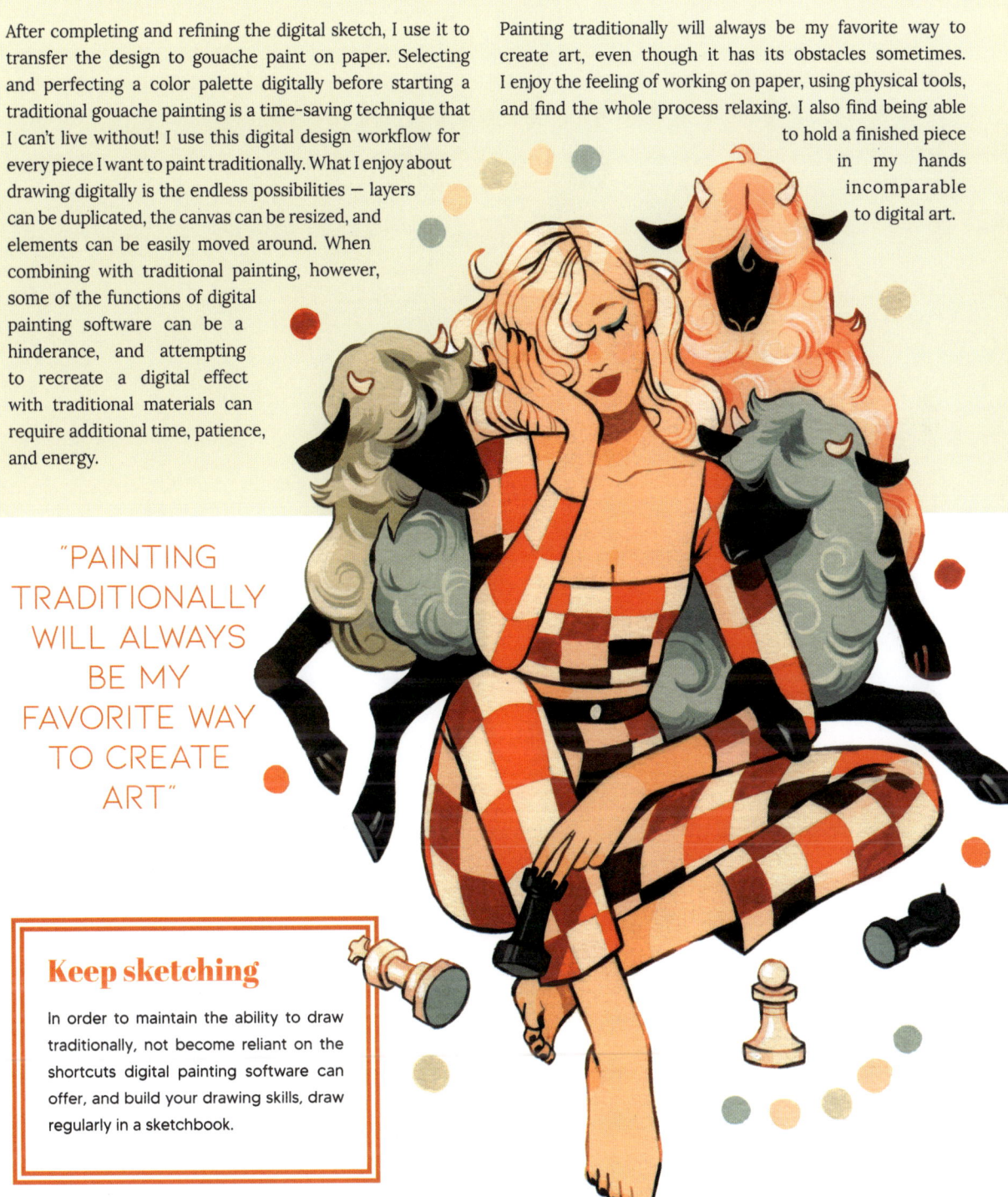

"PAINTING TRADITIONALLY WILL ALWAYS BE MY FAVORITE WAY TO CREATE ART"

Keep sketching

In order to maintain the ability to draw traditionally, not become reliant on the shortcuts digital painting software can offer, and build your drawing skills, draw regularly in a sketchbook.

tutorial
PAINTING WITH ACRYLA GOUACHE

In this tutorial, I paint a bust with Acryla gouache. I follow the same method for painting with Acryla gouache as I do when painting with regular gouache, but the finish is slightly different.

Here, I use Holbein Acryla gouache on my favorite thick paper, Canson XL Watercolor 300 g paper — its heavyweight thickness means it's strong enough to hold wet media such as watercolors, gouache, and other heavy paints. It also has a slightly grainy textured finish, which I enjoy. The brushes I use are all synthetic, and work very well with the paint and paper I use. They are affordable and the high quality means they are also durable.

As previously mentioned, I usually sketch the design digitally on my iPad first and print it out to trace the design on to watercolor paper with my light table. Using a light table isn't necessary but I find that it saves time and makes the workflow more efficient. I then have a quick and easy base drawing, ready for painting.

To create a similar finish to this piece, as well as your choice of gouache paint and watercolor paper, you will also need a pencil to sketch the drawing, an eraser, a liner brush to outline and paint details, and a bigger round brush to fill in large areas.

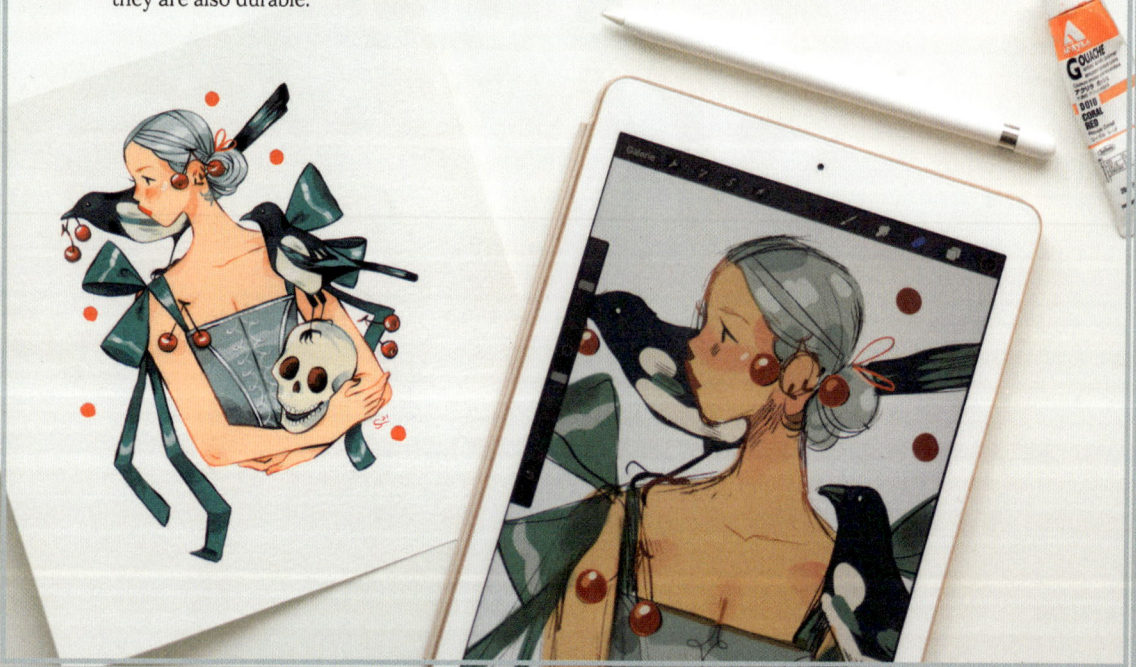

1. BASE DESIGN

I start by printing out the linework of my digital drawing (1A). To create this particular design, I use Procreate on my iPad. I then tape the printout to my light table with masking tape (1B), followed by a sheet of watercolor paper on top. I then trace over the drawing with a pencil and carefully remove the new sketch from the light table (1C).

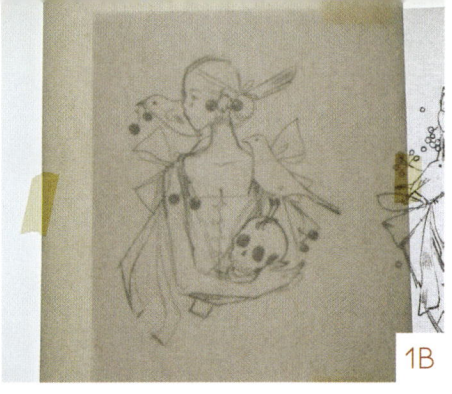

1B

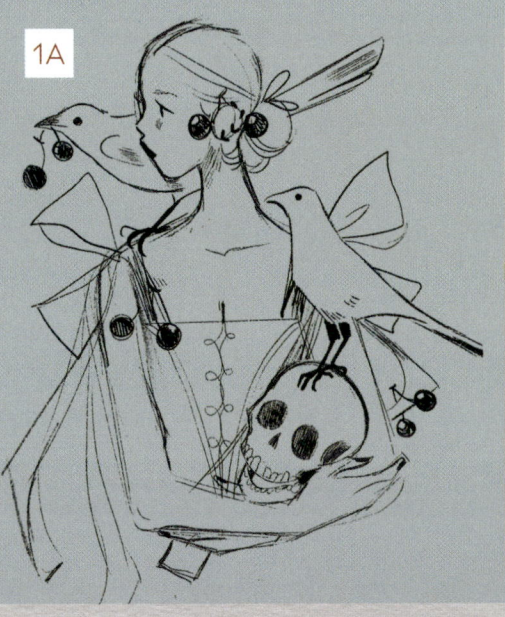

1A

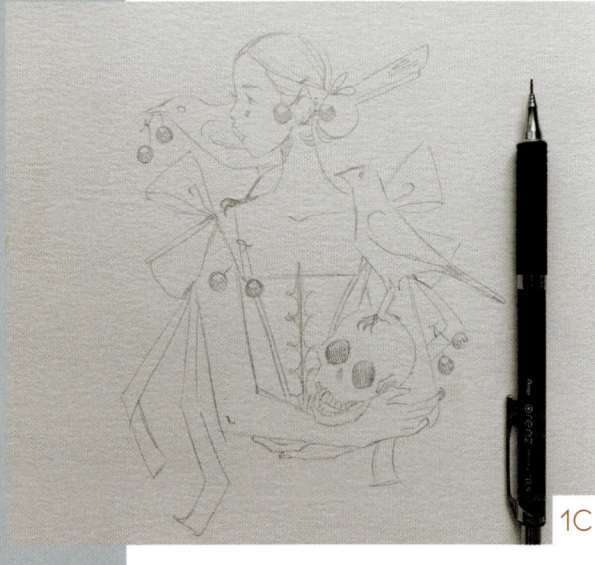

1C

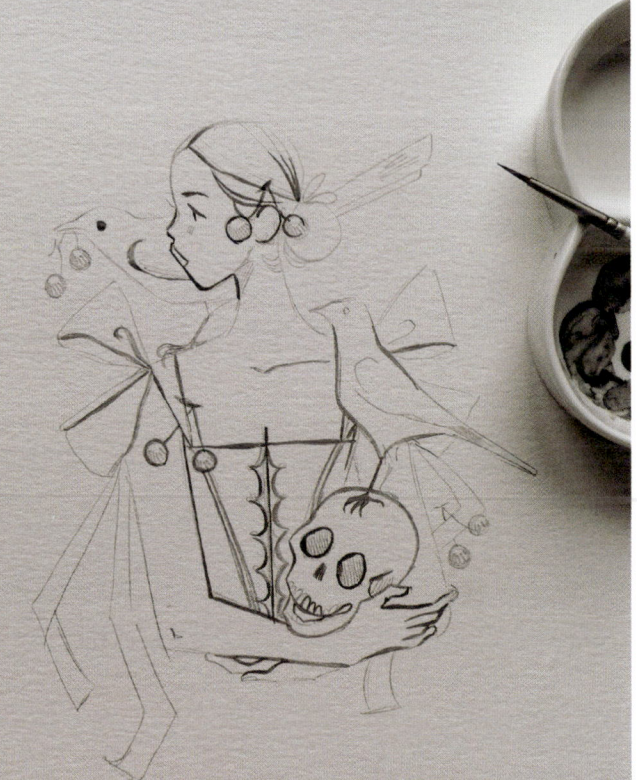

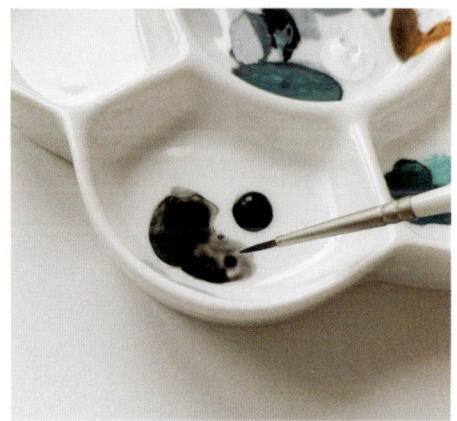

2. PREPARATIONS FOR PAINTING

With dilute black Acryla gouache, I draw the lines that are most important to me and the clarity of the design. This prevents the important details, such as the face and hands, from getting lost under the opacity of the Acryla gouache paint.

3. DIGITAL REFERENCE

Next, I open Procreate, where the finished digital drawing can be seen in full color (3A). As described in the previous tutorial, when creating the digital design, I decide upon the best color palette for the image, to save time when painting traditionally. I use the colored digital design as a guide as I start to paint on paper (3B).

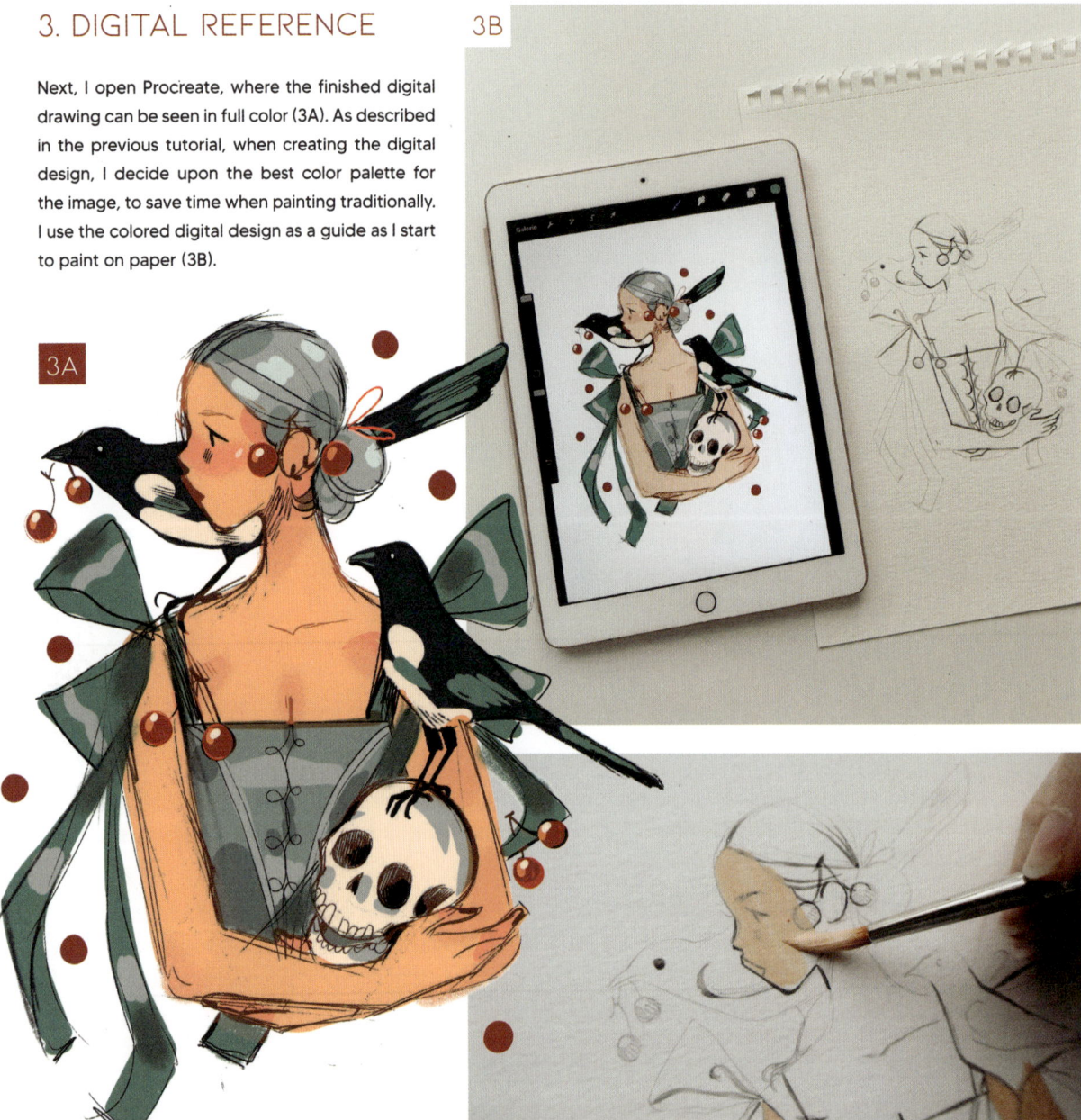

3B

3A

Layer from back to front

Acryla gouache is opaque, so I recommend that you start painting the elements in the background first. For instance, here, I could have started with the bird behind the girl.

4. FIRST COLOR LAYER

Acryla gouache dries very quickly. Usually, I try to cover all areas that will be the same color at the same time to avoid wasting paint. Here, I start with the character's skin. The paint is mixed with a little water, which is why the first coat is not completely opaque. With the application of a second layer of paint, the flat color is more opaque and harmonious.

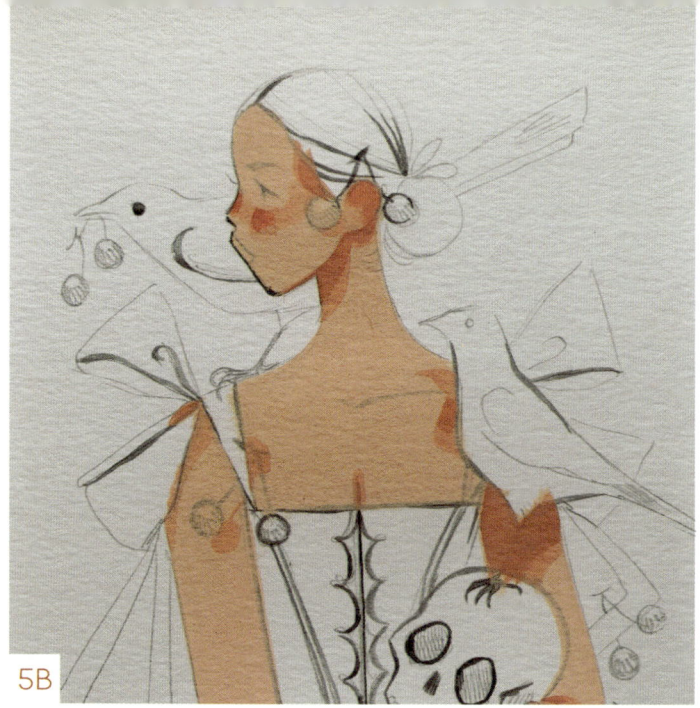

5B

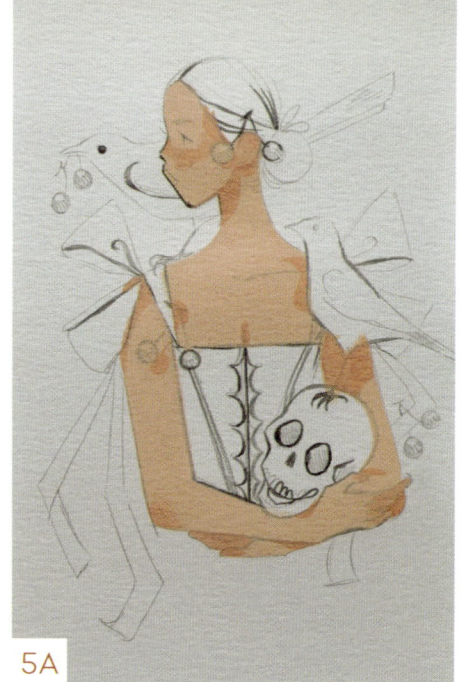

5A

5. SHADING

Using the leftover apricot-colored paint, I move on
to adding shadows and rosy areas of the skin. I add
a little red paint to the apricot tone for the areas
of redness (cheeks and fingers), and brown for the
shadows (5A). I then add depth with a brighter red
for the cheeks and a darker, pronounced shadow
with some brown (5B).

6. CHARACTER OUTLINES

As I have a small amount of brown paint left in my
palette, I take this opportunity to add brown outlines
to the character. The dark lines contrast against the
pale skin to give her form more definition.

Cut down drying time

To speed up the drying time between
layers of paint, use a hairdryer to dry
the painting. But be careful to check
that the paper and paint can handle the
heat, or the painting could be damaged.
Taping the drawing to a board or desk
also helps to avoid crinkling as it dries.

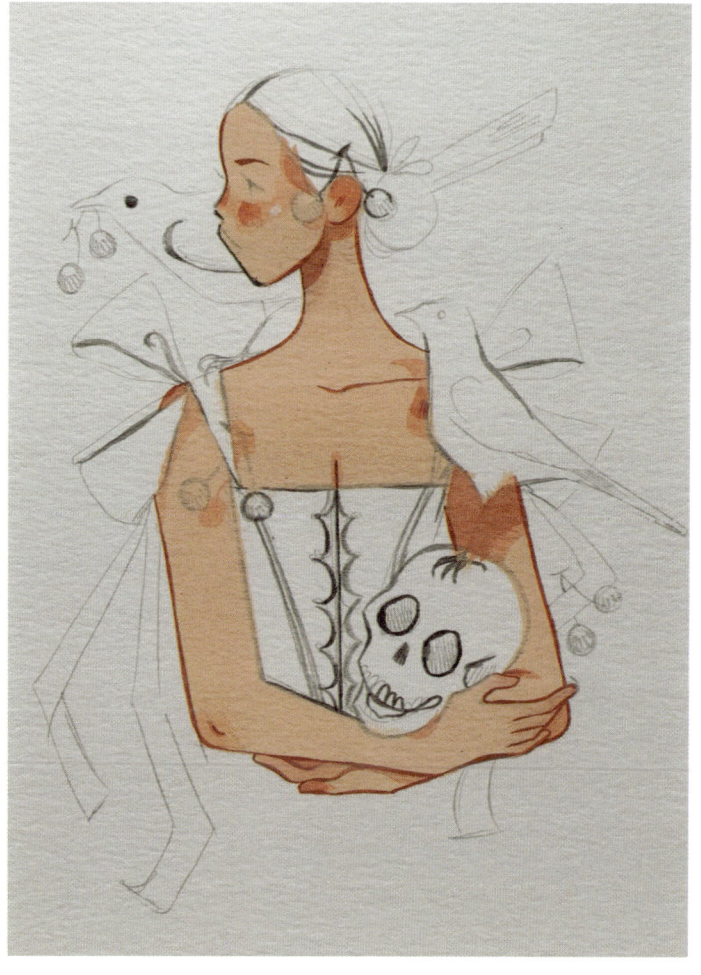

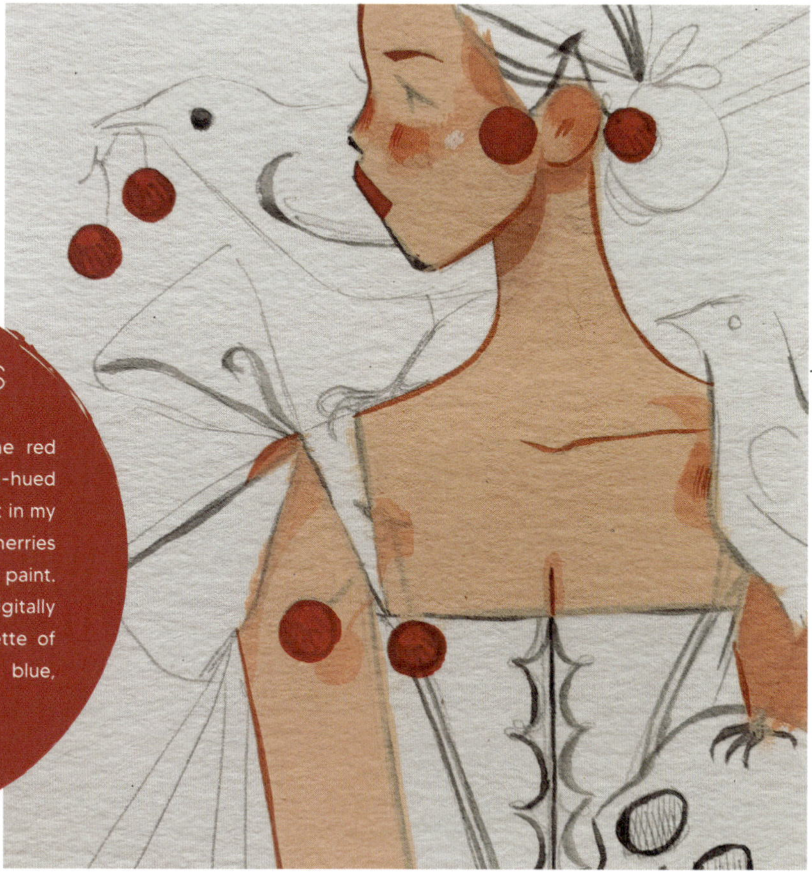

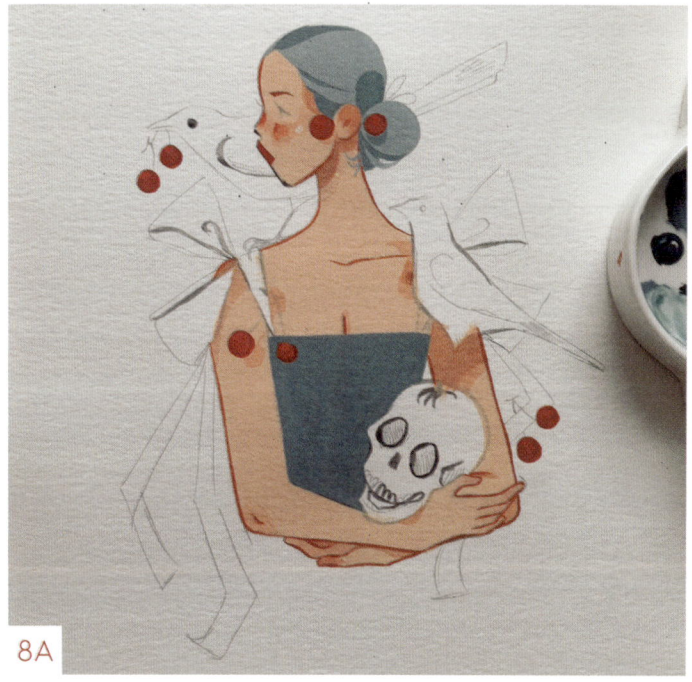

7. RED ACCENTS

Next, I decide to paint all of the red areas because I still have some red-hued paint that I used for the cheeks left in my palette. I simply paint the lips and cherries in place with one layer of deep red paint. Having designed the image digitally beforehand, I know that the palette of this piece will be predominantly blue, with a contrasting accent of red.

8. BLUE LAYERS

I then introduce blue, which will occupy large areas of the drawing. After applying a first layer of blue to the character's hair and clothing (8A), I add lighter blue areas by mixing varying amounts of white to the base blue (8B).

8A

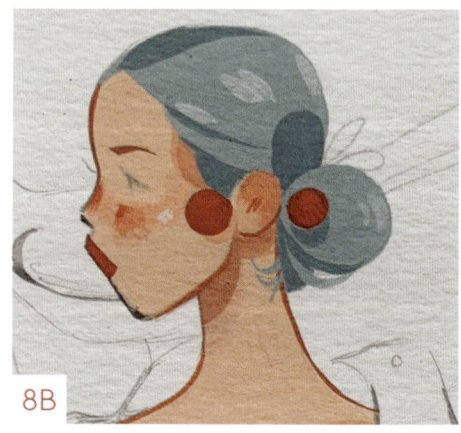

8B

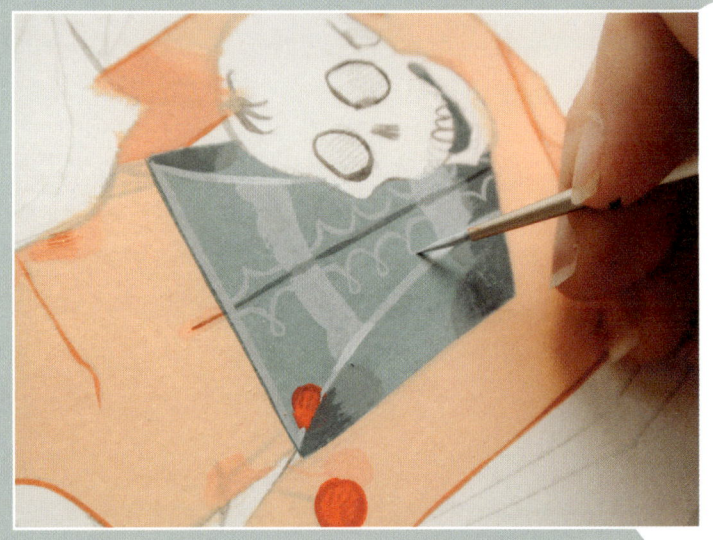

9. BLUE DETAILS

I create very light blue shades by adding more white to the base blue and use them to add detail to the clothing and hair. For the shadows, I apply a blue with the addition of black. Here, I use the "dry-on-dry" technique to produce a slightly grainy effect. To obtain this dry-on-dry look, you have to make sure as little water is on the surfaces and paint as possible. The application of the paint will also accentuate the texture of the paper.

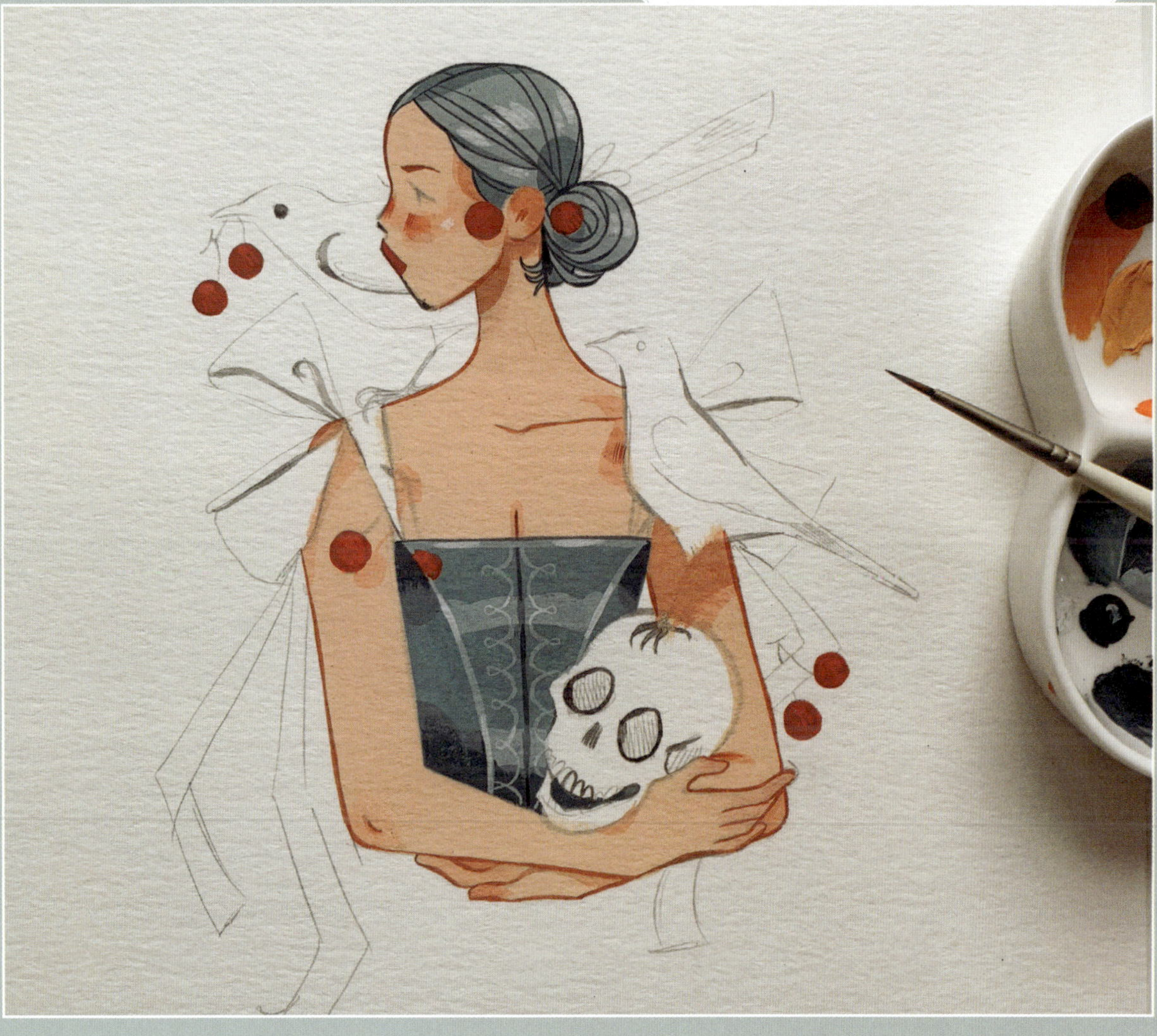

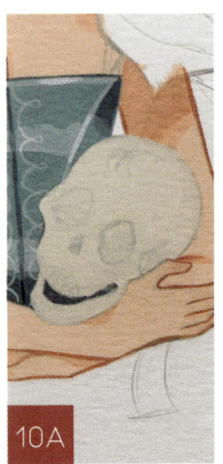

10A

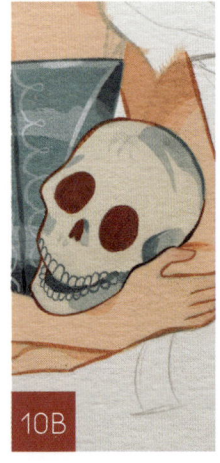

10B

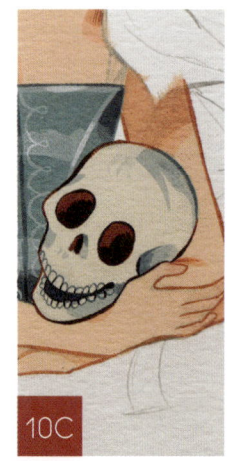

10C

10. PAINTING THE SKULL

Next, I focus on painting the simple skull element. First, I apply two layers of beige (10A) before introducing blue shadows in the same hue as the character's hair, and outlining the details (10B). To finish, I add depth to the deepest points of the skull with the application of black paint (10C).

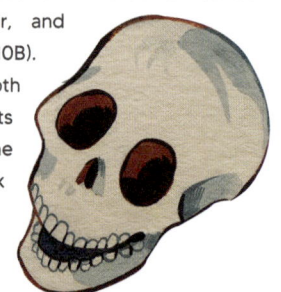

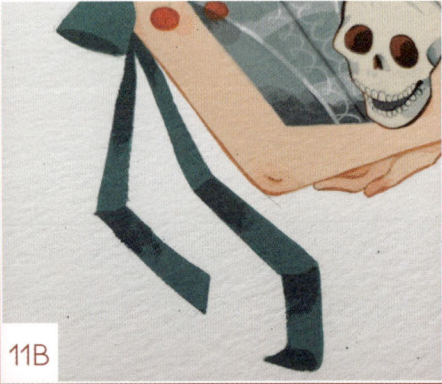

11B

11A

11. RENDERING RIBBONS

I then move on to rendering the large ribbons on the character's clothing. I apply two coats of blue (11A) and then add a darker blue for the shadows (11B). Here, I again use the dry-on-dry technique to bring out the grain of the paper and give a subtle texture to the shadows. I paint highlights on the ribbons with the color I used for the character's hair. The echoing of colors gives the piece a comfortable visual consistency.

As I have some blue paint left, I mix it with black and add deeper shadows, as well as outlines to the ribbons (11C).

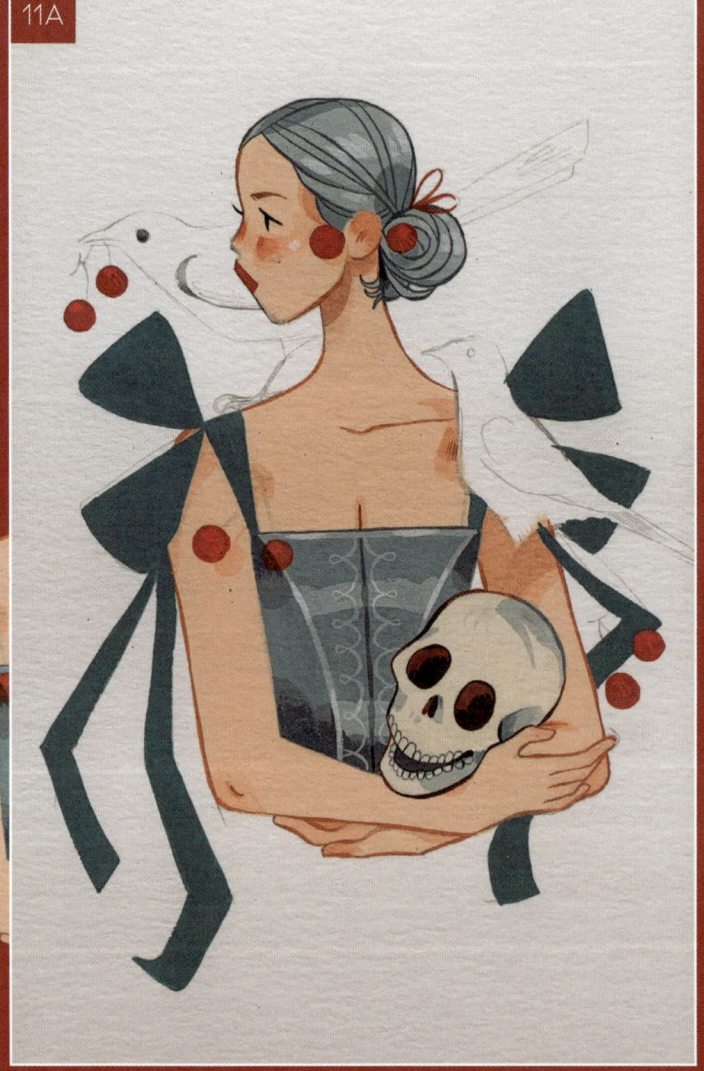

11C

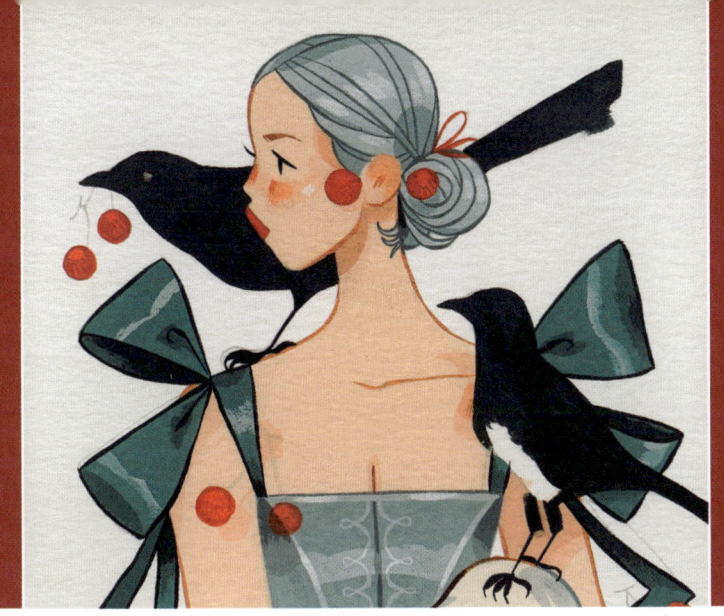

12. BUILDING THE MAGPIES

To paint the magpies, I start with a dark base layer. Using the beige paint I used on the skull, I add the characteristic magpie markings to the birds' wings, and with the blue used on the ribbons, I add accents to their feathers and beaks.

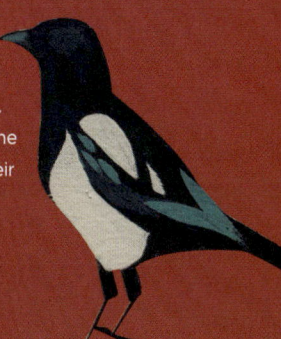

Easy corrections

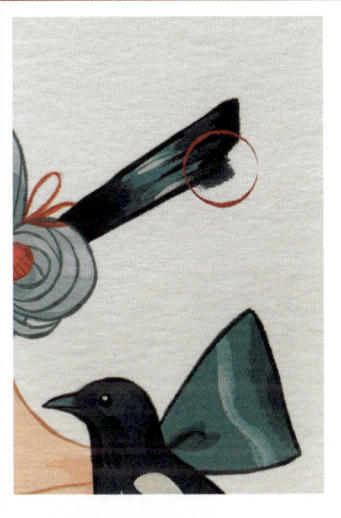
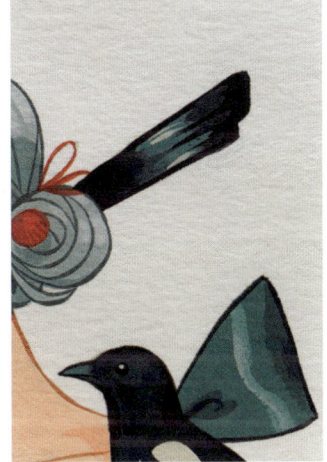
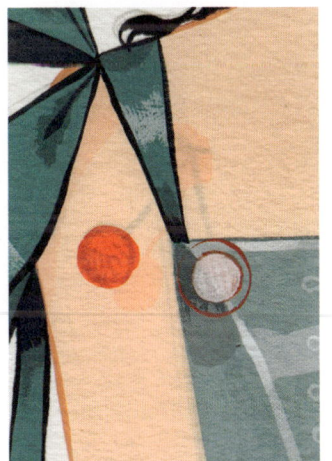
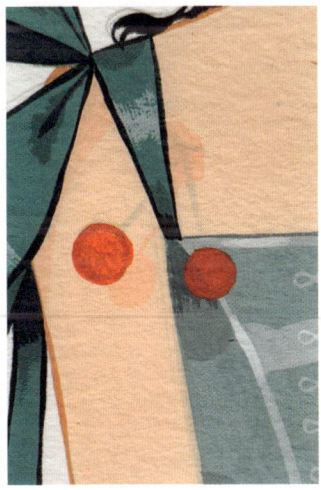

I accidentally smudge the paint on the magpie's tail while painting, but fortunately, as Acryla gouache is opaque, I easily cover it with white gouache to correct the error.

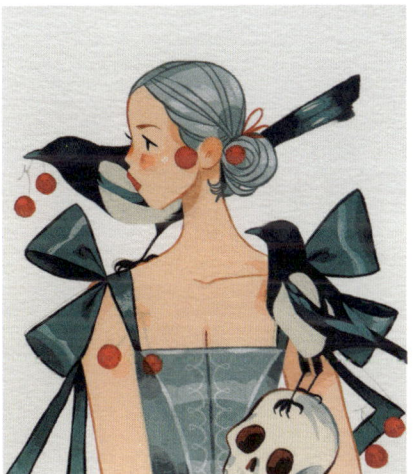

However, some colors are not completely opaque, such as yellow and red, so require additional layers to appear true to their hue. Here, the red cherry in front of the girl's clothing is too transparent, so I fill the area with white to create a neutral base and repaint red. The result is a solid and even color.

13. PERFECTING THE CHERRIES

After correcting the opacity on the base red of the cherries, I add a little black to the leftover red on my paint palette to create the color for the cherries' shadows. The simple shading on the cherries gives them dimension and brings them to life. Small white highlights and black outlines complete them.

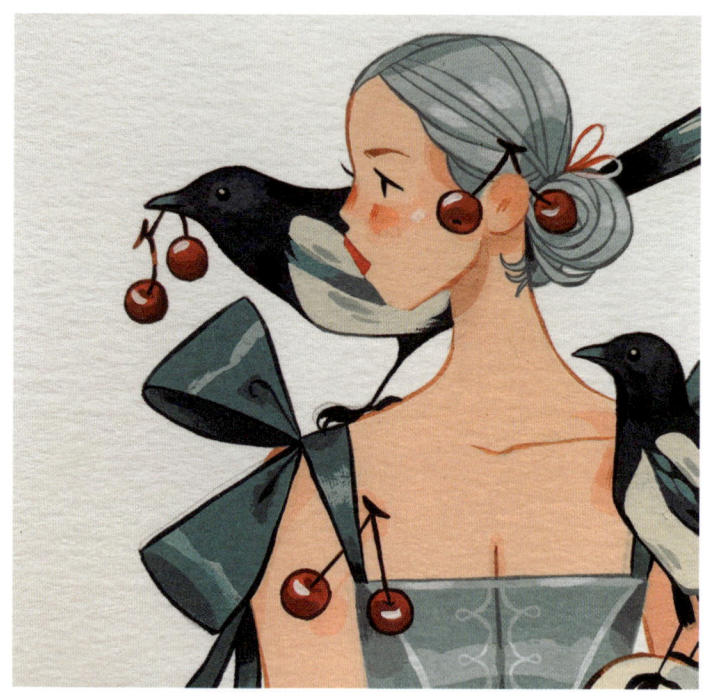

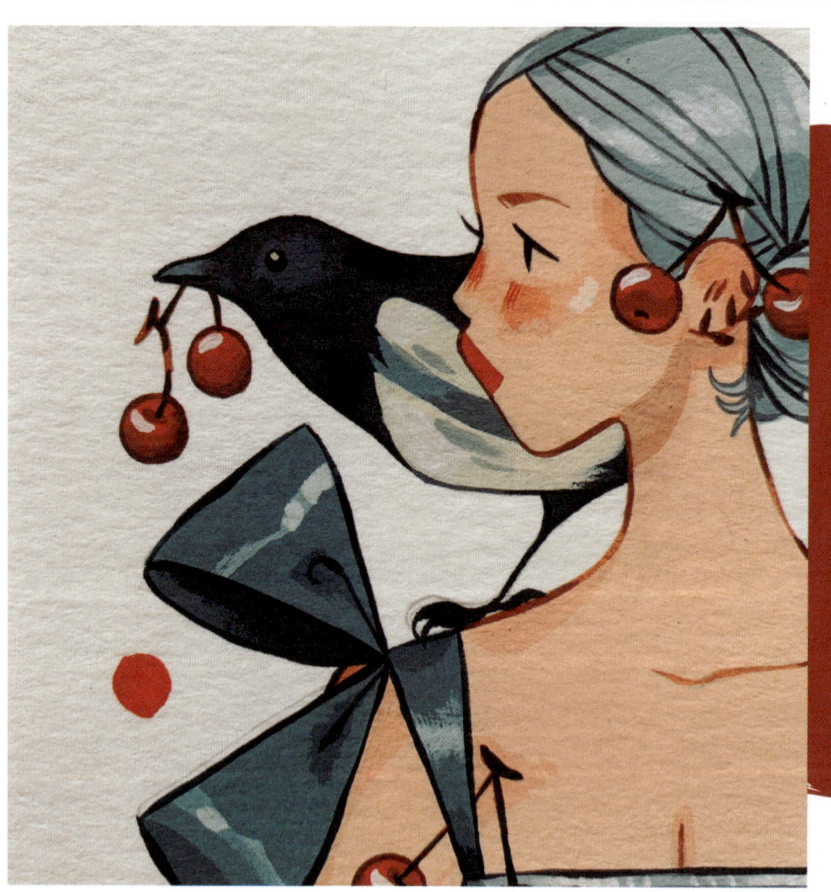

14. REFINING READABILITY

To give greater definition to the silhouette of the character's face, and set it apart from the body of the bird behind, I outline it in a reddish-brown color to match the existing outlines of the character.

15. FINAL DETAILS

I add some final shadows and highlights to the clothing. I also add outlines where there aren't any yet. When I used to outline with ink, I really liked the variations of intensity in the lines, which is why even using gouache, I like to add variations in thickness and color to my outlines.

Voilà! The illustration is complete.

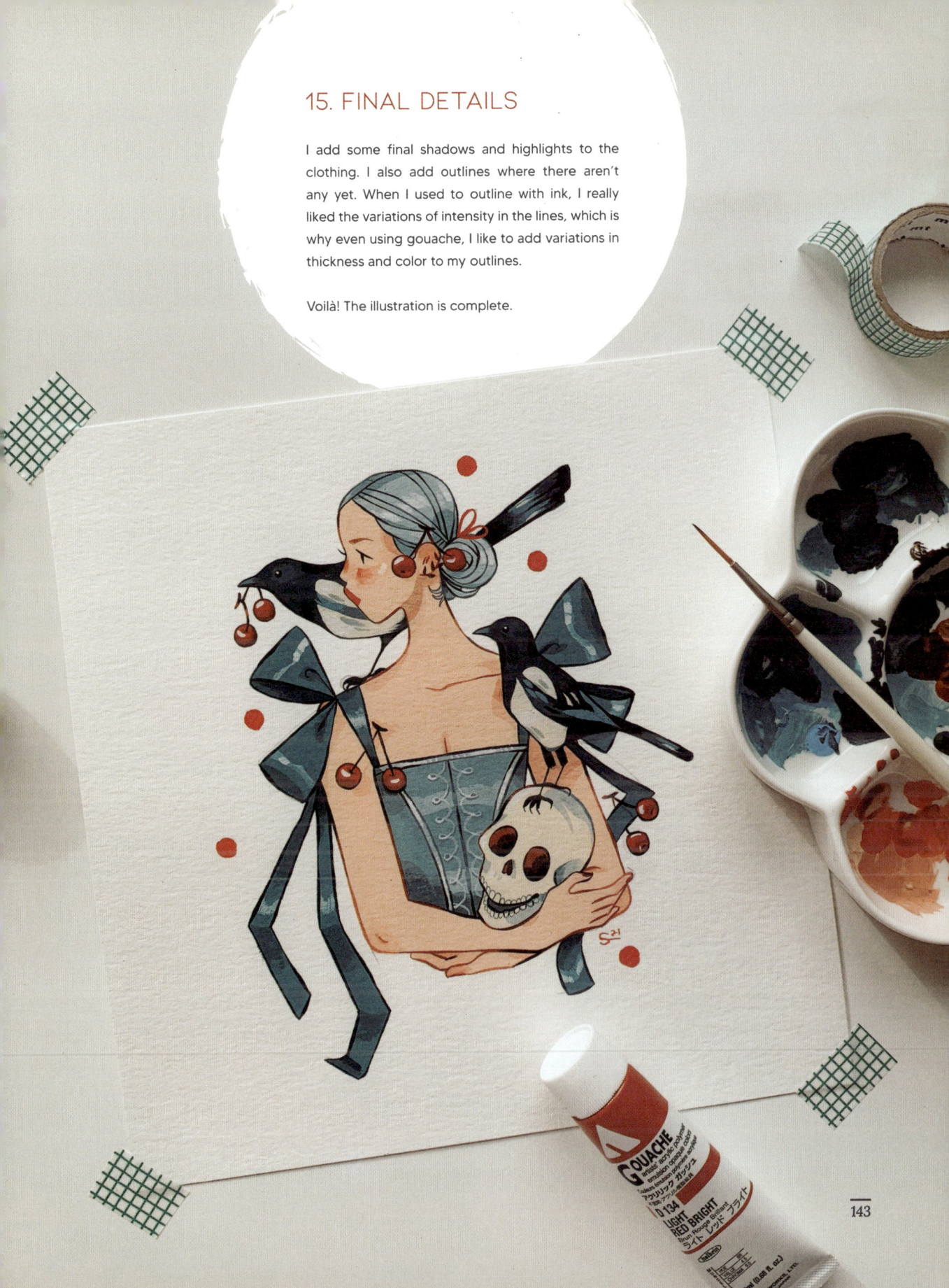

tutorial
STYLIZING A REAL SCENE

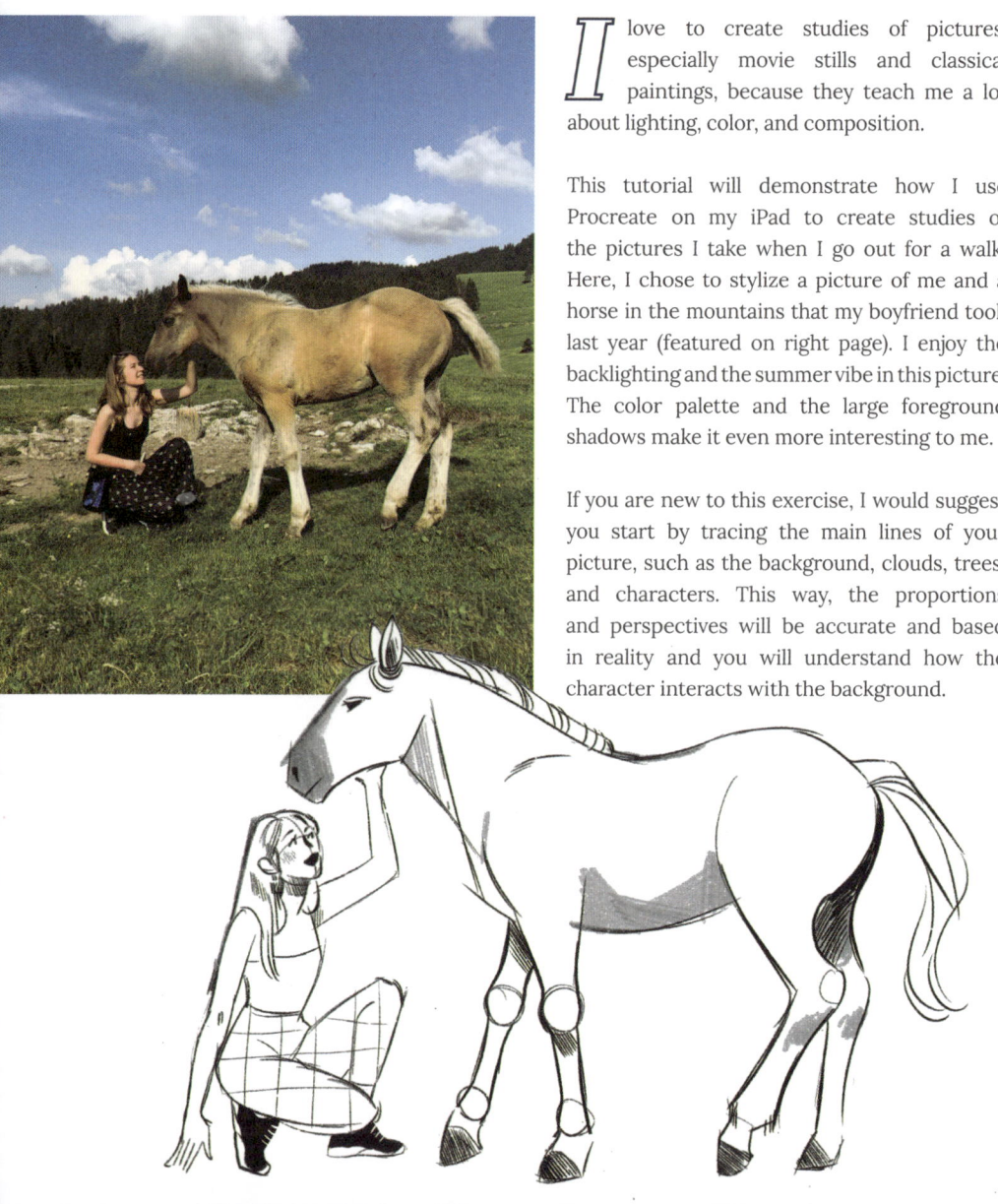

I love to create studies of pictures, especially movie stills and classical paintings, because they teach me a lot about lighting, color, and composition.

This tutorial will demonstrate how I use Procreate on my iPad to create studies of the pictures I take when I go out for a walk. Here, I chose to stylize a picture of me and a horse in the mountains that my boyfriend took last year (featured on right page). I enjoy the backlighting and the summer vibe in this picture. The color palette and the large foreground shadows make it even more interesting to me.

If you are new to this exercise, I would suggest you start by tracing the main lines of your picture, such as the background, clouds, trees, and characters. This way, the proportions and perspectives will be accurate and based in reality and you will understand how the character interacts with the background.

1. REFERENCE

Find a suitable reference image or photograph that ignites your creative fire. If you want to create from your own photographs, go out into nature at different times of the day and simply capture visually interesting moments.

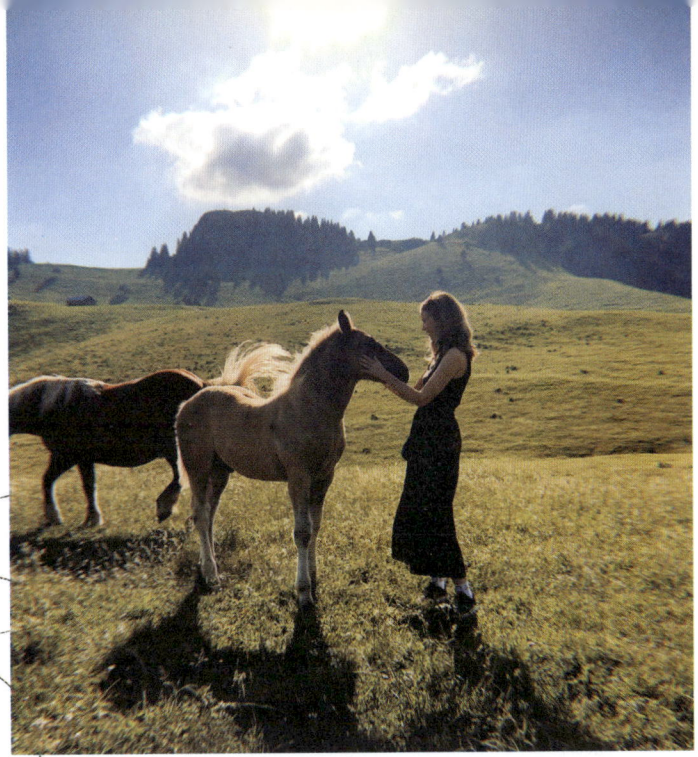

Find focus

Curate the composition and eliminate any useless elements to make the design more effective. For example, I want to focus on the character and the horse here, so decide to remove the second horse on the left.

2. GRAPHIC SKETCH

I draw the important lines of my picture with a sketching brush (I use the Dry Ink brush in Procreate). I like to sketch the main shapes in a geometric way (this can be seen in the graphic black shadows at the bottom of the frame). Geometric shapes help me understand how the picture is built. I usually start with big blocks and work into them as I progress the image. This is especially obvious in the development of the background.

3. COLOR PALETTE

I build a color palette based on the original photograph. My goal here is to draw something as close as possible to the original photograph. If I want to change the colors of a study, I usually alter them once I have finished drawing it by adding layers of colors on top of my finished illustration.

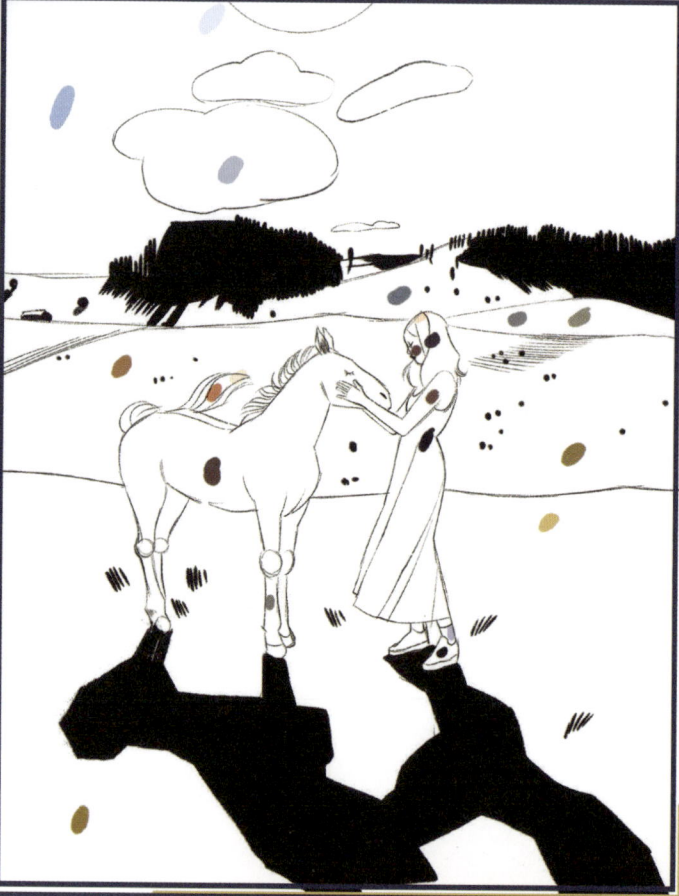

4. FLAT COLOR

Next, I fill the biggest spaces in the composition with the colors taken from the original image. I start by painting the sky and meadow. There is just a single layer of color, but already the depth of the background can be seen and felt.

Stylize!

Exaggerate some lines and forms to make the illustration easier to read.

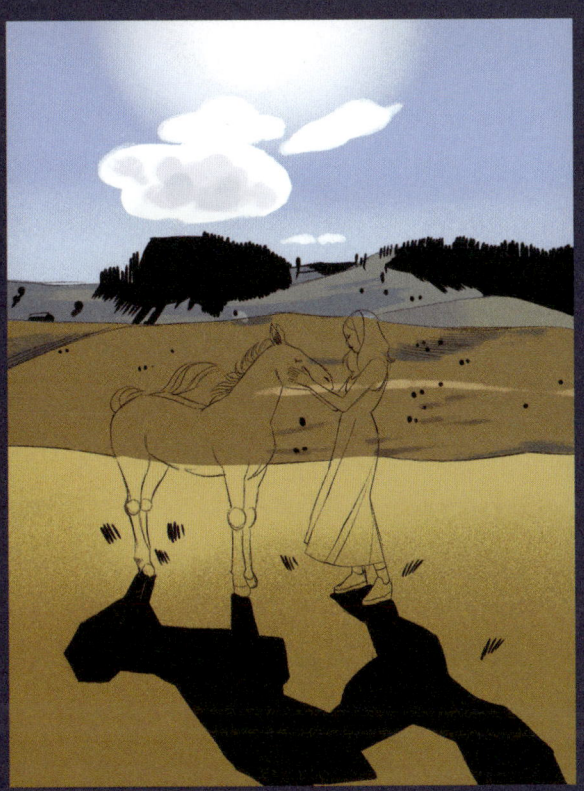

5. INITIAL LIGHTING PASS

I start to add light and shadows, also based on the original photo. During this step, I sometimes erase some of the initial black lines from my sketch to make the drawing easier to read — here I remove the linework for the clouds and sun entirely. With this lighting layer of color, the background is almost finished. I add the final little details later.

6. CHARACTER COLOR

I start to paint the characters by applying their key colors. In the original photo, the sun shines in from behind the characters, so I add highlights to their hair. I create a new lightened layer on top of my sketch using the following method: Menu > Layer > Lighten. I paint the remaining black shadow areas to blend them into the illustration — I add blue to the mountains in the background and a deep olive green to the shadow in the foreground.

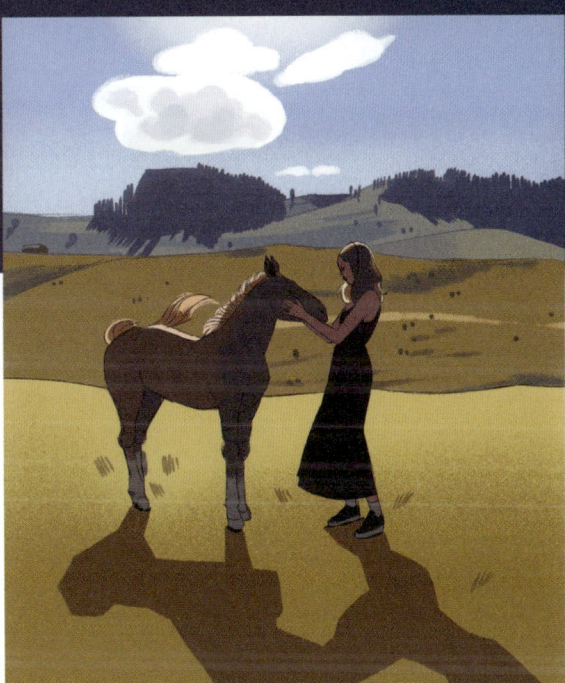

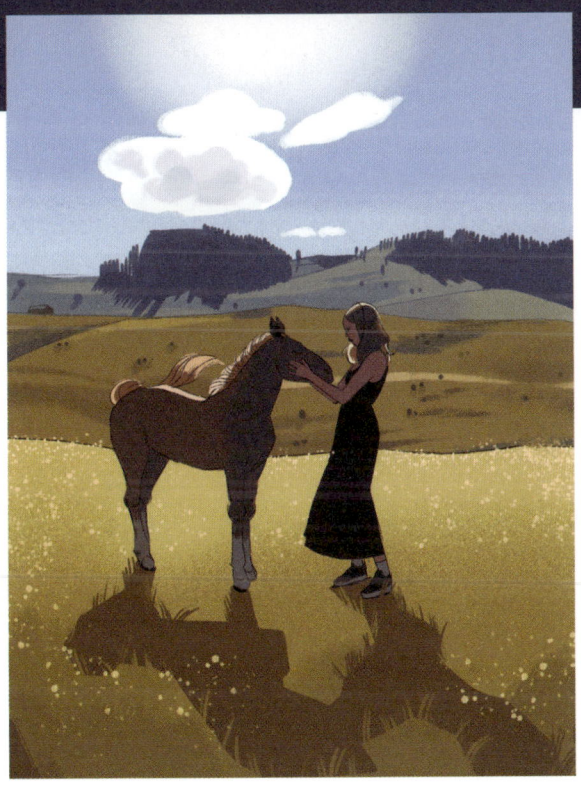

7. QUICK DETAILS

I add little details, such as flowers and grass. I like to paint details quickly but efficiently. Here, I used the Flicks spray paint brush to make the flowers (Brush > Spraypaint > Flicks). That way I don't have to draw each flower individually, and the render is pretty convincing too!

8. LIGHTING REFINEMENT

I add further lighting to my characters. Following the original photo, the light is brighter on the edges of the characters because the bright sun shining behind them creates a rim of light. A quick way to add appealing lighting in Procreate or Photoshop is to create a new layer, draw the lighting situation with a bright color (white is always a good choice!), and change the blending mode setting to Overlay. You can also play with the opacity levels to make your character glow subtly.

Make it your own

This is intended to be a fun exercise, so feel free to play with shapes, angles, light, and colors. It doesn't have to be an exact copy of the photograph you want to study.

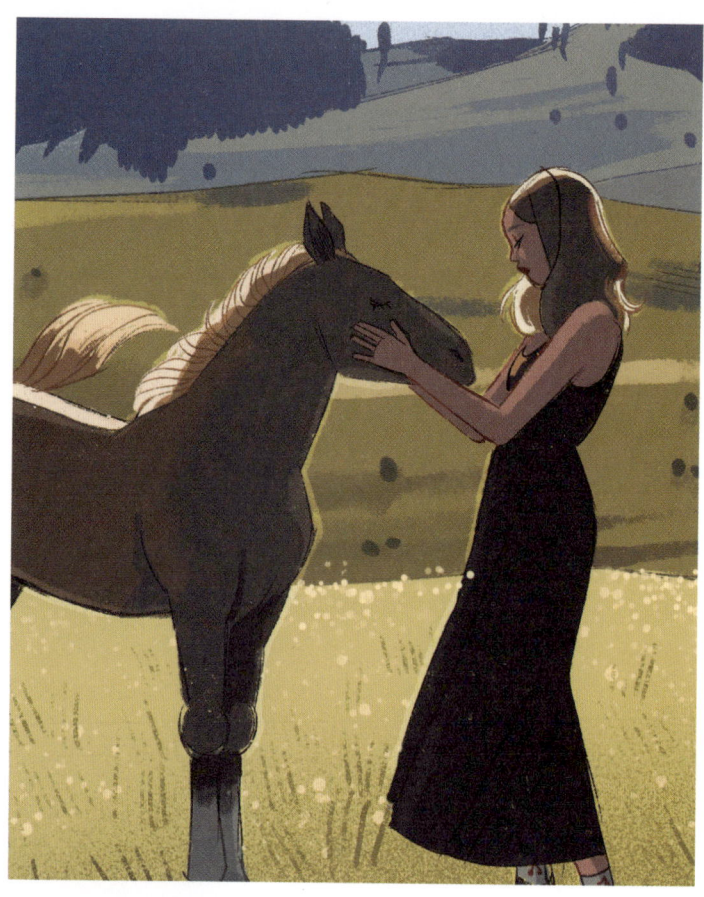

9. FINISHING TOUCHES

Next, I add flowers in the foreground and some hints of light in the background. I simply play with the spray paint brushes again to draw the flowers, and change my layer again to Overlay to make it pop.

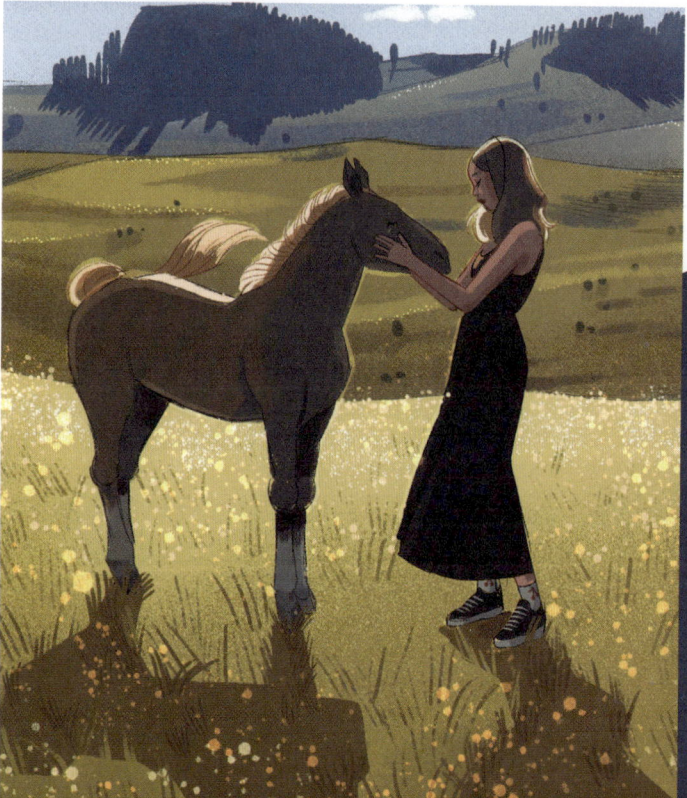

10. ADJUSTMENTS

I make final adjustments to change the colors slightly. I alter the grass and sky to appear more yellow and warm. I also find the overall colors too saturated, so I decrease the saturation a bit.

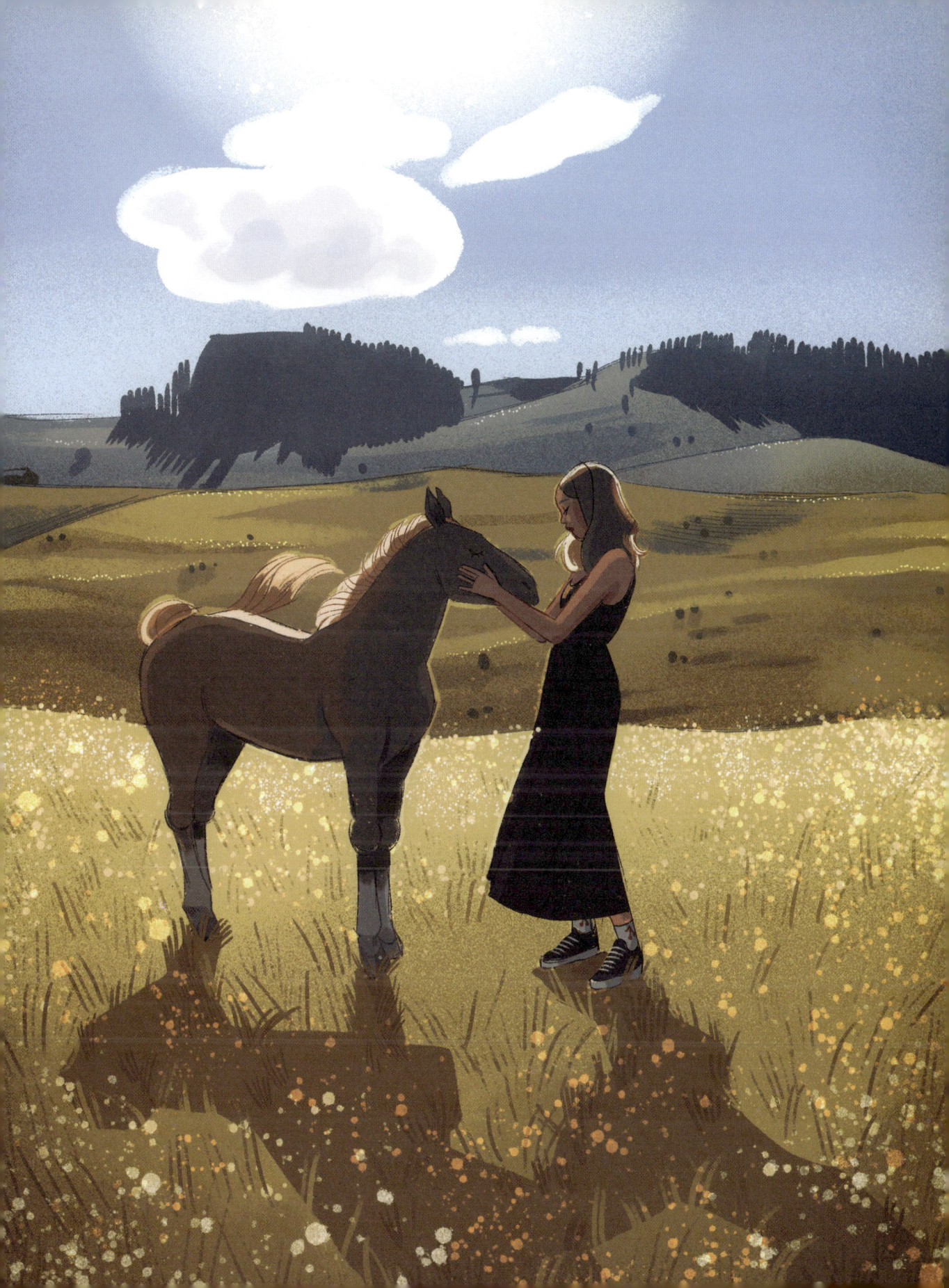

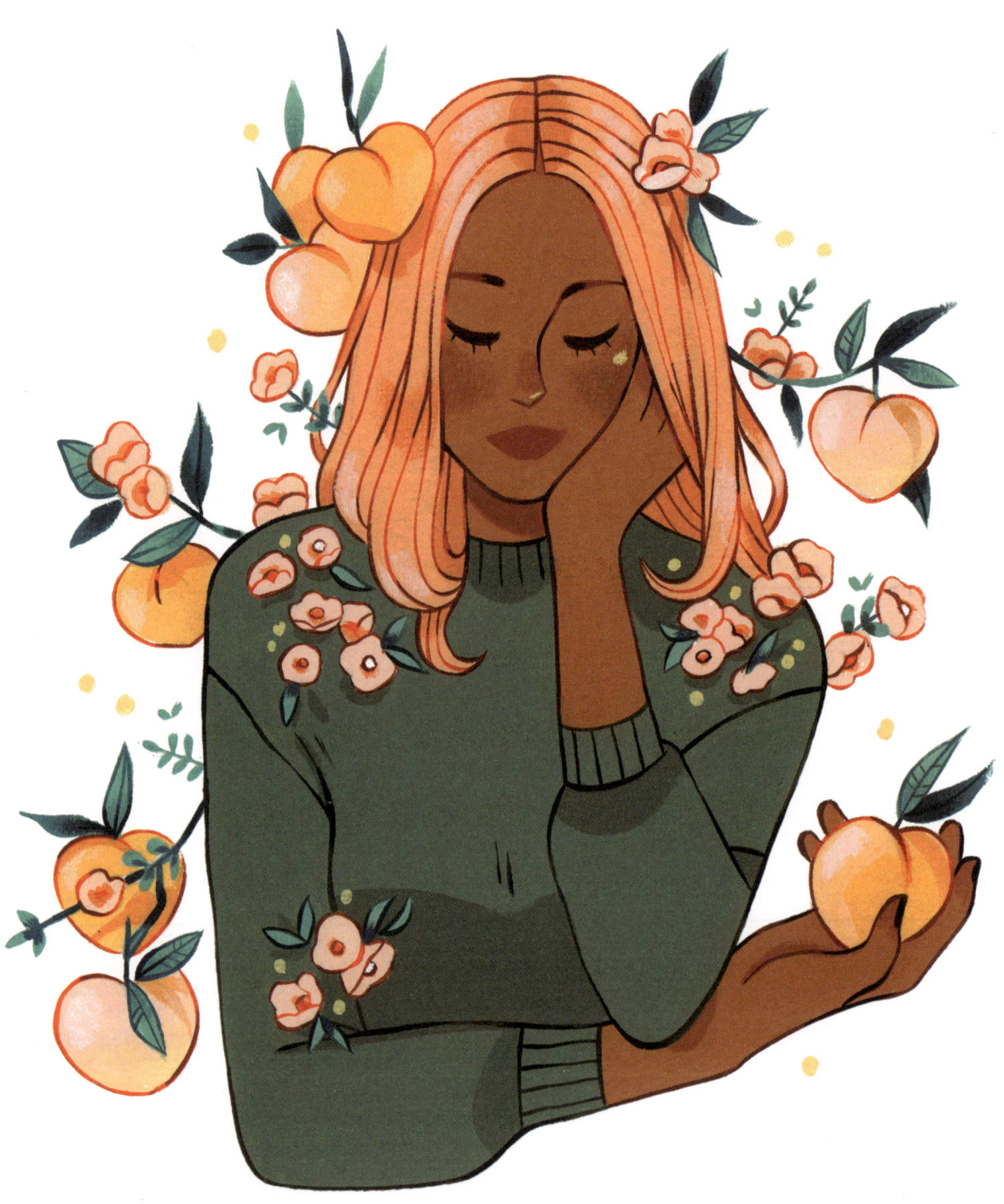

Peaches, Acryla gouache, 2019

THANK YOU

A big thank you to all of you who supported this project, made this book possible, and overall, for making this incredible adventure possible. Grateful doesn't even begin to explain how I feel. Your constant support, interest, and kind words mean the world to me, and make me want to keep creating for you, and to do better every day. Thank you for allowing me to tell my stories, to share what's in my mind with all of you. Who would have thought these little drawings would bring us together?

To my family, who supported my desire to become an artist since I was a kid – thank you. It's amazing to think that you never stopped believing in me.

Thank you to Apolline, for being my sidekick since day one. To Benjamin, for always being so enthusiastic about art, for helping me take the beautiful photographs seen in this book, and making my workspace look better than ever.

To Cyprien, for always being by my side when I am in doubt. For making me happy, and for making this journey more and more interesting through the years. Thank you for being my number one fan.

And of course, thank you to the lovely people at 3dtotal — Simon, Sophie, and Fiona. Thank you for giving me the opportunity to create such a beautiful book, for your brilliant ideas and precious help. Rêverie is everything I have always dreamed of; I couldn't have wished for a better team to make this book. Thank you!

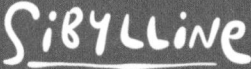

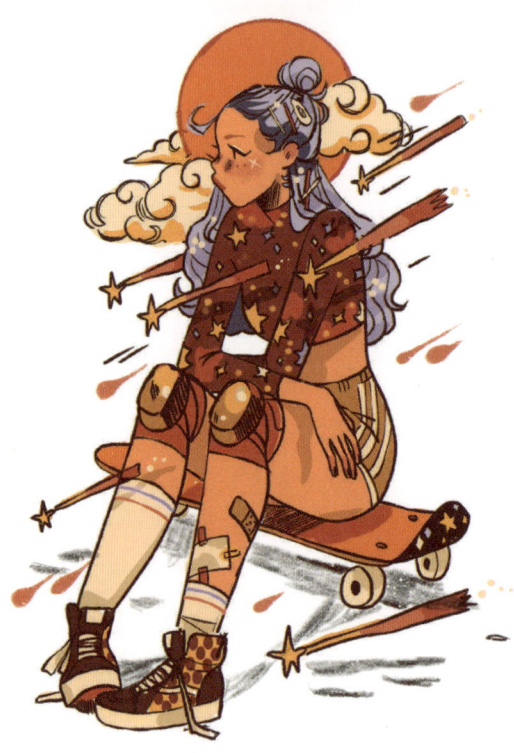

ABOUT 3DTOTAL

3dtotal Publishing is a trailblazing, creative publisher specializing in inspirational and educational resources for artists.

Our titles feature top industry professionals from around the globe who share their experience in skillfully written step-by-step tutorials and fascinating, detailed guides. Illustrated throughout with stunning artwork, these best-selling publications offer creative insight, expert advice, and essential motivation. Fans of digital art will enjoy our comprehensive volumes covering Adobe Photoshop, Procreate, and Blender, as well as our superb titles based around character design, including *Fundamentals of Character Design* and *Creating Characters for the Entertainment Industry*. The dedicated, high-quality blend of instruction and inspiration also extends to traditional art. Titles covering a range of techniques, genres, and abilities allow your creativity to flourish while building essential skills.

Well-established within the industry, we now offer over 100 titles and counting, many of which have been translated into multiple languages around the world. With something for every artist, we are proud to say that our books offer the 3dtotal package:

LEARN | CREATE | SHARE

Visit us at 3dtotalpublishing.com

3dtotal Publishing is part of 3dtotal.com, a leading website for CG artists founded by Tom Greenway in 1999.